Grit, Spit, and Never Quit

Grit, Spit, and Never Quit

A MARINE'S GUIDE TO COMEDY AND LIFE

ROB RIGGLE

GRAND CENTRAL

NEW YORK BOSTON

Grand Central Publishing
Hachette Book Group
1290 Avenue of the Americas
New York, NY 10104
grandcentralpublishing.com
@grandcentralpub

First Edition: November 2025

Grand Central Publishing is a division of Hachette Book Group, Inc. The Grand Central Publishing name and logo are registered trademarks of Hachette Book Group, Inc.

Print book interior design by Timothy Shaner, NightandDayDesign.biz

Library of Congress Cataloging-in-Publication Data
Name: Riggle, Rob author
Title: Grit, spit, and never quit : a Marine's guide to comedy and life / Rob Riggle.
Description: New York : Grand Central Publishing, 2025.
Identifiers: LCCN 2025028906 | ISBN 9781538769546 hardcover | ISBN 9781538769553 trade paperback | ISBN 9781538769560 ebook
Subjects: LCSH: Riggle, Rob | Comedians—United States—Biography | Marines—United States—Biography | LCGFT: Autobiographies
Classification: LCC PN2287.R534 A3 2025
LC record available at https://lccn.loc.gov/2025028906

ISBNs: 9781538769546 (hardcover); 9781538769560 (ebook); 9781538779064 (signed edition)

Printed in the United States of America

LSC-C

Printing 1, 2025

To my children, Abigail and George. I closed my eyes for a minute and you grew up. I'm not sad, though; that's what's supposed to happen. I remember every moment. I remember all the good times. I love you forever and ever, amen.

CONTENTS

Author's Note ix

Introduction xiii

PART ONE

WHEN I GROW UP, I WANT TO BE A LAWYER... I MEAN, FBI AGENT... I MEAN, US MARINE

1. Ready for All, Yielding to None: AKA Bring That Shit! 3
2. Whoops, the Microphone's On 19
3. Grave Hunting with Grammy 33
4. What Do I Wanna Be When I Grow Up? (Just Kidding, I'll Never Grow Up) 41
5. Grit, Spit, and Never Quit 53
6. Kidnappings and Comets 79
7. Flight School Follies 87

PART TWO

... I MEAN, COMEDIAN

8. F U, Fear! 101
9. How to Make a Good Impression 113
10. "Hold on Loosely ..." 129

11. There's No *T* in Team! 143
12. Be All In or Get All Out 155
13. Tomorrow Is Promised to No One 169
14. Focusing on the Mission.................... 183

PART THREE

TERROR, SPERM BANKS, AND BLESSINGS

15. Send Me 197
16. I Love You, Man.............................. 205
17. A Grateful American 213

PART FOUR

LEARNING TO BE ME—A GENERALLY HUMOROUS KNUCKLEHEAD FROM KANSAS

18. Are You Gellin'? Or, the Day They Broke My Sole . . . I Mean, Soul............ 231
19. Finding My Unicorn 239
20. My Way...................................... 257
21. Back in the Game 267

Guitar Picks and Goodbyes 275
Acknowledgments............................. 281
About the Author 285

AUTHOR'S NOTE

The events, experiences, and conversations related in this book are true. Pretty much. At least as the author remembers them. But the author barely remembers what happened yesterday, so . . . there you go.

Grit, Spit, and Never Quit

INTRODUCTION

We were dropping out of the sky—fast.

I was strapped into a cargo bay jump seat inside a Lockheed C-130 Hercules, a four-engine military transport. The bay was packed with pallets containing MREs (meal, ready to eat), bottles of water, and boxes of ammo and communication gear. Pallets, that is, plus six passengers—me, my gunnery sergeant, Andrew "Gunny" Lynch, and four gentlemen of unknown origin. Based on their accents, clothes, and equipment, and the stone-cold look of warriors about to do their business, I believe it's safe to say they were British special forces . . . but hey, what do I know?

It was an hour past midnight on December 10, 2001, just three months after al-Qaeda terrorists took control of four passenger planes on 9/11 and killed nearly three thousand Americans. I was a captain in the US Marine Corps, and we were descending into the terrorists' kitchen, otherwise known as Afghanistan.

There were no windows in the cargo hold. Other than a few red lights, the bay was nearly pitch black. I felt the G-forces twist my insides as the pilots maneuvered us into a downward corkscrew, to prevent us from being shot out of the sky by potential enemy fire—thank God I didn't get airsick. No one spoke. It wouldn't have mattered if someone had—it was near-impossible to hear anything over the whine of the engines and the creaks and groans of the fuselage. Like a tick on a raging bull, all I could do was hang on and pray . . . and that's exactly what I did.

Three months. Technically, eighty-nine days. That's how long it'd been since I'd first stood in disbelief on top of the devastation at Ground Zero along with hundreds of other military personnel, firefighters, police officers, and volunteers, moving rubble by hand, desperately searching for survivors we would never find. Eighty-seven days since a man in his fifties stopped me on my walk home from Ground Zero to ask, "How's it going down there?" When I told him it was slow work, the man calmly said, "God bless you." I don't know why—it was probably all the suppressed emotion that had been building up for days—but it finally came out. Right there on the street, I started to cry.

I wasn't just grieving. I was pissed. I felt violated. I lived in New York City; they'd attacked my *home*. Most of the victims died in the blink of an eye, so they never even had the chance to fight back. But I could do something about this injustice. I was a trained Marine officer who'd served during multiple overseas deployments. I was also a patriot. After my experience at Ground Zero, there was never a doubt in my mind that I'd be raising my hand to get back on active duty. This was the kind of moment Marines were made for. We were America's force in readiness, her first responders. So if not me, who? If not now, when?

The C-130's corkscrew tightened. We were close to landing.

The plan was for the plane to set down fast on a short, bombed-out desert runway. Our group was supposed to get picked up by Americans based at a compound near Mazar-i-Sharif, the largest city in northern Afghanistan. I'd already looked at maps to orient myself and mentally run through contingencies for what I'd do if the bad guys showed up before the good guys. Was I prepared to kill someone if I had to? Yes. Was I prepared to die? I'd rather not.

The runway we were aiming for ran east-west. The Hindu Kush mountains were to the east. The compound that would be our new home was six miles west of the runway. If the situation turned ugly, my egress would be to the west, which I could do on foot.

Just before takeoff, our pilot had told us, "Heads up, we're not stopping. The plane will not stop moving. We'll slow down as much as we can so you can get off, but we won't stop." Now, as the C-130 straightened out for its final approach, I remembered the pilot's words. *What exactly does that mean?* I thought. *Are we talking jump, tuck, and roll?* I pictured myself bouncing across the runway like a deadbeat just tossed from his bookie's car.

A minute later, I felt the bump of wheels touching down. The loading ramp had already been lowered. Instantly, the crew chief was up and rapidly pushing pallets down the ramp and into the darkness as the plane taxied down the short runway. I joined Gunny and the rest of the passengers in hurriedly unstrapping from my seat. As soon as the last pallet left the plane, I ran down the ramp with the others and jumped onto solid earth. Thankfully, the C-130 moved at a slow enough speed—so no bouncing Marines.

I looked back at the plane taxiing away from us. The crew chief stood in the doorway of the now-empty cargo bay. He gave a wave and a quick salute before the ramp closed. The C-130 circled around a crater at the end of the runway, picked up speed as it hurtled in our direction, and with a roar flew over our heads and into the night.

We were alone. The silence was deafening.

I'd already pulled out my sidearm, a 9-millimeter Beretta. The Beretta is a fine weapon, but let's be honest: It's a pistol. Effective to about twenty-five yards. I wasn't gonna do shit with a pistol. Unless the fight was in a closet or a phone booth, I was going be outgunned. But I was a staff officer, not a gunslinging operator, so the military in all its wisdom decided all I needed was a Beretta.

No M4 or M16 for me on this deployment. If the Taliban showed up they'd likely have AK-47 assault rifles, RPK machine guns, and rocket-propelled grenades. *Too late to worry about that now.*

The six of us took defensive positions by forming a circle around the pallets. I lay on my belly, a pallet behind me, the desert stretched out before me in the darkness. Other than the sound of wind blowing over me, the night was still and freezing.

Holy shit, I thought. *Just three months ago I was performing improv comedy in a little black-box theater in New York City. Now I'm lying on the cold ground of a bombed-out airfield in northern Afghanistan.*

To quote Ron Burgundy, that escalated quickly.

Yeah, improv comedy. I'd moved to New York in 1997, not just because of the Marines, but because I'd found the balls to pursue my dream—a life in the arts. When I wasn't on a deployment in Albania or Kosovo, I was a Marine by day and a comedian by night. People ask me all the time, "How do careers in the military and comedy fit together?" Well, they don't. But often, they do both require a talent for being in the moment and thinking quickly. I may not be good at everything, but I know how to focus and react to what's going on around me—whether it's a commanding officer suddenly barking orders or an improv colleague suddenly announcing we're a couple of goldfish in a toilet bowl. You gotta be ready for anything.

During my time in the city before 9/11, I'd taken all three levels of classes offered by the Upright Citizens Brigade, an improv comedy performance and teaching group founded by Matt Besser, Amy Poehler, Ian Roberts, and Matt Walsh. In 1999, I began performing with Respecto Montalban, an improvisational and sketch comedy troupe at the UCB. Was my name up in lights yet? Hardly. I was just another actor-comedian who was grinding away, learning the trade, refining my skills, and looking for the break that would launch me. Did I know if I would make it? Nope. However, more than a decade in the Marines had taught me a few important lessons—the most important being that as long as I didn't give up, as long as I stayed committed to putting in the work and preparing myself, I had a chance to succeed.

That lesson is where the title of this book came from. I spent a lot of hours debating and friend-testing titles. Some that didn't make the cut were *Die Hard or Die Laughing, Embrace the Suck, A Few Good Giggles, Gung Ho Riggle*, and *My Asshole Recruiter Lied.* Though *Grit, Spit, and Never Quit* isn't an actual Marine Corps motto, it might as well be one. It definitely matches our mindset and attitude. It's the same mindset I've tried to adopt in my comedy career and throughout my life—you keep going till the job is done or the show is over. No delays. No excuses. No refunds. And definitely no quitting.

That night in Afghanistan, we'd been on the ground only a few minutes when my musings were interrupted by the sound of vehicles. Suddenly, a convoy of white Toyota pickup trucks and vans raced onto the airstrip next to us. It was the moment of truth—were these fellow Americans arriving to transport us to the compound or al-Qaeda and Taliban terrorists about to open fire on us? I didn't know the answer yet—but I *did* know that no matter what happened, I had put in the work to prepare myself for this moment. I thought, *Bring it.*

Now that you've read the introduction to this book, it's *your* moment of truth. Are you prepared to join me on the crazy ride that's been my life so far? Here's what I say: No delays. No excuses. No refunds. Turn the page.

PART ONE

WHEN I GROW UP, I WANT TO BE A LAWYER . . . I MEAN, FBI AGENT . . . I MEAN, US MARINE

ONE

Ready for All, Yielding to None
AKA Bring That Shit!

I think all the funny people were bullied. —Chris Rock

Overland Park, Kansas, was a great place to grow up in the seventies and eighties. It was a time and a land of freedom. As a kid in the summer, I could get on my bike and ride for miles with my buddies. I was in excellent shape because we rode everywhere. Nobody had cell phones. There was no way to track me. I was just gone. My parents' only requirement was that I be back by dinnertime. If we had a problem when we were out riding, we had to solve it ourselves—a lesson that was driven home to me on more than one occasion.

I was far from a tough guy in those days (still true today). At most, I was average height and weight all through grade school. I was also a sensitive kid. When I got upset, the tears would flow. I once ran home bawling because I got mud on my brand-new tennis shoes. My vibe was closer to lover than fighter. And yet, somehow, I seemed to end up in more fights than Muhammad Ali.

Like the time I was six years old and playing football in my front yard with a couple of eight-year-olds—a dangerous and violent age for boys from that era. The scarier of the two, Chip, lived next door. Chip was a couple of inches taller than me, with long, shaggy blond hair. He was fast and quick. He was also wild and covered in dirt most of the time—the word *feral* comes to mind.

The worst part, though, was that Chip was mean. Imagine Kelly Leak from *The Bad News Bears*, only without the talent. This was a kid with no respect for authority. If his mom or dad told him, "Don't leave the front yard," Chip would yell back, "I gotta do what I gotta do!" I still can't decide if I should reveal Chip's last name. On the one hand, I want to protect his anonymity. On the other hand, there's a good chance he's on *America's Most Wanted*, and printing his name might lead to his capture.

That day in the yard, it didn't take long before Chip decided he'd played enough football and it was time to pick on me. When I wasn't looking, he stuck his leg out and tripped me. Then he did it again. And again. I wore my purple Fran Tarkenton jersey with the number 10 of the little Minnesota Vikings quarterback known for his ability to escape bigger linemen who were trying to pulverize him, but I guess putting on Fran's jersey wasn't enough to transfer his nimbleness to me.

Chip soon got bored with tripping me, so the next time I was on the ground, he started kicking my legs. Now I couldn't even get up.

"Stop! Knock it off!" I yelled. "Let me get up, jerk." As a first grader, my verbal acumen and ability to cuss with authority had yet to develop. I have to admit it—I was a polite kid with good manners.

My gentle protests accomplished nothing. If anything, they seemed to anger Chip, making him kick me even harder.

Remember, macho was not part of my makeup. When I would get to sixth grade, my teacher would show our class *The Velveteen Rabbit*. As the film rolled and I watched that rabbit's dream of becoming real turn to dust, I got more and more upset. I'm not talking about a little misty. This was hard sniffles and gasps for air. Then I realized that other kids in the class had started to notice. I had a desk with a lift top, so I raised the lid, stuck my head in the desk, and pretended to look for something. In reality, I was wiping tears and snot with a sheet of notebook paper . . . and fooling no one. I was not on anyone's list of neighborhood tough guys.

Which is why when Chip kept kicking me that day in the yard, I did what anyone who would one day aspire to a career in the military would do—I started to cry. I was hurt, scared, and humiliated. I had no idea how to handle a bully. I had no idea why he was doing this. After another kick, I pushed against Chip's leg, scrambled a few yards, then jumped up and ran across the yard to my house. Behind me, Chip and the other hoodlum, Jeff, just laughed.

Our big garage door was open, so I rushed inside. Mom must have heard me bawling because she met me at the doorway to the inside of the house.

"Rob," Mom said, "what's wrong?"

"They're being mean to me!" I blubbered. "They're tripping me and kicking me and knocking me down. I hate those guys!"

You need to understand that my mom, all five feet two inches of her, is one tough lady. Sandra Shrout Riggle was raised on a post-Depression farm in rural Missouri in the early 1940s. We're talking outhouses here. Her father, Fred, was away at war for the first four years of her life. Mom grew up fast and hard because she had to. She got her bachelor's and master's degrees back when women didn't do that sort of thing and became a junior high English teacher. Think back to what kids are like in seventh and eighth grade. The worst, right? Plenty of them are bullies. But those monsters were no match for my mom. When I was in high school, more than one of Mom's former students said she'd made them cry. She taught those little bastards—me, my friends, and others much meaner than we were—for thirty-one years.

So, let's just say that if I was looking for Mom to give me a comforting hug and invite me to sit down and eat of plate of fresh-baked cookies . . . yeah, that wasn't going to happen.

Mom cupped my chin in one hand, leaned in, and inspected my face for damage. Seeing none, she turned me around, put her hand on my back, and to my surprise walked me through the open garage door to the driveway.

"Rob, listen to me," she said. "If you don't deal with this, those boys will do this to you for the rest of your life. They will always pick on you and bully you. This will be your fate every day unless you go out there and take care of it right now."

I stood there, my mouth open and tears on my face, as Mom walked back into the garage and pushed the button that brought down the automatic garage door. Suddenly, I had nowhere to retreat. Just like Cortés, Mom had burned my ships.

I might have been only six, but I knew that something big—and scary—had just happened. *Mom, what the hell?* I thought. *You're supposed to protect me! Just what do you expect me to do?* It was the first time in my life that I had to deal with a serious problem all by myself.

I didn't have much time to think. As soon as they saw what had happened, Chip and Jeff began taunting me. "Hey, look who's back," Chip sneered. "You gonna cry some more for us, pussy?"

I felt like David facing Goliath, except I didn't have a slingshot and wouldn't have known how to use it if I did. Was I scared? You bet your Super Bowl tickets I was scared! But Mom apparently had faith that I could handle this on my own. I thought she'd gone crazy. Like truly snapped, gone bye-bye crazy, as in she was done being my mom and was inside packing her suitcase to run off with some slick-talking salesman she'd just met. Just playing the odds, I figured she was going to live in the Florida Panhandle with her new family. That's the level of insanity I was dealing with because none of the math was mathing. At the moment, however, it seemed I had no choice but to find out if she was right.

I walked back into the yard where Chip and Jeff stood with their hands on their hips, taunting me. These idiots looked like central casting's response to an order for a couple of child thugs—Chip wearing clothes that hadn't been washed in two years, looking like he'd just walked out of the jungle, and Jeff, a big boy standing with his mouth agape, per usual. Jeff didn't strike me as a conversationalist. If needed, I figured I could subdue him with a simple magic trick.

Chip's face twisted in an evil grin. "What's up, crybaby?" he said. "What are you gonna do?"

That was the moment when everything welled up inside me—the shame, the rage, and just enough courage to outweigh my usual good judgment. I had reached my limit. I was like a cartoon character with steam was coming out of my ears. I was Ralphie Parker in *A Christmas Story* facing off against his nemesis, Scott Farkus, when Ralphie morphed from bully victim to a whirling, cussing, fist-throwing Tasmanian Devil.

I bum-rushed the surprised Chip and tackled him as violently as I could. Which probably wasn't that violent, but we hit the ground and began to wrestle in the grass, both of us throwing rabbit punches to the body and shoulders. I was on top first, then Chip was on top of me, then I twisted away so I was on top again. It was like a cage match between Hulk Hogan and Stone Cold Steve Austin—only without the power, strength, coordination, or athleticism.

The scuffle seemed to go on forever, but it must have lasted only a couple of minutes—which, apparently, was already too long for Jeff's limited attention span. "Hey, you guys," he said, "knock it off. Let's either play or not play, but I don't want to just stand here watching you guys fight."

I got off of Chip, stood up, and realized I wasn't hurt. Then a wave of confidence overcame me—it was probably the adrenaline. I began talking some serious shit.

"I don't care!" I said, eyeing Chip warily. "We can keep going or we can play football. I don't care." I knew I was getting out of control. I was starting to sound like my grandfather when his tractor would break down and he'd smash it repeatedly with a hammer.

Chip stood up. His hair was even more unkempt than usual. He glanced quickly at me, then at Jeff, and mumbled, "Yeah, whatever. Let's play."

Say what you will about boys, but one thing we're generally good at is moving on from a conflict. My pop psychology take is that once the punches have been thrown, there's nowhere else to go. So we just started playing football again. Pretty soon a couple more neighborhood guys joined us. There were no problems. We played till dinnertime, then each of us went home. Nothing more was said about the fight. In fact, Chip never pulled any of that stuff on me again. He was still crazier than a shithouse rat, but he didn't pick on me anymore. I discovered that day that sometimes the best response to a bully is to just stand up to them.

I learned something else too. I already knew that Mom was tough, but I'd thought her son was more Chuck E. Cheese than Chuck Norris, a harmless weenie just trying to get through life without getting beat up. Maybe, however—just maybe—some of that maternal grit was in my DNA too.

When it came to parenting, my mom and dad were in lockstep. I guess that explains why when I was ten, my dad taught me almost the exact same lesson about bullies.

Robert "Bob" Riggle grew up in Iowa and Kansas City. He learned early the value of hard work. Dad had his own paper route when he was seven. Then he got a special work permit so he could be a car hop when he was twelve. He was the first in his family to go to college, which—you guessed it—he worked his way through. Dad sold group insurance for the Washington National Insurance Company for thirty years. He was good at his job, and his clients loved him. His colleagues loved him. His assistants loved him. Everybody loves him!

Maybe that was because Dad knows how to treat people. He is a gentle man and a great listener. His manners are outstanding. He is compassionate and patient. Throughout the free world he is known as "Smiling Bob." During my entire life, I've never seen anyone disappointed that Bob has just arrived.

This does not mean that Dad is a pushover. I have rarely seen him angry, but when I did, it scared me to death. All it took was the word *Hey!* in a low tone, and everyone knew things were about to get real. And like Mom, he also believed in standing up to bullies.

In my younger years, every Sunday our family piled into Dad's company car—usually an enormous Buick Regal or Oldsmobile Cutlass—and drove to Country Club Christian Church in Kansas City. Don't let the name fool you—this was a regular church, not a country club. There were no weddings on the tennis courts or baptisms taking place in an Olympic-size pool, though I did have to wear a suit and tie. The deal was that after attending church, my sister, Julie, and I were supposed to go to our separate Sunday school classes while my parents went to the class for adults. If Julie and I were good that morning, we got to go to McDonald's afterward. In those days, that was a huge treat. I'd order a Big Mac, fries, and a Coke, save my food till I got home, and then devour everything while watching *The Lone Ranger* (a lawman fighting injustice) and *The Rat Patrol* (four dudes in jeeps battling the Nazis in

Africa) on TV. Back then, this was as close to heaven as it got for a grade school boy.

On one of those Sundays, however, Dad found out I was skipping Sunday school. A friend of his must have spotted me wandering around the church when I was supposed to be in class and ratted me out. I spent most of each class session hiding in the bathroom.

After church that day, Dad sat me down at our kitchen table. "Why," he asked, "are you not going to Sunday school?"

The problem was another bully I'll call John P. He was a ten-year-old like me, but five inches taller and twenty pounds heavier, with a lot more muscles. For whatever reason, God wanted me to blossom last among every boy I knew. It seemed as though they all went through puberty early and with a vengeance. Everyone was stronger, faster, bigger, and better. Nerds, girls, everyone could take me down in those days.

Like a predator that can smell fear in other animals, I'm sure John P. could sniff out the dread dripping off me. I must have had BFE—big fear energy—because John decided to pick on me. He was always ready with a verbal jab. If I said, "I like Trans Ams," he'd quickly announce, "The Trans Am is a piece of shit car. Only rednecks who obsess about *Smokey and the Bandit* would drive something like that." This would draw laughter from everyone within earshot—he knew how to work a crowd.

John P. was not physically abusive. He just kept hitting me with putdowns. He was sophisticated—think a muscular, ten-year-old James Bond villain in a blue blazer, khakis, and penny loafers. He sorta had it all. He was physically well put together, he was smart, he was articulate, and he was charming. I actually liked him—I just didn't like being in his crosshairs. I felt like a tug boat going up against a battleship. I was outclassed in every way.

Mom's instruction on how to handle bullies didn't seem to fit here. Starting a fight at church felt out of the question, not to mention the fact that he'd beat the crap out of me. The only solution I could come up with was to skip class.

I didn't want to admit any of this to my dad. I was embarrassed and a little angry. Finally, though, my head down and my voice low, the story came out. Dad listened closely to every word, then thought for a moment.

"Rob, I want you to go back to class," he said. "If John says anything to you, I want you to ask him to step outside."

I looked up. "Dad, you're not listening to me," I said. "He's bigger than I am. He's stronger than I am. He'll kick my ass."

Dad shook his head. "I don't care," he said. "You stand up, you ask him to step outside, and you do it in front of everybody in the class. Just be ready. If you go outside and he comes with you, you're going to have to fight him."

"But... Dad," I said. "I don't want to start a fight. I don't want to get in trouble. I don't want to embarrass you and Mom. I don't want to get in trouble with the church. Plus... he's going to beat me up!"

Dad leaned back, a calm expression on his face. "I don't care," he said. "You're going to fight him as hard as you can, and you're going to give it everything you've got. He may win the fight, but he's going to feel it."

This was a revelation to me. I figured that starting a fight—especially at church—was one of the worst things I could do, a move that would bring serious consequences. Yet Dad was giving me the green light.

You would think that scenario would have scared the Happy Meal out of me. But it didn't. Dad had not only just given me permission to stand up for myself; he'd insisted on it. I doubt that I knew the word *empowered* at age ten, but if I had, that's what I would have used to describe how I felt. If I had the freedom to stand up for myself—even fight if necessary—in *church*, I had permission to stand up for myself anytime, anywhere. It was like being handed a lifetime supply of "Get Out of Jail Free" Monopoly cards. My new attitude was "Ready for All, Yielding to None" (the famous motto of the 2nd Marine Battalion, 7th Marines Regiment). I could not wait to go back to Sunday school.

After the church service the following weekend, I was ready. I said a quick "Bye, Dad," hustled off to the classroom, and sat down at a table.

Sure enough, John P., wearing a suit and tie like me, soon sauntered in and sat at another table. I was tempted to jump up and challenge him right then, but even at age ten, I realized that was the wrong move. If we were going to come to blows, I wanted him to be the aggressor. Do you have any idea how difficult it is to be patient when you're a young boy on the verge of battle? Nevertheless, I bided my time. Rather than provoke, I had to be patient and cunning, let him come to me. I was like a samurai warrior, Jedi master, and World Series of Poker champion, all rolled into one.

I didn't have to wait that long. Our teacher, Mr. Comer, told us to look up a Bible verse. A minute or so later, John glanced up from his table and spotted me. He then proceeded to make a smart-ass comment about me that I didn't even completely hear. But it made the other kids at his table laugh.

Booya. That was it. Now was my moment. The trap was sprung.

"What did you say?" I called across the room. The laughter abruptly stopped. Everyone froze.

John smirked. "You heard me," he said. I hadn't actually, but who cared. The game was afoot.

My senses were now on hyperalert. This was fight or flight, just like that dustup in my front yard with Chip. Now, though, it was different. Even though I knew this could go badly, I felt strong and confident. I was almost giddy with anticipation.

"Hey," I said, "if you wanna go, let's step outside." Some of the guys in class, shocked by my audacity, said, "Oooooh." They sensed that Rumble in the Jungle II was about to break out right there in Sunday school.

I'll never forget the look on John P.'s face. His mouth opened, but no words came out. For once, he didn't have a zinger to throw back at me. Then he recovered. "What the hell, Riggle," he said. "Chill out."

"Whatever," I said, doubling down on my challenge, "but I'm not going to listen to your shit anymore."

John shook his head in disbelief. "Whatever, man. Calm down."

At that point, Mr. Comer reasserted some control over his class. "All right, everybody calm down," he said. "Let's get back to the verses."

And that was it. I didn't have to step outside, and I didn't have to throw a single punch. John P. never gave me a hard time again. Much to my surprise, this drama wrapped up faster than an *Afterschool Special* episode. After that day, whenever I was around John P., we acknowledged each other with a nod or even made small talk. We were good. I'd put him on notice that I wasn't going to take any more shit, and I think he respected me for it.

READY FOR ALL, YIELDING TO NONE

—Motto, 2nd Battalion, 7th Marines Regiment

After the service, Dad was very interested to hear about how I'd applied his advice and how things had turned out. But he didn't gloat or say anything like "See, all you have to do to succeed in life is listen to your father."

All he said was "Great. Now you can go to Sunday school."

You might think that after all the great instruction I'd received on bullies by the age of ten, I would have figured out how to avoid fighting for the rest of my childhood. You would have thought wrong.

I was a seventh-grader and had been attending Indian Creek Junior High School for all of three weeks when I got into my next inadvisable altercation. I had just finished lunch and walked into the courtyard to kill a few minutes before my next class. Most of the guys already there were horsing around, giving each other little shoves and burning off energy.

One of the guys doing the shoving was Tony Aguirre, by far the biggest kid in my class. Tony looked more like the Incredible Hulk than a seventh-grader. He must have been at least six-foot-two and two hundred pounds. I think he shaved twice a day. He probably went through puberty in kindergarten. Tony was not a guy you wanted to cross.

Another guy there was a seventh-grader named Brad. He was half of Tony's size, closer to five feet tall and a hundred pounds—about the same as me at the time. I don't know if Brad said something Tony didn't like or if he was just in the wrong place at the wrong time, but Tony suddenly grabbed Brad and slammed him hard against the wall. To me, it looked like more than a playful push. It was a fighting move.

To this day, I don't know why I did it. I didn't even like Brad. But some instinct told me that Tony had crossed a line and that I could do something about it. Without thinking, I jumped between the two of them.

Surprise—Tony didn't like that. This time he gave *me* a hard shove. Suddenly, I was in the middle of a mob of bloodthirsty seventh, eighth, and ninth graders, all chanting "Fight! Fight! Fight!" At that point I started to go into shock. It was like I was starring in my own personal version of *Lord of the Flies*.

Oh my God, I thought. *What is happening here? I have to fight Tony Aguirre?*

To be fair, I don't think Tony was looking for a fight either. But we were surrounded. There was no escape and no way to save face. Tony put up his hands and closed his fists, so I did the same. My eyes must have been big as saucers as I looked up at Tony. It was game on.

The "game" didn't last long. We each threw a few punches. Then Tony uncorked a beauty, a straight jab that got me right in the nose. Blood—*my* blood—spurted everywhere. The crowd started screaming. I didn't know it at the time, but twenty years later, during a physical exam, I learned I had a broken nose. It had to have been from Tony's punch.

Then someone yelled, "Teacher!" As quickly as they'd gathered, the savage mob disbursed. Tony got out of there too. One moment, I was a gladiator in the Roman Coliseum. The next moment, a friend was escorting me alongside the escaping crowd.

What the hell? I thought. *What just happened?*

My hands trembled, but there was so much adrenaline pumping through my body that I didn't even feel the pain in my nose. I was guided into the bathroom, where I checked out my face in the mirror and tried to clean myself up. Despite the mess, I was relieved. I'd stood up for Brad, fought Tony Aguirre, and lived to tell about it. Other than a bloody nose, it seemed I'd survived the incident without any long-term repercussions.

You know how in every horror movie there's a scene where the soon-to-be victim looks in a mirror, sees nothing unusual, turns away for a moment, then looks back and sees the monster in the mirror standing right behind him? That's what happened that day in the bathroom. I was at the sink, cleaning my face. I looked down to pour more water onto a paper towel. I glanced back up at the mirror—and was shocked to see the ominous image of our vice principal just inches away from me.

Rob Winters was the school disciplinarian. I'm sure in his regular, non-school life he was a lovely man. He may have even had a loving family and been involved with his community in a positive way. I'll never know, because to the students of Indian Creek Junior High School, he was the Grim Reaper. He was six feet tall and stocky, with a bushy, jet-black mustache and hairy arms. We would often speculate on what happened to Mr. Winters's victims. We figured he'd stuffed the bleached bones and moldy retainers of troublemaking juveniles into the trunk of his car. The Reaper spent his days wandering the halls, looking for any excuse to torture preteens and young teenagers. If he was talking to you, it was bad news.

Mr. Winters did a sweep of the bathroom with his eyes. He didn't miss the blood all over the sink in front of me. The Grim Reaper put his ice-cold fingers on my shoulder—it was the grip of death. "Are you Mr. Riggle?" he finally asked in a deep voice.

"Yes," I croaked.

"So what's going on, Mr. Riggle?"

"Not much, sir."

"Right," he said. "Tell you what. Why don't we go to my office and talk about not much?"

"Ohhhkay," I managed.

The school rules about fighting were cut and dried—if you fought, you were suspended. *I'm going to the vice principal's office*, I thought. *I'm gonna get suspended! This can't be happening. What am I going to do? What am I going to tell Mom and Dad?* I'd just started junior high, and now I was about to get kicked out. That's when my emotions kicked in. Tears started flowing right there in the bathroom.

I have a hunch that at that point, the Reaper knew he had his man.

I spent the rest of that afternoon in Mr. Winters's office. Tony was there—he'd been fingered too. We both had to explain what happened. With classic 1980s male etiquette, Mr. Winters made us shake hands and apologize. I expected the scholastic death penalty—expulsion from school. Goodbye to my friends and my future. It was all over. I just hoped my folks wouldn't send me to boarding school. However, it wasn't quite that bad. Tony and I were both suspended from classes for the next day. That was it. I still had to go to school, but I spent the day in the principal's office. My homework was even delivered to me.

By the time Mr. Winters released me on the day of the fight, I had calmed down a little but was still in shock. School was out, and all the other kids were sitting on buses in the loading area, waiting to leave. I lived close enough to school to walk home, which took me right past those buses. It seemed like every kid in school had their face pressed up against the windows and was pointing at me and whispering things like "There he is. That's the guy from the fight. He looks mean." I was like an Old West gunslinger who'd lost his showdown with the sheriff and been forced to leave town—unarmed, but still dangerous. Suddenly, I was the bad boy in school, the troublemaker. I imagined the real baddies in school watching me and saying, "You think you're tough? Wait till I get a hold of you." If they only knew that a few minutes earlier, I'd been in Mr. Winters's office, crying like a baby.

To my surprise, my parents were cool about it. Well, Dad was, anyway. Mom wasn't pleased. She taught in the same school district, and I'm sure she thought I had sullied the Riggle name.

When Dad got home, he asked me to come upstairs. He was like Mr. Rogers—he'd come home and change out of his work suit and tie into jeans and a casual shirt. While he changed, I sat in a chair and gave him the whole story. All Dad said was "Yeah, I understand how these things can get out of control. You'll do better next time. Let's go have dinner."

That was it. I wasn't in trouble at home. For the rest of junior high and later, when we were around each other in high school, Tony and I got along fine. I served my one-day suspension at Indian

Creek, and as more kids got to know me, they realized I actually wasn't a wannabe gang leader.

Here's what I learned early in life: Bullies suck. Here's what I learned later in life: Bullies keep showing up in one form or another, and they still suck. It might be scary, but the sooner you confront 'em (if you can do so without getting killed), the better. Kick their ass and keep moving forward.

TWO

Whoops, the Microphone's On

I made an important discovery when I was a kid—I loved making people laugh. Science tells us that laughter releases endorphins, which makes us feel good. Shared laughter creates bonds between people. If you tell a good joke, it's a sign of intelligence. Laughter can even be a predictor of satisfying, long-term relationships.

Of course, I didn't know or care about any of that while growing up. I just knew that it was fun to make fart sounds when someone was giving a speech at school or delivering a lesson to my church youth group. It got my friends to laugh. Fart sounds are funny and always will be.

I think I first discovered the power of laughter at the two-story house Uncle Chuck and my dad were building on Lake of the Ozarks in Missouri. They were of that generation of men who just knew carpentry and masonry and how to build a home from the ground up (I, on the other hand, know how to write a comedy sketch about a masturbating storm chaser—not my best work, but I'll stand by it).

I was five years old when the lake house was finished enough that we started spending chunks of our summers there. It had no TV or telephone. This was way before the internet and cell phones. We had just each other. The result was that we ate every meal together and *talked* to each other. At least, that's what we did when we weren't water skiing, tubing, or swimming at the lake during the day, or playing charades, board games, or cards at night. I remember the adults playing cards for hours, telling stories and laughing so loud that it hurt my ears. Even though I wasn't in on the jokes, it just felt good to be near people who were having such a great time. (I also remember they were so busy playing and laughing that they didn't notice me sneaking Oreos from the kitchen—sorry, Mom!)

It was during those evenings at the lake house that I got my first tastes of show business and comedy. I blame my sister, Julie.

I better say something about Julie here, or she'll beat me up (kidding . . . but I'm sure she could if she wanted to). My sister is five years older than me. She is also smarter and far better looking. She's like my dad, universally loved by everyone who meets her. She graduated law school cum laude. She works full-time; she and her husband have raised three beautiful, well-adjusted daughters; she maintains a beautiful home; she volunteers at school and church; she hosts holiday parties . . . You get the idea. I was saddled with the curse of growing up as Julie Riggle's little brother. Every school year, on the first day of class, teachers would say to me, "Are you related to Julie Riggle?" I'd reluctantly admit, "Yeah, she's my sister." Then the teacher would say, "Julie is amazing! Such a great person, such a great student! I'm expecting big things from you, mister." By the end of the first week, those same teachers figured out they'd better start lowering their expectations.

One day during that first summer at the lake, after I interrupted my dad's work one too many times, I was banished from the construction site and told to "Go play with the girls" (Julie and our cousin Dawn were not excited to see me—don't ask me why). While the girls tried to ignore me, Julie suddenly said, "Hey, let's put on a show! We can do sketches, some jokes, some singing and dancing, entertain everybody, and then we'll pass a hat and get some quarters." It sounded like a great idea for raising money. We could take the change we earned to Dogpatch, an amusement park area at nearby Bagnell Dam, and blow it on arcade games, go-karts, water slides, and ice cream. Even so, I was a reluctant participant. First, as a five-year-old, I had no idea what they were really talking about. Second, I could see by the look in my sister's eyes that she already had diabolical plans for me. Third, we hadn't discussed what my split of the take would be!

Let's be clear about the performance standards for these "shows." We (that is, Julie and Dawn) wrote out a program of silly skits, jokes, and songs, most of it based on whatever church or Girl Scouts camp the girls had just attended. Our rehearsals lasted ten minutes at the most and usually consisted of three children yelling ideas at one another for eight of those minutes. The shows themselves were shorter than the rehearsals, usually performed by the three of us plus any other cousins who happened to be there. Our stage was the concrete dining room floor, while a few feet away, the audience of ten or so parents, aunts, uncles, and friends sat at the dinner table. Julie and Dawn were the stars. My role was more limited.

One Julie-Dawn act featured Julie's voice and Dawn's legs. Julie sat on top of Dawn, with Dawn's upper half and Julie's lower half hidden behind a skirt, so that Dawn's legs appeared to be Julie's legs. While Julie sang, Dawn "danced," complete with cancan kicks. It was so funny, for the performers at least, that Dawn started laughing, then Julie started laughing, then Dawn shouted, "Get up! Get up!" but Julie was laughing too hard to move, and Dawn ended up peeing on the floor, which really cracked up the adults. Comedy gold! It was the equivalent of *SNL* members breaking during a sketch on live TV. It was happening right there in the moment, and it was real. Fifty years later, we're still laughing about it.

After the cancan performance devolved into a puddle of pee, the girls ran from the stage to get Dawn cleaned up and ready for the next act. "Rob!" Julie half-whispered, half-shouted. "Get out there and do something!" She pushed me toward the adults and put on a record, Glen Campbell's "Rhinestone Cowboy."

You might think five-year-old Rob would be intimidated by this moment, but by then I was already a stage veteran. Earlier that summer, I'd danced in that same room in front of the same audience to the Village People's "YMCA." Yes, I spelled out every letter with my arms . . . and yes, I was proud of myself since I'd just learned my ABCs. The "crowd" was into it that day—at first. But I noticed that around the third time through the chorus, people weren't paying as much attention. They'd already seen all my moves. I realized that even my own family didn't want to watch me act out the alphabet through a whole song. I had to give them just a taste and then get out of there. My first lesson in show business: Always quit while you're ahead.

Now more confident because of my vast experience, I presented my enthusiastic dance interpretation of "Rhinestone Cowboy"—which mainly consisted of running in place, doing somersaults, and performing a modified Charleston, all to hoots of laughter. Then, halfway through the song, I bowed and walked off stage. It was so satisfying. I felt like a man who'd finally attained mastery of his craft. The applause was vigorous, appropriate for the dynamic performance the audience had just witnessed . . . in my humble opinion.

I can't say that a light bulb went on over my head during those summertime shows at the lake, that I knew I was destined for a career in comedy. I can say that it was great to make the adults smile and laugh. It felt powerful and fun and scary all at once. For a kindergartner, that was a lot to process, but I knew I loved it.

I might have realized that I enjoyed making an audience laugh, but you would not say that the comedy talent scouts were circling when I entered Indian Creek Junior High. My only stage performance during those years was in a Christmas program at our church. My dad played a shepherd, and I was his son (talk about casting to type). When the spotlight hit us, our job was to point up in amazement at the Star of Bethlehem. I may have oversold it—my mouth gaped, and I probably looked like someone who'd just been jabbed with a cattle prod—but c'mon, this was the Christmas Star!

That was the extent of my theatrical experience during junior high. The truth is, because so many of the guys in my class—not to mention more than a few of the girls—were a foot taller and could bench press me if they wanted to, I lived in fear at Indian Creek. I may have had a few moments of successfully standing up to bullies, but those moments were few and far between. In junior high, I spent most of my time evading situations and people that scared me. Which was almost everything and everyone. I always felt vulnerable to attack, like I might get my head shoved against a locker or into a toilet at any moment. I was a calf on the verge of being culled from the herd.

In ninth grade, however, I discovered a solution to my problem—one that would be highly useful to a future improv comedian, but one that also came with unintended side effects. I developed a razor-sharp tongue. If someone made fun of my size or my braces, I fired back, twice as nasty. Everything was fair game—their weight, their boobs, their clothes, their shoes. And I was good at it!

Julie L. was the first of my classmates to endure my newfound talent. In science class, when I was about to pick up a box full of Bunsen burners, she dryly observed, "Rob's gonna need help lifting that box. It's as big as he is." I hated it when people—especially girls—made fun of my size. Without thinking, I fired back, "At least I can bend down to reach the box. If you tried it with those huge knockers, you'd just tip over!" The group in my immediate vicinity roared with laughter. Julie L. shot me a mean look and it was over . . . and when I say over, I mean she never bothered me again.

The more I turned my acid wit on my obnoxious classmates, the more they kept a wide berth. No one wanted to harass me if they knew I might verbally cut them down at the slightest threat. After years of being Ponyboy, it was great to feel like Two-Bit for a change (sorry, *The Outsiders* was a big part of my life at the time).

Yeah, I was starting to feel pretty good about my life. Then came the fateful Presidents' Day weekend ski trip.

We were on a Greyhound bus, making the twelve-hour drive to Colorado's Breckenridge Ski Resort. Most of the students were playing cards, listening to music on their Walkman, or making out in the back. I was talking with a friend, Kim Hay, about a girl I liked. That's when she dropped a bomb on me.

"Rob, you probably need to know this," she said, lowering her voice. "Everybody hates you."

"What?" I said. "What are you talking about?"

"Yeah," Kim said, "a lot of people are pissed at you."

"What do you mean? Why would anybody be pissed at me? I'm nice to everybody."

"Oh my God, no, you aren't."

"What are you talking about?" I said again. I couldn't believe what I was hearing. "Give me an example."

"Remember that time in science class? You said Lisa was so fat, her dress size should be zeppelin."

I vaguely remembered being mad at Lisa for something she said to me and saying something back. "Yeah," I said, "I guess. But I was just kidding around."

"Well, Lisa was humiliated. Then she was mad. All the girls supported Lisa and hated you."

I was shocked. But over the next few weeks, my prepubescent brain began to connect some dots. *Oh, man*, I thought. *My words have a real effect on people. I'm putting some poisonous seeds out there.* After my cutting comments, all I'd heard and seen were the laughter and smiles by the kids within earshot. I hadn't noticed the embarrassed looks and hurt feelings suffered by my targets.

This was not good. All I was trying to do was keep the bullies from hurting me first. Instead, I had turned into a kind of bully myself.

Yeah, I'll admit it—I can be an idiot. But idiots can change. I'm living proof. For the rest of that school year, I made a focused effort to be nice to everyone at school—especially the girls. Girls had become very interesting to me by that point. I thought I might even want a girlfriend someday—which would be much easier to accomplish if all the girls at school didn't hate me. So, I decided I would not say anything mean-spirited, would not say a word that would embarrass anyone. Well, except for the dirtbags who were my best friends—those guys deserved to be harassed.

I started greeting people in the hallway with "Hey!" or "What's up?" If I saw an athlete, I said, "Hey, great game last night." It was humbling and led to some strange looks at first. But the more I put out positive comments—and the more I kept my mouth shut when I was tempted to snap back at someone (and there were ample opportunities, because junior high kids are shitty)—the more my classmates warmed to me. It was the first time in my life that I'd worked on improving my personality. As an athlete, I'd worked on my skills in football and basketball. But this was my first attempt at trying to become a better *person*.

Don't get me wrong, I didn't suddenly turn into Mother Teresa—as evidenced by my argument with Mike B., a fat asshole I didn't like who didn't care much for me either. One day before class, he announced, "Let me guess, Riggle, you didn't do your homework again? Ya fucking idiot." To which I responded, "Shut the fuck up, fat ass, before I fuck the fat rolls in the back of your fat neck." So original. Sorry, Mike.

Still, for the most part, I was a new man (or ninth grader, anyway). And people were noticing. Near the end of the school year, during a short break between classes, I was enjoying the smell of Pine-Sol in the hallway and retrieving a notebook from my locker when Kim walked up and leaned close.

"So, Rob," she whispered in her most gossipy voice, "I hear that Laura likes you."

Of course I tried to play it cool. "Oh, yeah?" I said. "That's interesting." On the inside, however, I was doing backflips. *Yes!* I thought. *A girl likes me! My positive approach is actually working!*

I learned a valuable lesson that year—life gets better when you're kind to others, when you start with a smile and try to lift people up and make them laugh rather than try to tear them down. I'm grateful I figured that out in ninth grade. Some people never do.

High school. Yeah, that was a different story. Thankfully.

That summer between junior high and high school, puberty finally took hold of one Robert Riggle, and once it corralled me, it didn't let go. I grew five inches over those three months. I added weight and muscle. My braces came off. My lopsided face settled into its form and started resembling the look of a male human being. Oh, and I finally got a decent haircut.

When I walked onto the campus of Shawnee Mission South High School for the first time, casual friends I hadn't seen all summer didn't even recognize me. They did a double take, tilted their head up at me, and guessed, "Riggle?" I was no longer the runt of the litter. It was great.

Thanks to my new-and-improved personality and Zeus-like body, I finally felt the confidence and freedom to just have fun, be a goofball, and entertain myself and my friends. Comedy films and laughing with my buddies were my bliss. By this time, I was really beginning to appreciate comedy. Just like some guys worshipped Van Halen or Metallica, I raised my hands for Eddie Murphy, Bill Murray, and Sam Kinison. I had already bought, loved, and memorized George Carlin's album *A Place for My Stuff* (he did a bit about selling a wheelchair and made it sound like he was selling a Trans Am—it always cracked me up). I'd watched and loved Eddie Murphy's stand-up special, *Delirious*. I'd seen and laughed at every eighties comedy ever made. My buddies and I would repeat lines from the movies, like "This is the worst-looking hat I ever saw . . . oh, it looks good on you, though!" Or if we were ordering steak in a restaurant, one of us would say to our waiter, "Tell the cook this is low-grade dog food," and then someone would add, "This steak still has marks where the jockey was hittin' it!" (If you saw Rodney Dangerfield in *Caddyshack*, you know what I'm talking about.) Every now and then, the waiter would recognize our reference and laugh along with us, but for the most part we just annoyed the shit out of people.

My favorite place to play, however, was in the school's radio booth. During my sophomore year, I successfully auditioned for the radio and television class for juniors and seniors. Once every month or two, we did a TV news show that aired on a local access channel. We also had this radio booth, which was basically a tricked-out closet with a pair of turntables, a mixing board, and two microphones. We didn't actually broadcast anything off campus. But at lunchtime, I and whoever my partner was that day acted as disc jockeys while spinning records that played on speakers throughout the cafeteria. We had a captive audience of about five hundred students and faculty.

Our teacher was Ms. McNamara. She seemed ancient compared to us but was probably in her late twenties. She was thin and wore a blouse, skirt, and heels every day. Ms. McNamara listened to our daily lunchtime show while in the cafeteria. Fortunately, she always warned us ahead of time if she was grading our performance that day. If she was, we'd keep it straight and do our best. But if she wasn't . . .

Record stores used to donate their throwaway albums to the high school, the stuff no one would buy. One day in the booth I picked up one of those albums. It featured one of the most obnoxious-looking hair-metal bands I'd ever seen, a group called Helloween. The stupid name and ridiculous glam pictures of guys with big hair and heavy makeup instantly put them in my crosshairs.

Soon I had a Helloween song blaring over the cafeteria speakers. I imagined everybody eating lunch in the cafeteria, frowning, plugging their ears, and saying to each other, "What *is* this shit?"

"Hey," I said into the microphone as soon as the song ended, "I know you guys have been dying to hear Helloween. Not only are we going to play more Helloween but, and you're not going to believe this, I've got Helloween on the phone right now! Let me introduce you to Ingo, the band's drummer."

"I'm not Ingo, mate, I'm Kai!" said a voice in a British accent.

Yeah, nobody was on the phone. The other voice was also me. I was interviewing myself. I thought the guys in the band looked Dutch, though I found out later they were German. But the only accent I could do was British, so on this day everyone in Helloween sounded like they were from London.

"Sorry, man!" I said. "So, everybody, I'm with Kai from Helloween. Kai, we are here listening to your latest album and everybody at school is just loving it. Can you tell us where the inspiration for the song 'Reptile' came from?"

"Yeah, mate," said "Kai" in that British accent, "it's a great song, it's about a lizard, y'know?" And on it went.

As DJ, one of my required roles for each show was to read the daily announcements, riveting news like "Don't forget that there's an ice cream social tomorrow" or "Let's all attend the girls' volleyball game Thursday and root them on as they try for an undefeated season." On the back of the announcements sheet would be a list of the day's faculty absences, titled in all caps with the phrase DO NOT READ. Think about that for a moment. You're handing a piece of paper to a creative, slightly rebellious, knucklehead high schooler—in this case, me—and providing him with juicy details that the people in authority say he is *not* supposed to read on the air. Just what do you think is going to happen?

"Well," I said into the mic one day in early April after reading the announcements and flipping to the back page, "it looks like Mr. Mentzer, everyone's favorite geometry teacher, decided not to come into work today. What do you all think he's doing? Hm, it *is* opening day for the Kansas City Royals. Any chance that Mr. Mentzer is out at Royals Stadium today? I'm willing to bet *yes*."

Jeff Robbins was my DJ partner that day and is still one of my closest friends. I first ran into Jeff while playing football in fifth grade. He is logical, wise, a great salesman, and one of the funniest guys I've ever met. To this day, he prank calls me, always in character, by leaving long messages that start with something like, "Hello, I'm part of a men's masturbation club, and your name came up as a perfect candidate for membership . . ." Jeff is always up for a little mischief, which I love.

In the high school radio booth, Jeff responded to my speculations about Mr. Mentzer with one of his own: "Personally, I think Mr. Mentzer has a hangover."

"What?" I said. "No, no, you can't say that, he's not a drinker. I think he's at the stadium. Of course, it *is* nice outside. He could be fishing. Anybody else out there have a theory? If you do, come on down to the booth here at KSMS and let us know."

Ms. McNamara was not pleased. She burst into the booth, her words spraying like machine-gun fire. "Seriously, guys, I've already reminded you about this!" she said. "Somebody get me the announcements." I handed the page to her. Ms. McNamara flipped the paper over and practically thrust it in my face. "What does it say right here?" She pointed to the paper. "Right here at the top? What does that say, Riggle?"

As softly and innocently as possible, I answered: "It says, 'Do Not Read.'"

"And yet you did read it, didn't you? You big dummy. It's very simple. Where it says, 'Do Not Read,' everything underneath that—do not read!"

As always, we told Ms. McNamara it was an honest mistake. We apologized and promised to never do that again. A promise we kept . . . for about two weeks.

The radio class was one of my first chances to explore my creative comedy instincts in front of an audience. It's where I began to hit my comedy stride. For example, I loved to play a game I called Whoops, the Microphone's On. One day, I was in the booth and said into the mic, "Hey you guys, don't forget the football game tonight. And speaking of that, you know what gets people in the mood for football? How about some AC/DC with 'Back in Black'?" I got the song playing on the turntable, then "accidentally" turned the mic volume up to ten. Soon, everyone in the cafeteria heard my voice blasting through the speakers, drowning out Angus Young's guitar riffs: "Whew, glad that shit's over with. I gotta take a huge fucking dump! Oh my God, Ms. McNamara has been busting my balls lately."

A few seconds later, we heard the sound of Ms. McNamara's heels clicking like popping popcorn kernels against the linoleum as she raced down the hall in our direction, screaming all the while, "The microphone's on! The microphone's on!" The door to the booth flew open. Ms. McNamara, gasping and wheezing from her record-breaking sprint, sputtered, "Guys, the microphone's on!"

"What?" I said as Jeff and I put on our most innocent faces. "What?" I looked at the mixing board. "Oh my God, the master volume's up!" I turned it down.

"Guys," Ms. McNamara said between deep breaths, "you have to be more careful. I heard everything you were saying and it was *not* nice."

"Ms. McNamara, I'm so sorry," I said. "I don't know what happened." Jeff also apologized.

"Just keep the master volume at three," Ms. McNamara said. "And pay attention to what you're doing, okay?" We promised to be more careful.

Yet the next week, somehow, the same thing happened again. And the week after that . . . and after that. Ms. McNamara never seemed to catch on. We did wear her down—her panicked hallway yelps transformed into lowkey, incoherent rants. Looking back, I feel bad for Ms. McNamara. We tortured that poor woman. She never knew what was coming next. She always smelled like cigarettes—no doubt she was stress smoking. We exhausted her every single day. I hope today she's not sitting in a nursing home somewhere, a cigarette dangling from her lips, thinking, *I could have had a life if it wasn't for those damn kids.*

Ms. McNamara may not have enjoyed our antics, but the cafeteria crowd loved them. They looked forward to our little games every week. I was told they were the lunchtime highlight of the year for the senior class. It's probably one of the reasons I was voted "most humorous" in my class at the end of high school. I wasn't the class clown, mind you. Those guys are jerks who interrupt class and need constant attention. I just liked entertaining people—starting with myself.

THREE

Grave Hunting with Grammy

You could say that military service is in my genes. Mom's father, Fred Shrout, was a staff sergeant in the 8th Army Air Corps in World War II. Uncle Dick, my dad's twin, served in the Army during Vietnam. I had ancestors who fought in the Civil War. My dad even discovered that an ancestor named Michael Riggle was a private on the payroll of the Continental Army at the beginning of the American Revolution. So my great-great-something-or-other was at Valley Forge, shivering along with the rest of George Washington's troops, during the long, cold winter of 1777–1778.

Dad tried to serve too. He put his name in for the draft during the early days of the Vietnam War, but he kept getting deferred. First it was because he was in college. Then it was because he was married with a job. Then it was because he was married with a job and a child. He never was called to serve, but he always said, "I'm ready to go." I grew up understanding that military service was a proud tradition in our family and an honorable thing to do.

The event that really ignited my interest in my family's military history, though, occurred during spring break when I was in ninth grade. That was when I went grave hunting with Grammy.

It wasn't as macabre as it sounds. Grammy—my grandmother on my mom's side—wanted to get into the Daughters of the American Revolution. To do that, she needed proof of a relative who'd fought in the war. She'd run across a reference to a potential relative with the last name Kelly who'd been a Minuteman, part of the colonial militia in North Carolina (I knew what a Minuteman was because the NFL's New England Patriots had one as the logo on their helmets). Now Grammy needed to do more research to confirm her theory—and she had a particular grandchild in mind to assist her.

As spring break approached, I knew nothing about my grandmother's plot. I was looking forward to sleeping in, hanging with my friends, taking in the latest movies, and playing the video game Galaga at the arcade. (Yes, I said arcade. Those were super cool in the eighties. Don't judge me.) Then Mom dropped the bomb: "Rob, you're coming with me and Grammy for spring break. We're driving to Kentucky. We're going on a genealogy hunt."

Genealogy? I thought. *Isn't that the study of rocks? Or some flat-earth conspiracy theory?*

Who cared? Either way, my vacation plans had just been crushed. All I said, though, was "Mom, seriously?" Again, this was the eighties. Kids back then were actually expected to do what their parents told them. I knew I didn't have a vote.

At least I was allowed to bring a friend with me. Bill Konen was and is one of my oldest friends. We share the same twisted sense of humor. Bill also laughs like Eddie Murphy in *Beverly Hills Cop*—long and drawn out, like a honking goose—which is hilarious and contagious. You could be listening to a sermon at church, and if Bill started that laugh, it would be impossible not to join in. It was easy to get Bill to come on the trip. His choices (as I described them to him) were to hang around Oak Park Mall for another cold, gray Kansas spring break . . . or to explore the wonders of the bluegrass state, land of the Kentucky Derby and Fort Knox, where every citizen is required by law to bathe or shower at least once a year (That's actually true!).

On the Monday of that spring break, the four of us piled into Grammy's white Cadillac Eldorado. That Caddy was huge and high class, with red leather interior. If there was such a thing as a two-door limousine, it was the Eldorado. Mom drove. Grammy smoked. Her cigarette of choice was Vantage menthols, and she had one lit up the entire trip. Bill and I sat in the back seat, trying not to cough, barely visible to each other through the gray cloud.

This was in the days before computers and family histories that could be accessed with a few clicks on a keyboard. At our first stop, Lexington, Grammy did more genealogy research at a library. Then we were off to a local cemetery, where Grammy directed us to the proper section.

When the car stopped moving, it was our cue. Bill and I stumbled out of the Eldorado, which had so much smoke streaming from the open doors, it looked like an oversized slow cooker at a barbecue joint. Freezing rain fell from the sky, but we paid no attention. We gulped fresh air like scuba divers who'd run out of oxygen and breached the surface just in the nick of time.

When I recovered enough to breathe normally, I glanced at the car. Grammy was frowning at me and pointing toward the graves. Time to get to work. Bill took one section and I took another. Through the pouring rain, we weaved among the headstones, scanning the names. "We're looking for John Kelly," I reminded Bill.

"There's a John McCormick over here," Bill called back.

"That doesn't help!"

Finally, I did find the guy on Grammy's list. Since none of us had a cell phone in those days, we had to rely on more primitive methods to record our findings. From a bag I carried, I pulled out materials to make a grave rubbing of the headstone with wax paper.

Our mission complete and our bodies going numb from the cold and rain, we returned to the Eldorado smoke pit.

"Give me the paper! Give me the paper!" Grammy snapped as soon as I slid into the car. I extended the wax paper to her in a shivering blue hand, wondering if frostbite had already set in. Grammy snatched it and examined it closely. Her lack of concern for her foot soldiers was concerning. Apparently, our efforts passed muster, because we were soon on our way to another section of the cemetery.

That five-day road trip to Kentucky wasn't exactly my dream vacation. I became far more familiar with the cemeteries in Lexington and Frankfurt than any ninth grader should ever be. In truth, though, the trip wasn't so bad. Bill and I had a room to ourselves at the Holiday Inn Holidomes where we stayed. We swam, played pool, and generally ran amok. One day we were even allowed to get in a round of golf on a local course while Grammy did more library research. I'd just started golfing and had fallen in love with the sport. Bill wasn't a golfer at all, but he still played with me. It probably helped that he had nowhere else to go. It was either the golf course or Grammy's smoke chamber.

More important than refining my golf game, though, was that Grammy and the genealogy hunt in Kentucky inspired my interest in history—our family's background, military history, and history in general. Whether they're funny, dramatic, or tear-jerkers, I've always loved stories. When I learned I had a relative named Kelly who'd been a Minuteman, I thought, *We've got a touch of Irish in our family—how fun is that? I wonder what his story was? I bet he was a farmer who kept his musket on the porch, so whenever a rider showed up, Paul Revere style, and yelled, "The British are coming!" he dropped what he was doing, grabbed his musket, and went off to fight the British.* This wasn't like reading a textbook. I was picturing something close to what had really happened to someone from my family's history. This wasn't just Kelly's story—it was my story too.

Today, I read military books, world history books, leadership books, biographies, autobiographies, battlefield histories—everything I can get my hands on. The one book I have read twice in my life is David McCullough's *1776*. Some people are nerds about Dungeons and Dragons or chess. I'm a history nerd. If I had a full week to myself, I would spend it in Gettysburg, Pennsylvania. Every morning I'd get on my bike and ride all over the Civil War battlefield, doing my own study of that conflict. To me, that's about as fun as it gets.

As a kid, I was already a big fan of the TV show *The Rat Patrol*. I'd seen and loved John Wayne in *The Sands of Iwo Jima* and Bill Murray in *Stripes* (each heroic in his own way). During high school, I would take in darker and more realistic interpretations of military life in movies like *Platoon* and *Full Metal Jacket*.

While watching war movies, I was always impressed by the sacrifice demonstrated by the sailors, Marines, soldiers, and airmen. I admired their courage and their commitment. These people risked everything for their country.

It was during those teenage years that I began to think about what being an American citizen meant to *me*. I already felt a measure of pride when I said the Pledge of Allegiance at school each morning or took my hat off and sang the national anthem before a game. My parents explained how lucky we were to live in America, that so many in the world didn't have the freedoms we did. At school, I learned more about other nations, places with brutal dictators and terrible poverty. I realized that compared to the rest of the world, America kicked ass in every way possible. Freedom of religion, freedom of speech, freedom of the press, the right to bear arms were all just the start. As an American, you could choose where and how you wanted to live. You could criticize the powerful. You could pursue your dreams. You even had the freedom to breakdance as an uncoordinated white guy!

Since I grew up during the Cold War, the threat of the Soviets launching nukes to wipe us out was always in the back of my mind. We had annual drills at Trailwood Elementary on what to do in case of nuclear attack—get away from the windows, walk down to the basement, and sit in the hallway with our heads between our legs (I'm not sure how much good that would do during a real attack, but at least the drills got us out of solving math problems). Nearly every news broadcast, movie, TV show, or pop song referenced the tension of the time. *The Day After*, a movie portraying a nuclear exchange between America and the Soviets, was set primarily in Lawrence, Kansas, just a short drive from my house.

It was scary stuff. But my thinking began to shift a couple of months before I turned ten, when I watched the broadcasts of the Olympics at Lake Placid, New York. The US hockey team—made up of college players—took on the Soviet Union, a team of professionals who'd won the last four gold medals. Like just about everybody, I was prepared to be disappointed—I didn't think our college guys had a chance. But to the shock of everyone, the US won the game, 4–3, in one of the biggest upsets in sports history. I chanted "USA!" right along with the crowd on TV. I loved it.

All right, I thought. *We're gonna be okay.* My ten-year-old mind decided that if a bunch of our amateurs could beat the Soviets at their own game, maybe they wouldn't be able to destroy us with bombs after all.

If you consider that I grew up in the eighties . . . during the Reagan era . . . in Kansas . . . maybe it's not a big surprise that I became a patriot. Even as a kid in the seventies, I noticed that everyone seemed depressed about Vietnam. But in the eighties, the economy got better, gas lines disappeared, and people started to realize that Vietnam vets had served their country with honor. It just felt cool again to be an American. Even the movies were better and often funnier—you can't beat comedy classics like *The Blues Brothers*, *Beverly Hills Cop*, *Stripes*, *Caddyshack*, and *Ghostbusters*!

The more I learned about America's strengths, the more I felt like, *Yeah, we're doing this right.* Of course, as I got older, I began to see that our country has flaws too. Even so, I believed as a teenager—and still do today—that we're the best thing going on this planet. Generally speaking, you don't see Americans flocking to the borders, trying to escape. It's the other way around. In oppressed nations around the world, America is still the place that people dream of calling home, that they will risk their lives to get to. The US and its freedoms remain a symbol of hope to billions.

Ronald Reagan once said, "Freedom is a fragile thing and it's never more than one generation away from extinction." I agree. I feel each generation has a responsibility to safeguard the freedoms we have and not let America turn to socialism or a dictatorship. As a teenager, I wouldn't have been able to put it in those words. I was lucky to put three intelligible sentences together. But still, I had a sense of it.

Did my family's history and my growing feelings of patriotism make me think of joining the military myself? Sure, it was in the back of my mind as an option. I liked the idea of serving my country. Given my family background, I was sure my parents would support me if I wanted that. But in high school, I wasn't ready to think that far ahead. I was on cruise control. My focus was on getting along with my girlfriend, having fun with my buddies, playing sports, making life miserable for Ms. McNamara, and getting good enough grades to graduate. I just wasn't thinking about my future.

But that was about to change.

FOUR

What Do I Wanna Be When I Grow Up? (Just Kidding, I'll Never Grow Up)

My mom went to college at the University of Kansas. My sister went there too. Most of my high school class, including my girlfriend and all my friends, were going there. The idea that I'd become a Kansas Jayhawk after high school always seemed like a foregone conclusion. And that was fine with me. I loved KU.

I'd visited my sister at her sorority several times and liked the picturesque old buildings on campus. The university sat atop mighty Mount Oread, altitude one thousand feet (in Kansas, anything over a hundred feet is a big deal). As a bonus, KU had a ton of beautiful girls and a great basketball team. Lawrence was forty-plus miles away from Overland Park—close to home, but not so close that Mom and Dad could easily check up on me. The perfect scenario.

Of course, I had no idea what I wanted to do with my life. Does anyone when they're eighteen? But during the summer between high school and college, I realized it was time to start figuring it out. My motivation arrived courtesy of the Pioneer Container Corporation.

Granddad (my mom's dad) believed that getting a taste of the hard life would be good for my sister and me. He had a friend who ran a bag factory down by the river in Kansas City, Missouri. Julie was the first to go. She lucked out—she spent her bag factory summer in the admin department doing clerical work. The summer after I turned eighteen, however, I was assigned to work on the factory floor. My job was to load and unload pallets full of huge bundles of bags designed to contain feed, grain, and dog food. The pay was minimum wage. In 1988, that was $3.65 an hour, which bumped up to a whopping $4.10 an hour if—and only if—you put in forty hours that week. Not thirty-nine and a half; it had to be a full forty. It was grueling work, especially on those hot and humid summer afternoons. If it was 100 degrees outside, it was 130 degrees inside the truck trailers that delivered those pallets.

My coworkers were the strangest, scariest, and goofiest bunch of characters I'd encountered in my life. They were like the cast from *The Longest Yard*. Vernell, five-foot-ten and muscular, was quiet. He was on a work release program from prison. He was in for murder. Duane, six-foot-two and sporting a scraggly beard, was more talkative, the salesman of the group. He'd been in a gang called the Money Dogs and did fourteen months' time for forgery. He'd also done what he called "some light pimping"—a hobby, apparently. Jimmy was an eighteen-year-old high school dropout who smoked weed every chance he got. Luther showed up every morning wearing an Adidas sweat suit and a wrist purse. He'd punch his card in the time clock at the beginning of the day, then disappear into the labyrinth of the warehouse. We never saw him again until quitting time, when he mysteriously reappeared, punched out, and went home.

Then there was Danny, a Vietnam vet with no teeth. Danny would freak out every now and then. He'd scream, stomp his feet, and then run off into the warehouse. Sometimes he'd come back before the end of the day, sometimes not.

One day some of us were wrapping and securing bags on a pallet to prepare it for shipping. Danny, who was supposed to be helping, was missing. Without notice, he emerged from the shadows, walked by us without saying a word, and grabbed a heavy metal grain shovel that had been leaning against the wall. For reasons known only to Danny, he started spinning in place, holding the shovel out with his arms extended like he was a hammer thrower at a track meet. His form was impressive.

I watched this unexpected development from about twenty feet away. *What the fuck is he doing?* I thought. *Is he trying out for the Olympics? Is he trying to make himself puke?*

In mid-twirl, Danny let the shovel go. It soared through the air, past us, and into the warehouse, landing with a *Cling! Clang! Ding!* as it bounced along the concrete floor. Danny screamed, "Mrrrauuuuuuugh!" Then he walked away without moving his arms, as if he were Arnold Schwarzenegger in *The Terminator.* It was confusing and somewhat terrifying. Needless to say, we didn't see Danny again till he punched his time card at the end of the day.

Danny's unpredictable behavior fit right in with the rest of these characters. I felt like I was surrounded by a pack of wild dogs that could turn vicious at the drop of a shovel.

That was the crew at the bag factory.

Our foreman, Gary, was a big, doughy guy with thick glasses who always walked on the instep of his orthopedic shoes. Partly because of his oafish appearance, no one in our crew respected him—not even Gary himself. The other reason Gary got no respect was that some of the guys wanted to get fired so they could stop working and collect unemployment. Whenever Gary tried to make us do something, the crew either told him to go smoke a turd in hell or paid no attention.

Except me. Since I was the one guy who still respected authority, I didn't challenge Gary. The result was that I didn't really fit in with the rest of the crew. Making friends at the bag factory proved tougher than I'd imagined. On our daily thirty-minute lunch breaks, the rest of the guys would take off somewhere, and I'd sit by myself on top of a pallet with my little Playmate cooler and down my Diet Coke, sandwich with the crust cut off, apple, and Oreos. Good times!

Then one day late in the summer, Duane's car wouldn't start. I was just about to pull out of the parking lot when Duane applied his salesmanship skills and talked me into giving him a ride home. On the way, naturally, he wanted to make a "quick stop" at this other apartment. To borrow five bucks? To talk to his bookie? To arrange a hit? Who knew? I didn't, and I didn't want to. But I pulled into the apartment complex parking lot anyway and watched Duane from the car. He knocked on an apartment door. He knocked some more. The door cracked open. He had a brief conversation on the steps with whoever was inside, which involved much waving of arms and ended with a "Fuck you!" Then Duane returned to my car, scowling.

"That asshole won't open the door 'cause he thinks you're a narc," Duane said when he sat down.

I laughed.

"Don't worry," Duane said, "I know you're not a cop." He stared out the window a moment, then glanced at me. "You're not a cop, right?"

"No, Duane. I'm eighteen years old. I'm just a guy working for the summer at a bag factory."

"That's what I thought," Duane said, nodding his head. "That's what I thought."

That broke the ice. The next day at lunchtime, when I grabbed my cooler and headed for my usual spot, Duane saw me. "Hey, man, we're going out for lunch," he said. "Come with us."

Out for lunch? Where could these guys possibly go for lunch? There were no restaurants for miles. This sounded insane to me, especially since we only had thirty minutes, and if we took too long, we'd fall short of our forty hours for the week and lose our eighteen-dollar bonus. (Eighteen dollars in today's money is $10,486. I didn't check my math, but I'm sure that's right.)

This is a terrible idea, I thought. *We're going to get back late, we're going to clock in after lunch late, and we're all going to get fucked out of our bonus. How stupid can you all be? I'm a kid just out of high school, and I know this is a bad idea.*

And yet . . . they had graciously invited me to join them. At last, I had a chance to make some work friends! I wanted to be part of the gang. If they were reaching out, I had to at least meet them halfway, right? Why it mattered to me to be in with that group of knuckleheads is a question I can't answer. I guess there are times when you just gotta play hooky with the boys. So instead of listening to my doubts or telling Duane what was going through my head, I said, "Lunch? Sure."

I followed the guys into the parking lot and saw them head for a beat-up, two-door '77 Mustang—not the big, badass Mustang from those years, but the little four-cylinder job they used to drive in *Charlie's Angels.* Jimmy got behind the wheel. Vernell called shotgun. Duane, Danny, and I ended up in the back, with me somehow stuck sitting with my cooler on the hump over the drive shaft. The five of us were packed into that little Mustang like the dudes jammed into the Durango 95 in *A Clockwork Orange* (yeah, pretty much everything reminds me of a TV show or movie from the seventies or eighties).

As soon as the doors shut, someone shouted, "Let's go!" Jimmy backed up, then laid rubber as we hauled ass down an industrial access road. We must have been going a hundred miles an hour as we flew over the beer cans and broken glass that littered the pavement.

I'm dead, I thought. *I'm going to die with these idiots from the bag factory. What a stupid way to go.*

Four minutes later, we fishtailed to a stop in front of a liquor store. Like an Indy 500 pit crew springing into action, everybody jumped out of the car, leaving the doors open, and ran inside—everybody, that is, but me. The wild intensity in their eyes had all the earmarks of trouble, so I decided it was wise to stay in the car. The tires hadn't even had a chance to cool before the guys were rushing out of the store and back into the car. I was relieved when they came out with smiles on their faces and nothing but beer and liquor in their arms.

Duane divided the spoils by ripping a pair of twelve-packs in half. Each guy—again, except for me—ended up with a six-pack of Old Milwaukee beer and a half pint of Seagram's Extra Dry Gin, which they began consuming immediately and with gusto. Jimmy burned rubber back to the factory, at least as fast as before, and we sat in the parking lot. To my utter amazement, we were still alive and still had twenty minutes of lunch break left. Those remaining twenty minutes weren't wasted. Each of the guys drained every can of their beer and all the gin.

Truly, it was phenomenal what these ne'er-do-wells had just accomplished in thirty minutes. Some mornings, it took me thirty minutes just to brush my teeth, but these guys had completed a road trip and three nights' worth of drinking. It just shows what a little motivation can do.

As I punched back in for work, another realization hit me. *This explains it*, I thought. *I've cracked the code!* Every morning, my crew was the surliest, meanest bunch of hombres this side of the Mississippi. But every afternoon, they laughed and gave each other shit as if they didn't have a care in the world. Because of my teenage naïveté, I'd never understood it—till now.

It also explained why Duane appeared to be trying to kill me. In the mornings, whenever Duane drove the forklift, he was meticulous, as if the cops were watching his every move. But when he maneuvered that forklift in the afternoons, it was a different story. He was a maniac. I'd be in a semitruck trailer, waiting for Duane to drop pallets. He'd come roaring at the trailer like he was in a demolition derby and dump a pallet weighing a few thousand pounds at my feet, nearly crushing me every time. If I hadn't kept my head on a swivel, I have no doubt I'd be dead today. *Of course*, I thought at the end of our high-speed liquor run that day. *Duane's not trying to kill me. He's just drunk out of his mind.* It put my mind at ease knowing it wasn't personal. It didn't make me any safer from Duane, but at least I finally knew what was going on.

Now that I think about it, though, the real brains of that group was probably Luther. One day I was deep in the warehouse, trying to find some pallets I was supposed to load, when I came across him. He was racked out in a hammock made out of factory bags that was strung between a couple of stacks of pallets—fast asleep. *This* was where he went every day. If anyone ever did a "Where are they now?" piece about my crew at the bag factory, I bet they'd find out Luther was a company CEO. He'd figured out how to make money while he slept—this guy was a natural entrepreneur!

Needless to say, by the time that summer ended, my appreciation for the value of higher education had risen dramatically. Even though I'd already planned on getting my college degree and having a career, now there was no doubt. *No way*, I thought, *do I want to spend the rest of my life working in a bag factory.* For that motivational kick in the ass, I owe a big thank-you to my grandfather, along with Duane, Jimmy, Danny, Luther, and the rest of the crew at the Pioneer Container Corporation.

I'd done it. I'd set a firm goal—I would graduate from college. But I still had no idea what I'd do after that. The concept of planning a future was sinking very gradually into my (maturing?) teenage brain.

As a freshman at KU, I had to declare a major. Since the TV show *L.A. Law* was hugely popular at the time and since my sister was an attorney, I thought, *How about becoming a lawyer? They make good money. If my sister can do it, why can't I?* It helped that I was interested in politics, and political science was a prerequisite for a law degree. I declared as a poli-sci major. But after falling asleep while reading several poli-sci books, I knew I had to be honest with myself—I wasn't going to practice law. The academic requirements for a law degree were incredibly tough, and I was not what you'd call a model student.

One other lesson I learned from the bag factory crew and their crazy lunch breaks: Life is short, so you gotta embrace the moments you get. They lived for those beer and liquor runs. I believed in the value of hard work, but I also wanted a good work/play balance. Mind you, I already knew how to have a good time, but now I was even more ready to embrace my moments. You know how every dude says he was a "wild man," the "party guy," back in college? He wasn't. He was a nerd. *I* was the wild man. (To my kids if you're reading this: Not true. I was always studying at the library, pursuing academic excellence. To everyone else reading this: Yeah, I partied well and had a blast. They were the best four years of my life.)

Sadly, however, campus parties and games of beer pong do not pay for a mortgage. It seemed I needed to come up with another plan for my life.

Early in my sophomore year, I thought, *How about the FBI? That sounds exciting. Those guys are always catching spies and investigating kidnappings and bank robberies.* I liked the idea of being one of the good guys and protecting society. I also liked the way "Rob Riggle, FBI agent" rolled off the tongue.

One day I called the FBI field office in Kansas City. They were nice enough to connect me with a special agent. I introduced myself and asked what it took to become an agent.

"Well, are you an accountant or lawyer?" he asked. "We really love those guys."

"Nope."

"Any chance you'll become one?"

"I doubt it," I said, thinking of my grades. To me, writing a paragraph, let alone a paper, was like extracting teeth. "Is there any other way to become an agent?"

He paused. "You know, we really like Marine Corps officers."

"Oh, really," I said. "That's interesting."

I didn't know it at the time, but that short phone conversation with a G-man I'd never met in person would change my life.

As I pondered my family's military experiences and my own fascination with the military and military history, the thought of becoming a Marine started growing on me. After all, I loved my country. Plus, I was strong physically, and thanks to lots of practice with a .22 on my grandpa's farm, I could shoot the ears off a frog at a hundred yards.

The few. The proud. The Marines. *Could I be one of those guys?*

At KU, I was a member of the Phi Gamma Delta fraternity—a Fiji. Two of my older fraternity brothers there were in the Marine Corps officer program. When I asked them about the Marines, they encouraged me to talk with their recruiter. Marine Corps recruiters are the best in the business. They could sell barbecue ribs to a woman in white gloves. This guy sized me up and said, "Rob, the Marines will make you a stronger man physically and mentally. They will challenge you. They will push you beyond your limits. How does that sound to you?"

Push me beyond my limits? I thought. *Sounds to me like you'll end up with a broken dude who's more like a quivering pile of shit in the middle of the road. How's that going to work?*

Yet the recruiter had sensed I was ready for a challenge. I secretly *wanted* to push myself. Then he asked if I was interested in flying and said he likely could get me an aviation contract. *A pilot!* I thought. *How cool would that be?* I figured I'd be a good candidate. I had excellent vision. Heights didn't bother me. I'd been in small planes and on roller coasters, and they didn't make me puke. Plus, I hoped I'd look badass in a patch-covered leather aviator's jacket.

The more I talked with the recruiter and my Fiji friends, the more the Marines started sounding like the experience of a lifetime. It felt like something I might actually want to do.

One crisp Sunday in October, just a few weeks after my call to the FBI, I drove home from campus so I (okay, Mom) could do my laundry and I could talk to my parents about my new idea. After serving a wonderful chicken dinner, Mom left the kitchen—probably to wash my clothes. I was in my usual spot—sitting almost against the wall, with a view of the little black-and-white TV on the cubby next to the fridge—where I'd sat for meals nearly my whole life. Dad was in his regular seat too, at the end of the kitchen table on my left.

I wasn't nervous. I'd always been able to talk to my parents about anything. But I did wonder if they would think of some important question or obstacle that hadn't occurred to me. I cleared my throat.

"Dad," I said, leaning forward, "I'm thinking of signing up for the Marine Corps officer program. Got any thoughts on that?"

My dad stayed calm. He didn't jump up and start singing, "My son might amount to something after all!" He also didn't pound the table and shout, "Are you crazy?"

Instead, he took a deep breath and asked a few "dad" questions. "Are you sure you know what you're getting into?" Yes, I said. The recruiter said they needed pilots, so I had a good shot at getting into flight school. "Are you sure you know what this means? We're at peace right now, but if our country goes to war, you could be called to serve." I said I understood that and was prepared to serve if needed. "Why do you want to do it?" I wanted to give back, to serve my country. I also thought this offered a chance at entry into the FBI.

My mom soon joined the conversation. You have to understand that Mom is old school, as in a schoolmarm from the old country—Germany in this case. Verbal expression is not her thing. She communicates mostly through harrumphs, *hm*s, sighs, and exhales. A layperson would never know the difference, but over the years, I'd developed a skill for translating the meaning behind each.

As I continued to lay out my plans, Mom offered several *hms*. I mentally tallied the number that translated to *Interesting* and the number that meant *Well, that's bullshit.* Fortunately, the "interestings" were winning.

"You've clearly done your homework," Mom said when I was done. "It sounds like an amazing opportunity."

"I just want to make sure you finish college first," Dad said. I assured him that was my intention. I could start my officer training in the summers and still go to classes at KU the rest of the year.

My parents were supportive. They were treating me like an adult. Given my lack of attention to my future up to that point, I had to wonder what the hell were they thinking. This was the first real decision I was making about the course of my life, and they were allowing me to make it. I was both relieved and shocked at their judgment.

What I didn't say to my parents that day in the kitchen, of course, was that the soundtrack of *Top Gun* was playing in my mind and I thought pilots had a better chance of getting laid than waiters. "Who me? I'm a Marine, a naval aviator," seemed like a better pickup line than, "*Hey!* Don't puke there! You girls want another bucket of beers?"

But I have to admit there was a little more to it than that. I'd always liked the mentality behind John Kennedy's famous words, "Ask not what your country can do for you. Ask what you can do for your country." I think that's part of what drove me to (foolishly) step in to defend Brad against Tony Aguirre. I wanted to be the kind of guy who helped people who couldn't always stand up for themselves.

In other words, I wanted to be cool. Heroic. *A badass.*

There was another factor as well. Guys almost never talk about it, but I believe that every man, if he's honest with himself, wants to know what he's capable of, what his limits are, what he's made of. Could I be an officer and leader of men? I'd had my scuffles, but how would I handle a *real* fight? How would I do in a battle if people were shooting at me? Could I face down the fear? When the moment arrived, would I turn into jelly or would I take charge like John Wayne? For me at age nineteen, these were burning questions.

I had so much respect for the men in my life, especially my dad. This was a guy with a rock-solid work ethic. He not only was unafraid of a hard day's work; he preferred it. He was a white-collar traveling salesman by day, but when he got home from work, he put on jeans and fixed whatever was broken around the house. He meticulously washed our cars every weekend, whether they were dirty or not. He worked with Granddad on his farm, sometimes coming inside with bloody cuts all over his arms and knuckles that he barely seemed to notice. It seemed like Dad could do anything. He did triathlons with his brother, fished with his buddies, and still made time to watch his kids play sports or whatever they were doing. If anyone was a man's man, it was my dad.

Bottom line: Like any male who's barely out of his teens, I wanted to know if *I* was a real man, like my dad. Joining the Marines seemed like a great way to find out.

And if I met a few ladies along the way, well, that would be pretty cool too. Sorry, but it ain't *all* altruism . . . a man's got needs!

FIVE

Grit, Spit, and Never Quit

Never quit. Never, never, never, never. —Winston Churchill

I think I've made a big mistake.

It was three in the morning. I was lying on the top rack of some random and forgotten barracks in some random and forgotten corner of a place called Quantico, Virginia. It was ninety-something degrees indoors, and the dress shirt and khakis I'd worn all day were soaked through with sweat and salt stains.

The Quantico area was one of the early American settlements, distinguished by plantations rooted along flatlands near the Potomac River in northern Virginia. *Quantico* is a Native American term that's been translated to mean "by the large stream." To me and the young men around me, however, Quantico meant "place of pain and stress by the swamp."

Quantico's history, however, was the last thing on my mind on that humid night in July 1990. Instead, at the tender age of twenty, I was confronting the consequences of the first big decision of my life—which was also starting to feel like the worst mistake of my life.

How the fuck am I going to do this? This SUCKS.

I knew I would get no sleep that night. I'd been on top of that rack (otherwise known as a bed), thinking about what I'd done, for exactly one hour. In exactly one more hour, I would be expected to jump up and start my first full day of Marine Corps Officer Candidates School (OCS).

If I had been on the enlisted track, I would have started with boot camp—a grueling thirteen weeks of training. But I was attempting to become a Marine officer. OCS was like boot camp on steroids. For me, OCS would be twelve weeks long, divided into two six-week segments over two summers.

There was another key difference between the two tracks. If you enlisted, you were committed to the Marines for four years, and they were committed to you. If you failed boot camp, you kept getting sent back until you figured it out or the Marines figured out what to do with you. But the mission of OCS was to screen and evaluate potential officers. The evaluation criteria were 25 percent academic, 25 percent physical fitness, and 50 percent leadership ability. The Marines came up with every fiendish method they could imagine to test you—they were *trying* to get rid of you. If you couldn't hack OCS, you didn't deserve to be a leader in the Corps. And if you failed OCS, your time with the Marines was probably done.

No pressure.

My journey from home to Quantico had been a blur. The goodbyes to my parents were short, no tears, just a "Go do your best; I know you will" from Mom and a "It's going to be tough but you've got this; stay strong," from Dad. They dropped me off at the military processing station in downtown Kansas City, Missouri, and I and the other candidates spent the night in a Travelodge on Main Street, down by the river—at the time, not the best neighborhood in KC. The disproportionate number of men getting out of Cadillacs in the parking lot, wearing wide-brimmed hats and full-length fur coats, seemed odd for such a low-budget motel.

It wasn't long before the ten of us officer candidates gathered on the balcony connecting our rooms. Though we were scheduled to have an early start the next day, no one wanted to go to bed. What followed was like a macho version of speed dating—ask short questions, try to project competence and strength, then move on. We tried to act like it was no big deal, but we all knew we were in for a long summer. This was a chance to make a quick friend—for all we knew, the only friend we'd have over the next several weeks.

"Hey, where you from?" I asked the first guy I met, a tall dude with blond hair. "What's your specialty?"

"Kansas City. I'm studying astrophysics."

"Oh," I said, thinking, *Well, this guy's obviously a lot smarter than I am*. "I'm from Overland Park. I've got an aviation contract."

"Cool. What's your major?"

"Umm . . . theater and film?"

"Mmmm. Well, good luck with that."

Eventually, I approached a five-foot-five African-American who was built like a brick house. *Oh my God*, I thought. *I bet this guy can do a hundred pull ups and a thousand push-ups. I have trouble getting my gangly ass over the bar ten times. What am I doing here?*

"You look like a football player," I said.

"I am."

"Don't tell me . . . fullback."

"You're right!"

"I knew it. That's kind of my thing. I can tell what position people play just by looking at them."

I did know my sports. I played them all in high school—football, basketball, baseball, golf. I even wrestled for a season. But my best sport was football. I was one of several team captains my senior year and was named to the second-team defense as a cornerback for the Sunflower League (the league name was referencing our home state rather than us being delightful).

The fullback on the balcony's name was Sam Judy. I learned he played football at KC's Central High School. Central wasn't in our conference, but we had common opponents, so Sam and I started swapping game stories.

"Yeah, I don't like to brag," I said, "but I did score ten touchdowns in the second half of my last game. Almost broke the scoreboard."

I might have been exaggerating. Just a little.

Sam listened patiently to my description of how I steamrolled over the other team's would-be tacklers, nodding as if he could picture my moves. Then he returned serve.

"I know what you mean," he said. "I don't usually like to talk about the game where I scored eleven touchdowns."

I knew Sam and I were destined to be friends.

Like me, Sam was in the flight program. He ended up in a different platoon at Quantico, but he graduated and got his aviator wings. We didn't stay in touch because it was much harder then (no email, no cell phones) and we were both young, straight men who had higher priorities than writing letters to each other. We did go out drinking in Kansas City a couple times. It was always fun. He even puked in my car once—if that's not male bonding, I don't know what is.

I finally said good night to Sam and got into my bed at the Travelodge, but sleep was impossible. *What am I getting myself into?* I wondered for about the millionth time. I wasn't completely naïve. I knew OCS would be extremely difficult. I expected to be yelled at and pushed to my physical limits. I imagined Gunnery Sergeant Hartman (played by Lee Ermey, an actual Marine drill instructor) from *Full Metal Jacket*, in my face like he'd been with

Leonard "Gomer Pyle" Lawrence, screaming at the top of his lungs.

You're so ugly you could be a modern art masterpiece! What's your name, fat body? Riggle? What kind of dumbass name is that? You'll be wriggling like a worm before I'm through with you!

My self-torture was interrupted by a muffled scream from somewhere beyond the motel. The locals were entertaining themselves.

Do you suck dicks, Riggle? yelled the drill instructor in my mind. *I bet you could suck a golf ball through a garden hose!*

Now I heard sirens and what sounded like distant gunshots. This was definitely not the high-rent district.

Riggle, wipe that disgusting grin off your face or I will gouge out your eyeballs!

Yeah, I was not going to get much sleep this night.

Early the next morning, I opened my bleary eyes to get ready for the flight to Reagan National Airport in Virginia, where we were herded onto buses for the trip to Quantico. Few of us spoke. I looked at the rest of the wannabes sitting on the bus and thought, *Who are you? What's your story? Actually, I don't care. I don't have time for this. I'm just trying to survive.*

Then we drove through the iron gates and saw the replica of the World War II memorial of Marines raising the flag on Iwo Jima that marked the entrance to Marine Corps Base Quantico. I was completely intimidated. This was the last time I'd be a regular US citizen. Whatever was going to happen . . . was about to happen.

The bus pulled to a stop. An extremely trim man in a Marine uniform boarded. He wore a Smokey the Bear hat, angled down so you could barely see his eyes. He gave us a brief, icy stare that sent a shiver of fear into my gut.

"Listen up!" he shouted, gesturing with straight-fingered hands that cut the air like knives. "When I say 'move,' you all will jump up and get off this bus! You will drop your bags and put your feet on the yellow footprints that are painted out here so you idiots know where to stand! It's very easy—do not screw it up. Move!"

I was unnerved. In just a few seconds, this Marine sergeant had my adrenaline pumping harder than Evel Knievel's during a motorcycle jump at Caesars Palace. But I was also a tiny bit relieved. He was exactly what my college Marine buddies had told me to expect. At least my intel was good.

We spent the next several hours filling out forms, waiting in lines, giving blood and urine samples, and getting yelled at. That evening, while I waited in yet another line, I realized I hadn't been to the bathroom for hours. The need to pee was suddenly a top priority.

Throughout the day, I'd listened when other guys asked to go. Some requests were granted without incident. Others got their heads chopped off (not literally, though a couple times I thought they might). The successful ones spoke loud and proud.

I practiced for a minute under my breath, mumbling what I believed were the proper words. I'm sure the people around me thought I was praying. I probably should have been. Finally, I was out of time. *If I don't say something right now, I'm going to piss my pants. That would not be good. Whether I'm ready or not, here I go.*

I stepped out of line and approached our drill instructor. "Sergeant Instructor Staff Sergeant Stevenson!" I shouted, trying to not let my voice quiver. "This candidate requests permission to use the bathroom!"

The sergeant jumped toward me, his face two inches from mine. His eyebrows lowered and his nostrils flared. The look in his eyes communicated, *You have just personally insulted me. I hate your guts. Get ready for death.*

"*What* the hell do you want?" he roared. "Marines don't have *bathrooms*, they have *heads*! Are you trying to piss me off, candidate? It's not that fucking hard! Aren't you supposed to be in college? How can you be in college and be this fucking stupid?"

I knew it would happen sooner or later, but I hadn't expected it so soon. I was shocked and afraid. Even so, I knew better than to glance around and see if the other guys were laughing at my misfortune. I stared straight ahead, focusing on those angry eyebrows. *I've just got to get through this so I can pee!* To borrow a phrase from *The Office*, I was at threat level midnight—I was ready to burst.

When the sergeant paused to breathe, I tried again: "Sergeant Instructor Staff Sergeant Stevenson, this candidate requests permission to use the *head*!"

Apparently, the sergeant decided he'd wasted enough time on me. "Go, moron," he said, shaking his head. I sprinted to the nearest *head*. Taking a piss had never felt so good . . . or lasted so long.

Finally, at 2 a.m., we were directed to the barracks, where each platoon had its own area, known as a squad bay. In my bay were rows of bunk beds—no sheets or blankets. We were told that reveille was at 4 a.m. and ordered to get some sleep.

Yeah, right.

As I lay there in the dark, tired and hungry, surrounded by strangers, the self-doubt, anxiety, and fear kicked in. I'd always had people around me—my parents, my sister, friends, a girlfriend—who I could count on for support. That wasn't going to happen this time.

It was a cold feeling.

Part of me wanted to give up right then and go home. But as soon as I had the thought, I realized that wasn't going to happen. Quitting was not an option. I'd learned that when I was thirteen years old.

The memory came flooding back like an overflowing toilet. I'd been at home, upstairs, when the phone rang. I answered it in my parents' bedroom. "Hi, Rob," the caller said, "this is Coach O'Neill."

Why, I wondered, *is Coach O'Neill calling me? He's the B team football coach.*

Then it dawned on me. My heart sank.

I'd been playing tackle football since fifth grade. I loved the game. All my friends played. We'd been on the A team every season. But a funny thing happened during that summer before eighth grade. Everyone in my group of buddies went through puberty—everyone except me. My friends turned into hulking young men, and I was still a skinny, prepubescent twerp. Even so, I never gave it a thought during tryouts. I always made the A team.

Until now.

On the phone, Coach O'Neill was talking about what a great season we were going to have and how much he looked forward to me being on his team, but I barely heard him. The room was spinning. I felt like Alan Rickman falling off the skyscraper in *Die Hard*—how was this possible? Quietly, I began bawling my eyes out. I couldn't believe this was happening. The shame! The shame!

I got off the phone and went downstairs. My mom saw I was upset. Pretty soon she and my dad were trying to calm me down.

"I don't even want to go back to school," I said. "All my friends are on the A team. I'm a loser. It's official. I'm the biggest loser in history. I've lost all my friends. My life is over."

"All right, Rob," Dad said. "I know you're not happy. But let's try to focus on the positive. It sounds like you're going to get a lot of playing time."

Fuck playing time! I thought. *You're not listening to me. I'll ride the bench on the A team!*

Finally, through sniffles, I said what was most on my mind: "I don't even know if I'm going to play at all."

That was the moment. Dad sat up straight in his chair and locked his eyes on mine. Remember, this was a man who'd been employed since picking up a paper route at age seven, who'd worked his way through college. When Dad started something, he saw it through.

"Oh, you're playing," he said in a low tone indicating there would be no discussion. "You are gonna play."

That's when I realized that before tryouts, I'd told my parents I was committing to play. It was an unwritten rule in our family—if you made a commitment, you stuck to it. You could try something and fail. That wasn't an issue. You could play football for a season and give it up the next year. But quit? That wasn't an option.

Those first few days at Quantico were overwhelming. I got my head shaved and discovered my cranium is lumpier than a bowl of oatmeal. I traded my civilian clothes for a uniform—at least it wasn't a prison uniform. I was given a footlocker and shown the precise military method for making a bed—several times, since I wasn't used to making my bed. New information came at us nonstop. It was like drinking from a firehose. The idea was to strip us of our identity and turn us into green machines that thought, spoke, and acted like Marines.

Not that I had a problem with that. I understood that the success of the Marine Corps on the battlefield depended on teamwork. You couldn't have guys doing some kamikaze mission on their own—we had to operate as one unit. You subjugated your individual self for the greater good.

No matter how well I understood the philosophy, though, I was out of my element when I arrived at Quantico. It was a constant struggle to keep up. In fact, I was so stressed out I couldn't take a dump. For real, I didn't go number two for a week. Now I was scared because I couldn't shit. It wasn't natural to eat three full meals a day and exercise without using the toilet. *Where is all that food going?* I wondered. *This doesn't make sense. Something must be very wrong with me.* Finally, I got the courage to ask the platoon corpsman (medic) in a whisper, "Is this normal? Or am I in trouble?"

"It's normal," he said, "but a week *is* also a long time. You probably need to take a shit." No kidding, Doc! He said he didn't want to give me a laxative because he couldn't guarantee when it might activate and didn't want me to unload while running the obstacle course (I'm sure the candidates following me up the rope climb didn't want that either). The best the doc could do was offer some advice: "Eat as much fruit as you can at dinner and then before lights out try to force a dump . . . but don't force too hard or you'll get a hemorrhoid and then you're really fucked. Good luck." Thanks, Doc.

That night I wrestled a demon out of my body. It was as terrible as you might imagine . . . and then some. I sat in one of the barracks stalls to do my dirty work. None of the stalls had doors, mind you, so my efforts to bomb the bowl were fully available to the viewing public. The heat and humidity were unbearable. Soon I was pushing hard, my outstretched hands flat against the metal walls, sweat pouring from every pore (If we meet in person someday, you can thank me then for putting this image in your brain). It was like another workout—I was actually winded.

It's almost impossible to equate the experience with anything from this earth. I stood at the gates of hell and saw the devil laugh with delight . . . but I handled my business. When it was over, I felt like buying cigars for everyone in my platoon. I'd recorded my first major accomplishment as a prospective Marine.

I wasn't the only stressed-out candidate. I saw a guy lose it the first week. Our sixty-four-man platoon was marching in formation one evening from the chow hall across the parade deck. It was ridiculously hot and humid, a "black flag" day, which meant we couldn't train outside during peak hours because of the heat.

As we marched, one of the guys suddenly broke formation and sprinted toward the woods. He just took off. It was so completely shocking that we didn't know what to do. After stealing a glance at the escaping candidate, who was running like a rabbit on amphetamines, I stood in formation and kept my eyes straight ahead.

The drill instructors were just as surprised as we were. They yelled at the guy and then started chasing him, but this poor, heat-stroked candidate had too much of a head start—he disappeared into the trees. Pretty soon they had Marines, helicopters, and the county sheriff out looking for him.

It wasn't a surprise that a candidate had snapped—that happened almost daily during the first two weeks. I remember this one kid, a stereotypical California surfer dude. We all knew we'd be getting our heads shaved upon arrival, so everybody, me included, showed up with a crewcut or really short hair. Except this guy. He arrived with a tan and blond, rock-star-long hair. He looked like he'd just walked off the beach. He was so laid back I had the impression he could fall asleep during a march. I think he even called a drill instructor "dude" once.

At the beginning of our second week, surfer boy screwed something up during physical training, so of course a drill instructor got in his face and began yelling. We'd all learned our first night that we were expected to comport ourselves with "military bearing," which meant addressing our superiors by their rank or as "sir" and referring to ourselves in the third person. So, I was shocked when the California dude started talking back to the drill sergeant.

"I don't know what your problem is, man," he said. "This is bullshit."

Uh-oh, I thought. *Dude, why did you come here? This is an elite branch of the military. They're going to be sending us to the worst hotspots in the world. If you can't handle somebody yelling at you, you shouldn't be here.*

He soon wasn't. The drill instructor said, "Come with me." The sergeant didn't even invest energy in yelling anymore. He just wanted to remove surfer boy from our sight. By the time we finished our session of physical training and got back to our squad bay, his bunk was stripped down and his footlocker was gone. We'd seen the last of him.

The problem with the heat-stroke runaway, meanwhile, was that when he snapped, he took off with an M16 rifle. Thank God he didn't have any ammunition on him at the time—I could picture him, in a delirious state, going Rambo and taking on the entire forest. I heard they found him lying in a ditch on the side of I-95. He was fine, at least physically. Whether it was the pressure or the heat that got to him, I'll never know, because I never saw him again.

We never talked about candidates who dropped out. We just went about the cold business of closing ranks as each man disappeared. It only bothered me if it was someone I thought was gonna make it. I remember guys who were physical gods. I was sure they were total badasses . . . and then they were gone. I realized that so much of victory or defeat, success or failure, is in your mindset. The battle is most fierce between the ears.

The primary way guys were eliminated from OCS was getting "boarded." The platoon commander, a drill instructor, or anyone on the staff could send you to appear before a board of Marine officers. I always imagined a Star Chamber vibe, where a panel of distinguished Marines sat on thrones and pelted you with impossible questions. You might be charged with substandard performance for loss of bearing or for an integrity violation. You were automatically boarded if you failed two or more exams (classroom, field, drill) or if you failed enough inspections (such as rifle, footlocker, field gear, or uniform). You could make your case to the board to stay in the program, but only about one in ten candidates were allowed to come back. If you got to that point, you were probably gone.

I did not want to get boarded.

I remember one candidate, I'll call him Hansen, who was a physically huge football player from Louisiana. He just looked like a Marine—square jaw, big muscles. He was boarded for an integrity violation. During physical fitness tests, we had two minutes to do eighty sit-ups. We self-reported our number. At one test, Hansen said he did eighty, but a drill instructor watching him said he did only seventy-seven. It was the instructor's word against Hansen's. The instructor's word won. I felt bad for the guy. There were only a couple weeks left in the program.

I did screw up plenty, but usually it was something minor, never enough to get me boarded. Once, though, I thought I'd fatally blown it. My platoon was running at port arms, which meant we carried rifles, to form up on the company road in front of our squad bay. A captain from another platoon—the meanest officer in the entire company, Captain Timberlake—was walking in the other direction. As hopeful officer candidates, we were expected to salute any senior officer. The problem was that there two correct ways to salute while carrying a rifle, and I didn't know either one. It was week 3, right? I couldn't be expected to learn everything *that* fast! When I got near the captain, I took my right hand off my weapon and saluted while jogging past. That was about as dicked up as it could be. Proper salutes are a big thing in the military. What I did was the equivalent of sticking my tongue out and giving the captain a raspberry.

Captain Timberlake exploded. "What the hell!" he shouted. "You," he said, pointing at me. "Get over here! Do you know what the hell you just did? You don't even know how to render a simple salute?"

Most captains don't bother much with candidates from other platoons, but I think this one secretly wanted to be a drill instructor. He was brutal, and I was in trouble.

I stood at attention. "This officer candidate thought he rendered the proper salute!" I said. "This candidate does not know how to salute!"

"You fucking idiot!" the captain shouted back. "I swear to God, all the candidates they're sending us are shit!" He continued to dress me down as the rest of my platoon watched. My right leg began to shake.

Oh, shit, I thought. *I'm fucked now. This is it. I'm outta here, all because I rendered an improper salute.*

Eventually Captain Timberlake's disproportionate rage began to wane as he exorcised whatever demons he was carrying around that day (obviously someone had pissed in his cornflakes). "Candidate," he said, "I want a three-hundred-word essay on leadership and the proper way to salute, on my desk, in exactly one hour!"

The captain then marched me to my platoon commander's office. While I stood at attention just outside the door, the captain went in and related to my commander what an asshole I was.

"What's this guy's story?" Captain Timberlake asked. "Is he a piece of shit?"

I knew the brass talked among themselves about candidates all the time. These conversations often led to a candidate's swift exit. In that moment, all it would take was a nod of agreement from my platoon commander, and I'd be gone. I held my breath. My future in the Marines was on the line.

"No, he's doing fine," my commander said. "He's not bad."

Thank God for my platoon commander. Thanks to him, I avoided disaster. The comedian in me immediately wanted to print T-shirts that read ROB RIGGLE: HE'S NOT BAD. It's funny how the comedic mind never goes away no matter how desperate the situation.

Fortunately, that salute incident was an exception during my time at OCS. Most of the time when I made a mistake, I got "corrected" on the spot—chewed out by a drill sergeant—with a little something extra thrown in to help me remember what to do next time. The consequence usually involved doing pushups until muscle failure set in and I couldn't move my arms anymore.

Speaking of arms that don't move . . .

At Quantico, our mornings started just like you see in the movies—at 4 a.m., drill instructors burst into the squad bays, banged on garbage cans, and shouted "Get on line! Get on line! Count off!" Everybody jumped off their racks, stood at attention on the line, and snapped their heads from the left to straight ahead as they shouted out their number in order. We counted off at night too. If the number was fifty-two at the end of the day, the number of candidates better be fifty-two the next morning. It was a military tradition, no doubt a holdover from colonial militia days when deserters who got tired of risking their lives for meager rations and even more meager pay decided to sneak out and go home.

The other thing you need to know is that despite the summer heat, the barracks started getting cold about two in the morning. We left the windows open and had six-foot-high fans running 24/7 at both ends of the squad bay. We were colder still because we slept on top of our sheets and blankets. It wasn't because we enjoyed freezing our asses off. Every morning, each rack had to be made to exact regulations—for example, sheet and blanket folded evenly, fourteen inches from the headboard, with the pillow centered on top of the sheet, four inches from the fold. Which took forever to do. Since we often had as little as five minutes to make our beds, dress, and prepare our space for inspection, it made more sense to keep the rack made and sleep on top of it. Most guys tried to stay warm by curling up as tight as possible. At night, our barracks looked like it was populated by oversized bowling balls.

The problem for me one particular morning was that to fight off an especially freezing night, I'd slept on my belly with my arms under me. When the garbage can symphony started, I jumped up like most mornings, only partially awake, except this time I promptly fell onto my back on the floor. I couldn't move my arms to catch myself. They were completely numb. As in useless. Not just a little tingly, mind you—they were 100 percent useless.

My disoriented brain tried to make sense of what was happening. *Where am I? Why am I on the floor? Why won't my arms move?* My frontal lobe was firing orders to my body, but my body wasn't listening. I couldn't get up.

What else could I do? I used my legs to wiggle my body forward until my head reached the line. Picture a room full of Marines in shorts and skivvies, standing ramrod straight—and one half-paralyzed, very stressed-out dude lying on the floor. The guys closest to me had noticed my predicament and were holding back giggles.

The count-off had already started. My turn was coming.

"Forty-seven!"

"Forty-eight!"

I was next. "Forty-nine!" The unmistakable and unusual sound of someone shouting from the floor filled the room.

"What in the blue fuck," the drill sergeant roared, "is going on back there?" He raced down the aisle and stared at me in disbelief.

From my vantage point on the floor, I looked up at the upside-down giant with bulging neck muscles who towered over me. I would have laughed if I hadn't been terrified. I tried my best to appear nonchalant, as if to say, "Oh, good morning drill instructor, was there something you needed?" I fantasized that he wouldn't mind my little problem and that the whole thing would just go away. However, his bulging forehead vein and utter astonishment at what he was seeing made it clear I'd better start explaining.

"Sergeant instructor, this candidate can't get up!" I said.

"What do you mean you can't get up? Candidate, I want you on your feet *now*!"

"Sergeant instructor, this candidate can't move his arms!"

"What do you mean you can't move your arms?"

"This candidate's arms are asleep, sergeant instructor!"

"Bullshit!" he said, shaking his head. "Don't move." He looked down the aisle and gestured to another sergeant. "Come down here—you've got to see this."

Pretty soon I had two perplexed and angry Marine instructors staring and yelling at the pathetic blob on the floor—me. Finally, the sergeant turned toward the nearby candidates still standing at attention. "Get him off the floor," he said, "and on line!" I couldn't be sure, but for the briefest moment I thought I saw him stifle a smile.

Somehow, thankfully, I didn't get boarded for that memorable incident. I did pick up a nickname from my rackmate, though: Candidate Dead Arms.

You don't want a nickname when you're in Officer Candidates School. You don't want *anything* that makes you stand out. Anything that is different about you or your behavior, anything that attracts attention, creates another excuse for someone to focus on you and yell at you. The trick is to blend in, to be anonymous.

In our squad bay, we had a space on one wall where guys put up pictures of their sweethearts. These were head shots, nice yearbook-style photos. Then one of my squadmates, who already had the nickname Candidate Suck (his last name was Hoover), made the mistake of posting a photo of his girlfriend in a bikini, in a sexy pose—an image clearly meant for his eyes only.

When our platoon commander saw it, he was not pleased. "What the fuck is this?" he shouted. "Who put this up?" He made the entire platoon gather around for a teachable moment.

"This is not cool," he said, pointing to the bikini photo before turning to Candidate Suck. "Don't put your girlfriend on display for everyone to ogle! Did you ever think about her coming to graduation? We're all going to meet her. *If* you get out of here, you're going to be educating young Marines someday. You've gotta teach them right from wrong. I don't think this is right—do you?"

Candidate Suck did not blend in that day.

I wanted to blend in. But maybe it was the performer in me. I just seemed to have a knack for getting noticed.

There was the morning we did a combat conditioning course right after reveille. This was an intense, four-mile run while wearing boots and utes (camouflage utility trousers and a skivvy shirt). We climbed through tunnels and up ropes. We ran over hills and mountains and through valleys and streams. When we got back to the base, we were covered in mud. We had five minutes to shower and get ready for the next activity.

For some reason, I felt really good at the end of that run. Maybe it was the endorphin high from being in prime physical shape. Maybe it was the sense that I was starting to get the hang of this Marines thing. Whatever it was, I was *euphoric*.

The shower room had sixteen shower heads. We lined up and moved through them like we were on a conveyor belt, trying to hit as many streams of water as we could while rubbing and scrubbing. All I had with me was a towel and the flip-flops on my feet.

Other than my good mood, I still don't have an explanation for what I did next. I don't really know what I was thinking or why I did it. But I did.

I started whistling.

Remember what I said about blending in?

I didn't even know what I was whistling. I wanna say it was the "Marines Hymn," but I think it was actually "I've Been Working on the Railroad."

It didn't take long for my solo turn to get interrupted. One of our drill instructors was from Jamaica, so everything he said was delivered in a Caribbean Island accent.

"Whistling?" he exploded. "Who's whistling? Who's working on the gah-damn railroad in *my* head?"

I was so lost in my pucker performance that I only half heard the sergeant's words. But I did notice that everyone around me suddenly froze, then looked at me.

"What?" I said.

The guy standing next to me whispered, "You're whistling, dickhead."

Uh-oh.

The sergeant's voice echoed through the shower room. "*Who is whistling?* Somebody better answer me!"

I had to respond. I ran out of that shower room and toward the sergeant like an Olympic sprinter. Of course, even a kindergartener can tell you that running in the shower, in flip-flops no less, is a bad idea. The sergeant stood in the doorway to the shower room. My intent was to come to a sudden stop and stand at chagrined attention in front of him.

That isn't what happened.

When I stopped running, my flip-flops skidded on the wet floor. Instead of coming to a halt, I did a naked wipeout into the unprepared sergeant, sliding underneath his legs in the process and taking him down. It was a tackle that any Premier League soccer player would have been proud of.

The sergeant was up quickly, sputtering, furious, and looking like he was on the verge of a heart attack. I just lay there, naked and humiliated. *Well, shit,* I thought. *Just kill me now and get it over with.*

"*What da hell?!*" the sergeant shouted. "Candidate, get on your face! You don't work on the railroad in my fucking head! Start pushing!" As in, start doing push-ups until the sergeant instructor is satisfied . . . and a sergeant instructor is never satisfied.

So, there I was on the floor, counting off push-ups, my pecker sinking into a puddle of water with each one. The sergeant ignored me while berating the rest of the platoon for taking too long in the head. By the time I reached fifty-six push-ups, my arms were shaking and my chest was on the ground. I couldn't push myself back up.

This, I thought, *is the most ridiculous thing that has ever happened to me.*

The sergeant finally noticed. "Get up, dummy!" he yelled. "Get up and don't ever whistle in my head again!"

Amazingly, I didn't get boarded for that incident either. But in all the years since that morning, while in the Marines and after, I have never again whistled in the shower.

Not even once.

Remember how I said two fails during the program got you boarded and kicked out of OCS? If you had to drop out during a ten-mile march with all your gear on, that was a fail. If you didn't pass the physical fitness test, that was a fail. Same if you didn't complete the obstacle course on time or didn't pass combat conditioning.

During my fourth week, disaster struck. I failed night land navigation.

My objective was to locate five ammo boxes that had been strategically placed in the woods. We gathered near the parade deck. I'd been given a compass, azimuth figures (a direction on the compass), and a distance in meters for finding the first box, along with an index card to record the numbers on the boxes to show I'd found the right boxes in the right order. I shot my first azimuth and started marching into the woods. It wasn't long before I was alone—alone, that is, along with the snakes, spiders, ticks, and other creatures of the night you'll find in the Virginia woods. I didn't have time or energy to worry about them, though. My fear of land nav failure was far greater than my fear of death by spider bite.

When I located the first box, I got more azimuth and distance figures to help me find the next one. I walked up and down hills and around a pond as I took my compass bearings. Crickets chirped and owls hooted. Once, I heard a distant "Oh, shit!" when a fellow candidate stumbled into a creek bed. But I kept my focus. After I identified the fifth box, I worked my way back, again using the compass. I was walking tall and looking good, as the Marines often say.

Navigating in the woods at night is slow and tricky work, but I'd been doing great in land nav up to now, so I was confident of success. I made it back within the time limit. Everything seemed right. But when I handed my index card to the drill instructor, he rolled his eyes and grunted.

"Nice job, idiot," he said. "What ammo boxes were you looking for? You failed. Get back to your platoon. Next!"

To this day, I don't know what I did wrong. One of the ways the instructors try to trick candidates is to position boxes near each other. Most likely, when I got to what I thought was the second-to-last box, I stopped a little short of the correct one. It didn't really matter. What mattered now was that I was in trouble. If I recorded another fail, they'd kick me out of the program—an all-too-real possibility, because I was struggling with close order drill, and that test was just a couple weeks away.

We all had to learn how to lead the platoon in close order drill, which is how we moved a formation from one place to another. It involved calling out commands like "Platoon! Atten-hut! Right . . . Face! Right shoulder! Arms! Forward! March!" When the platoon was on the move, you needed to give your commands while on the correct foot and in the right cadence. It was like learning how to dance. If you got the footwork and the timing wrong, you could send the entire platoon into a tree or a wall, just like that marching band in *Animal House.*

It should have been easy for me. I wasn't your typical white guy. I had rhythm. I could dance. But close order drill intimidated me. When you're leading the platoon in a march, it isn't just the drill instructor who's watching. Every eye is on you. I could just feel the guys thinking, *All right, Riggle, don't make us look bad. Let's see what you've got.* It was like facing off against Chip in my front yard all over again. Nothing made my heart pound like leading close order drill.

It didn't help that we never had time to practice. My one opportunity was fire watch. Everyone had to take their turn on fire watch, which meant you patrolled the squad bay for an hour in the middle of the night, alone and armed with a flashlight, to keep an eye on the platoon and to, well, watch for a fire. When your hour was up, you woke up the guy who was next in line and went back to sleep.

I quietly practiced my footwork and commands during my fire watch shifts, but I still wasn't getting it, and time was running out. I looked like Willard in the movie *Footloose*, a big, uncoordinated dude who couldn't tell his right foot from his left. I was getting nervous. If I messed this up, I was out.

Thankfully, this was the moment that my inner drill sergeant showed up for the first time. We all have one. Mine accepts no excuses. I can't hide from him or lie to him because I *am* him. He knows all my dreams and all my fears. He knows exactly what I need and shows no mercy. This guy's a real son of a bitch.

INNER DRILL SERGEANT: *All right, Riggle, you've got a situation here. You want to be a Marine officer, but you suck at close order drill. The solution is obvious—you need to take extra fire watches to get in more practice.*

ROB: *Oh, I dunno about that. Sleep is important. I like sleeping.*

IDS: Sleep?? *What is wrong with you! Why did you even come here? Quit dicking around! Time is running out! Getting more practice is as easy as saying, "I've got your watch."*

ROB: *But . . . that means losing sleep. I don't get enough sleep as it is! It would be like giving up food . . . or women . . . or . . . food!*

IDS: *Save the drama for your mama, pussy boy! Just shut up and do it. You need the practice, and it's just another hour of sleep.*

ROB: *Yeah, but—*

IDS: *Do you ever want to get laid again?*

ROB: *What?*

IDS: *Do you want go home in shame? Do you want the whole world to know you're a quitter? A piece of garbage? A loser? Do you want to be a Marine officer or not?*

ROB: *I . . . do. Okay, okay, I do. You're right. Fine. Let's start drilling!*

We weren't supposed to do it—go figure, the drill instructors said we needed our sleep—but I started doubling up my fire watch shifts. I'd tell the guy who had the shift after me, "Hey, I'm going to take your fire watch tonight."

It was not a hard sell. "Are you serious?" my fellow candidate would say. "Yeah, sure. You got it, sucker."

So, there I was every night, quietly marching in the darkness up and down the walkway between two rows of bunk beds and foot-lockers, with about thirty-five exhausted officer candidates snoring away on both sides of me. "Atten . . . hut!" I whispered. "About . . . face!" I must have looked like the most zealous fire watcher the Marines had ever seen, but I had to get this down.

Did I miss the sleep? Oh yeah. Training to be a Marine was challenging enough when I was fully rested. But regularly putting in two back-to-back hours of night practice started making a difference. I got more comfortable with the steps and commands. I was definitely feeling it. Now I was the coordinated, got-the-moves Willard after the "Let's Hear It for the Boy" montage. I actually had a chance of passing this thing.

Even so, I was nervous on the morning of my drill test. My rackmate was a guy named Dan Taylor (this was before *Forrest Gump*—I have no doubt that after the movie, Dan's nickname in the fleet became Lieutenant Dan). Dan was from Seattle, also twenty years old, and at six feet, a couple inches shorter than me. He was easy to talk to. We didn't have deep conversations—no one had time for that, plus I never knew when someone would get boarded and be gone, so I wasn't looking to get too close to anyone. But Dan and I got along well, and we found small ways to encourage each other.

Dan knew my test was set for that afternoon. "Hey, you got drill today," he said. "Good luck."

"Thanks, man," I said. Dan must have heard the fear in my voice.

"You're gonna do fine," he said. "You know this stuff." I appreciated the support.

My drill test would be conducted on the parade deck, the huge, all-asphalt open space that resembled a stadium parking lot, otherwise known as the "grinder" (a place for marching, calisthenics, and parades, not the gay hookup app). The heat and humidity were so bad that my camo uniform had soaked through and my sweaty hands could barely grip my rifle. I marched in formation with everyone else as one candidate after another took his turn at leading the platoon. Finally, I heard the words I'd been both hoping for and dreading.

"Candidate Riggle, front and center!"

I broke out of formation and stepped in front of the drill sergeant. "Candidate Riggle reporting as ordered, sergeant instructor!"

"All right, dummy," the sergeant said, "let's see what you can do." He handed me a card with my test instructions.

It was the moment of truth. I faced the platoon with an expression that I hoped communicated confidence and command.

"Platoon! Atten . . . hut!" I shouted. "Present . . . arms!" In unison, everyone snapped their rifle up from rest position to across their chest. Now I could move 'em. "Left . . . face!" Each member of the platoon made a sharp quarter-turn to the left.

This was happening. I had some momentum and rhythm going. *Yeah, okay, I got this*, I thought. *I know what I'm doing.*

"Forward . . . march!"

About twelve minutes later, my close order drill exam was over. It felt so good to hand the card back to the sergeant instructor and get back in formation. I'd killed it.

Afterward, I got a fist bump from Dan. "See, what did I tell you?" he said with a wink. A few other guys in the platoon congratulated me. I was stoked I'd passed and that the guys were happy for me. I'd made a commitment to do this and pulled it off. I was proud of myself. It was another deposit in my self-esteem bank.

A lot of people don't really understand self-esteem. They blame somebody else for their low image of themselves. But self-esteem is what you think of yourself. It's *yours*. Nobody can fuck with your self-esteem but you. It comes from keeping the promises you've made to yourself.

After I passed the drill test, though, the most satisfying thought of all was that I wouldn't have to do any more two-hour fire watches. At last, I could go back to getting some real sleep—that's what I'm talking about!

Out of the sixty-four candidates who started in my OCS class in July 1990, thirty-two—exactly half—made it to graduation six weeks later. The other half washed out. Of the thirty-two graduates, twenty-five were prior enlisted, which meant they'd already been through boot camp and knew the ropes. Just seven of the graduates from that platoon started out as total boots, green as their uniforms.

Yes, I was one of the seven. I graduated.

I told my parents to not worry about coming out for the graduation ceremony. It's not like our family could afford to go flying around the country every week. "We'll have a parade, some people will say some nice words, and then everybody will go home," I said. My grandmother's cousin—we called her Aunt Nancy—lived in Washington, DC, and did attend, which I appreciated.

Colonel Wesley Fox, the OCS commander and a combat veteran who'd been awarded the Medal of Honor for heroism in the Vietnam War, was our speaker. Just a few days earlier, Iraq had invaded Kuwait. It looked like the US military would be mobilizing for war. It would be a few years before I would complete my training and could be sent overseas—but if the war was still going, I'd be ready.

"Every generation," Colonel Fox said, "whether they like it or not, whether it's fair or not, has a duty to fulfill. When that duty comes knocking, it's each generation's responsibility to answer. The men standing behind me are this generation's answer to that knock. We should be grateful to them." The colonel's words that day filled me with pride. It was an honor to hear him speak.

After the speech, we made our "pass and review," marching past the stage and saluting in unison. Minutes later, we were dismissed. And just like that, it was over. I'd done it. Was I excited and proud? You better believe it! On my own for the first time, I had persevered through the toughest tests I'd ever faced. My "big mistake" had turned out to be one of my biggest triumphs.

Even my inner drill sergeant was happy.

SIX

Kidnappings and Comets

In college, a funny thing happened on my way to becoming a dedicated Marine and a serious, responsible adult. I discovered there was something called a theater and film major.

Movies were my thing growing up. I could quote them chapter and verse. I enjoyed figuring out what made a movie unique. When I watched *Ferris Bueller's Day Off*, I loved how John Hughes used slow motion, music, sound effects, jump cuts, and breaking the fourth wall to give that film its signature style. But I had no idea how to analyze these techniques or even what they were called.

Enter a jocular gentleman named Chuck Berg. With his goatee and expressive, erudite speaking style, Chuck reminded you of either a jazz musician or a professor. Which was no coincidence, since he really *was* a jazz musician (saxophone) as well as a professor at KU.

During my sophomore year, while knowing virtually nothing about Chuck or the class, I signed up for his introductory film course. From the moment he opened his mouth that first day, I was hooked. "We are going to examine some of the greatest films of all time," he told us. "We're going to understand what is great filmmaking, what is groundbreaking, why certain techniques work, and why others don't."

This is amazing, I thought. *I already love this stuff! We get to study films from the seventies and eighties, and classics from the forties and fifties? We get to* watch *movies? In* class? *It's like getting paid to be Claudia Schiffer's massage therapist!* (Nailed it—this early nineties reference is so spot-on for the timeframe we're discussing . . . booya!)

Truly, this was my dream course. The only thing that would have made it better was if I could've worn pajamas and munched on a huge plate of nachos all through class. Actually, I did come close—by the end of the semester, I was wearing sweatpants and hiding a small Doritos bag in my notebook.

I loved that class and studying films so much that I switched my major from poli-sci to theater and film. As far as my career went, my major didn't matter much. I was going to be a Marine and maybe an FBI agent. I just needed a degree, any degree, to uphold my family honor.

Since I'm sure you're a sharp reader, you'll have noticed that only half of my new major had to do with movies. The other half, theater, involved being onstage and acting—which as you'll recall, I hadn't done since junior high, during my impressive but brief turn as an open-mouthed shepherd's son in a church program. To fulfill the requirements of my new academic focus, I needed to take some acting classes.

My initial impressions of the world of college theater instruction were not favorable. To warm up, our teacher had us all stand up. "Put your arms out and imagine you're holding an energy ball," she said. "What does it feel like? How heavy is it? Is it hot or cold?"

I mean, for fuck's sake. I was a nineteen-year-old, fairly macho dude who'd just completed his first officer training program with the Marines. I was getting ready to lead men into combat. Now I had my arms in the air, holding nothing? *What is this Stanislavski method shit?* I thought. *You want me to tell you how it* feels? *I'll tell you how it feels—it feels fucking ridiculous! I look like a douchebag!*

But when we stopped the silliness and got to the scene work, even though I had no idea what I was doing, I loved it. It felt natural. I am not a natural musician. If I picked up a guitar today, all I could do with it is make noise—the kind of noise that hurts your fillings. It would take me days to learn the technique to create something that sounds like music. Yet right away, acting just felt right. I loved making an audience laugh or making them feel angry or sad. I also loved storytelling. I could spin a story from a character's perspective better than most (in my opinion). It was like wearing this weird shield where it didn't matter what people thought of this Rob Riggle dude, 'cause I wasn't him.

I remember in one of those early classes doing a scene from the play *Frankie and Johnny in the Clair de Lune*. I played Johnny, who was dancing with Frankie in her one-room apartment. My objective was to seduce her. (This was one character whose motivation I could relate to!) Frankie, on the other hand, was undecided about where she wanted our dance and our relationship to go.

At one point in the dance, I tried a simple thing that wasn't in the script, an idea I made up on the spot. As I guided Frankie into a twirl in the direction of her bed, I gave a little smile that only the audience could see, and glanced briefly at the bed. My classmates watching the scene immediately responded with nods of understanding and "Ohhhhh!"

After the scene was done, our instructor asked the class to give us feedback. "Oh, man," one guy said. "When you looked over at the bed, we knew exactly what was going on!"

"Yeah," another classmate said, "that was awesome!"

I was proud that my instincts had worked for the scene. It also made me realize that acting was about more than just saying the lines. I had a part in this too. You started with the writer's words on the page, but it mattered what *I* brought to the character and the scene. I was excited that acting could be that dynamic and personal.

Given how much of a ham I was, I shouldn't have been surprised that I actually liked real acting. After all, I'd always enjoyed entertaining myself and my buddies, whether it was reenacting scenes from comedies or conducting fake interviews on the high school radio station. When I got to college, I found new outlets for entertaining myself that other people—*some* other people, anyway—also enjoyed.

For example, at a chapter meeting at the Fiji house one day, a fraternity brother named Dave stood up. Dave was nerdy and serious (he would go on to Notre Dame law school), which made him a natural target for hooligans like me and Jeff Robbins, my former high school DJ partner who was now my roommate. Our nickname for Dave (don't ask me why) was Diamond Dave the Love Slave, or Slave for short. Dave complained to the group that someone had stolen his laundry basket. No one wanted to hear it. "C'mon, man, sit down!" yelled a voice in the back (no, it wasn't me). "We've got things to do." For the rest of the guys in the house, Slave's complaints were an irritation. To Jeff and me, they were entertainment gold.

As soon as the meeting was over, Jeff and I got together. "Are you thinking what I'm thinking?" I said. Jeff grinned and nodded. We ran upstairs, located my plastic laundry basket, and tore off several pieces. The next move, obviously, was to put one of the pieces in an envelope and mail it to Slave, along with a ransom note in block letters that read IF YOU EVER WANT TO SEE YOUR LAUNDRY BASKET AGAIN, LEAVE TEN DOLLARS IN SMALL, UNMARKED BILLS IN A BROWN PAPER BAG AT THE BASKETBALL COURT. We giggled like little girls as we finished the note and stuck the envelope in Slave's mail slot at the house. More notes and threats followed.

Did we stop there? Of course not. We then took turns calling Slave. To disguise my voice, I imitated Deep Throat and said in the lowest tone possible, "Dave—I know where your laundry basket is. Look outside your window." When he did, he discovered another piece of my basket dangling from a string. "It's time to get serious," I said. "We're watching you. Don't go to the cops if you want your laundry basket back."

This went on for weeks. At house meetings in our huge dining room, we all gathered around tables. Slave would stand up. "Brothers," he'd say in a monotone, "my laundry basket is still being held hostage." Everyone in the room immediately cracked up. Slave waited patiently for the laughter to die down before speaking again. "The ransom notes continue. I want to make it clear that I am not going to pay a ransom for my laundry basket. I am not giving in to terrorists. I simply want it returned."

What made it so hilarious was that he just didn't get it. *This guy is either the most highly skilled dry humorist I've ever seen,* I thought, *or he really is completely unaware of how funny he's making it.* All signs pointed to the latter. The more Slave talked about our shenanigans, the more everyone in the house loved it, and Jeff and I kept it going. It might have been the most fun I ever had.

For Jeff and me, torturing Slave was just a way to amuse ourselves. The fact that everyone else (except Slave) found it so amusing was a bonus.

At the end of every school year, KU hosted a scripted benefit show called Rock Chalk Revue. Fraternities and sororities paired up and auditioned to perform. Each of my first three years, my house had tried and failed to make the cut, but we finally got in my senior year.

Our mini play was a love story between the sun and the moon (classic stuff, right?). For some reason, I was given the role of comic relief. I played Halley's comet. My part involved skating onto the stage on Rollerblades—cutting edge at the time; no one had Rollerblades—saying something gossipy to one of the players, then gliding off again. I wore a helmet with silver wings that extended back from my head, a white T-shirt with sparkles on it, and a silver cape that fluttered when I skated. I looked like a cross between Superman and the FTD florist.

I was a hard-charging Marine now, which meant that, as silly as it sounds, I intended to be the best comedic Halley's comet that Kansas had ever seen. I'd never been on Rollerblades before, so I practiced endlessly, first in the parking lot and then onstage during rehearsals. I wiped out a few times, but when you're a comet, you get used to crashing and burning.

The big decision I had to make was the voice for my character. I wanted something funny and unique, so I went for an impression of Paul Lynde, who was famous for TV shows like *Hollywood Squares* and *Bewitched* and for delivering one-liners with a hitch in his voice. Would the audience go for it? How did I know—I was making it up as I went!

It was standing room only for opening night. It looked like there were a thousand people out there. I was nervous, but not too nervous. I knew my lines. My part was easy. One, skate on the stage. Two, say my lines. Three, skate off to peals of laughter and the adoration of everyone present.

When my moment came, I skated up to Rosa, the character who was playing the sun, and said in my quivering, Paul Lynde voice, "Careful, Rosa, this guy's a real piece of work." (Or something like that. You had to be there.)

The crowd's response hit hard and fast. The laughter boomed through the auditorium like an eruption. It actually scared me for a moment. *Holy shit! What just happened? I guess they loved it!*

I skated offstage. One of the other actors waiting in the wings silently mouthed, *My God, that was amazing!*

I know! I silently answered back.

Our show ran for four nights, and my drive-bys as Halley's comet killed it every time. The whole theatrical experience was a blast—the camaraderie with the cast and getting that massive dose of laughter and approval from the audience.

Did I ever dream of trying to make it as an actor or comedian? Yes—but it was more like a pipe dream. I mean, my life was set. I had a job waiting for me when I got out of college—a guaranteed flight contract. When I talked to friends, I was like, "I'm going to be a lieutenant in the Marine Corps. I'm flying planes. What about you guys? Oh, you're still looking for jobs? That's too bad." I had it going *on*.

Until I raised my right hand and took the oath of office, I still had the option of not accepting my commission as a second lieutenant. But pursuing a life in the performing arts would mean I'd be a waiter or bartender while I took classes, performed in community groups, and learned how to become a comedian and actor. That would be a tough sell to my modest, hardworking Midwest family. Even though I loved the idea and was studying for it, making a career of acting or comedy seemed unrealistic to pretty much everybody I knew. It seemed unrealistic to me too.

And yet . . . it was so much fun!

What I hadn't learned just yet was the importance of passion. Howard Thurman, a theologian and civil rights leader, once said, "Don't ask yourself what the world needs. Ask yourself what makes you come alive, and go do that, because what the world needs is people who have come alive." Starting a new tech business is what makes some people come alive. For others, it's teaching young people how to read.

For me, it was cracking jokes while skating on Rollerblades and pretending to hold a laundry basket hostage. Somewhere in my heart of hearts, I sensed the potential that I could do more, that I had a real passion for performing. But I wasn't ready to admit it to myself yet. I was too busy getting ready to put on a flight suit and become the next top gun.

SEVEN

Flight School Follies

I was sixteen years old when Tom Cruise, as Maverick Mitchell, climbed into the cockpit of his F-14 Tomcat to pull off daredevil stunts and shoot down Soviet MiGs in *Top Gun*. I and just about every teenage guy I knew thought he was the biggest stud in the world. He was cocky, he was cool, he got the girls, and he could fly. Who *wouldn't* want to be that guy?

That's why, three years later, I was all in when my Marine recruiter first mentioned that they needed pilots and he could probably get me an aviation contract. My grandfather loved the idea too. I think Granddad wanted to be a pilot during World War II and was disappointed when they made him an intel sergeant instead. In me, he saw a chance to relive a dream.

"Listen," he told me one day on his farm after I'd explained my hopes to be a Marine aviator, "if you want to get your pilot's license, I'll help you. I'll pay for it."

That was an offer I couldn't pass up. I found out the airport in Lawrence had a one-man flight school. I started taking lessons on a little Cessna 152, a two-seater with an engine that would probably fit in my lawn mower. I was exhilarated during my first flight at the controls as I sat shoulder to shoulder with the instructor in the tiny cockpit. Within five months, I had my license.

I'd rent a plane for $58 an hour and fly my friends over their hometown or my girlfriend to see the Plaza lights in downtown Kansas City at Christmastime. I'd fly to Grammy and Granddad's farm near Boonville, Missouri, and buzz low over the house till they came out and waved.

None of my other friends knew how to fly, which made me a cool date. I enjoyed the open space of the sky. I liked having an understanding of the basics of aerodynamics, how thrust overcomes drag to create lift. I trusted myself to know what to do in an emergency. It all gave me a feeling of competence and confidence.

Which helps explain my attitude when it came time for me to start flight school in fall 1993—I was ready to rock and roll. I'd graduated from college, completed the second course of Officer Candidates School, and survived six months of The Basic School. Like Maverick, I was going to be a macho, courageous, patriotic American taking out bad guys in the air and wooing the ladies in the bars. It was a foolproof plan. What could go wrong?

I was definitely feeling the need . . . the need for speed.

What I discovered, though, is that Naval Flight School is not just a fun step on the way to becoming a top gun. It's not nearly as glamorous as guys like Tom Cruise make it look. I'll let you in on four reasons why.

Six Wild and Crazy Guys

When I reported for flight school at the Navy's base in Pensacola, Florida, they weren't ready for the new class yet. I had to find another job there for a few weeks. I ended up being a physical fitness instructor for would-be pilots from Saudi Arabia. Let's just say their military operated a little differently than ours. They had more of a blue-blood selection system—these guys were the sons of oil tycoons or somebody connected to the royal family. Perhaps not surprisingly, they were in terrible physical condition. They didn't understand engines, weather, or aerodynamics—or much English, for that matter. Two other Marines and I were supposed to get them in shape and teach them how to swim.

This turned out to be a challenge.

On our first day, I told our group of six Saudis, "Meet me at 0630 in the parking lot tomorrow for a two-mile run. Then we'll do some basic calisthenics. Easy morning, guys."

"Okay, you got it, boss!" said one.

"We'll be there!" said another.

In the predawn darkness at 0630 the next morning, the instructors and I stood by ourselves in the parking lot. We were still by ourselves at 0645. And 0700.

Finally, about 0710, a bunch of Corvettes and IROC-Zs, with music blaring, sped into the lot. The Saudis turned off their radios, crushed out their cigarettes, and leisurely exited their cars. That should have been my first warning. Our initial lesson that morning was on the subject of military discipline.

The run didn't go much better. One guy named something like Rakmal (we gave him the nickname Rocky, which he loved) was a soccer player. He was fast. The rest of the guys were dying after a mile. They couldn't even finish the two miles. *What,* I thought, *have I gotten myself into?*

Our afternoon was dedicated to swimming lessons. The guys showed up in one-piece bathing suits that reminded me of something Buster Keaton would wear. When we waded into the shallow end of the pool, their eyes got wider with each step. These desert-dwellers were terrified of the water.

When we tried to teach the guys to float, they sank. The guy closest to me, Farouq, literally dropped like a rock to the bottom of the pool. We stared at each other through three feet of water before I finally reached in and pulled him up. I explained again that he needed to take a deep breath and use his arms to stay on top of the water. We tried again. No movement or effort at all. He just sank.

"What are you doing?" I asked after again rescuing Farouq from drowning in the shallow end of a pool. "Why aren't you trying to stay afloat?"

He blinked the water out of his eyes. "Inshallah, inshallah," he said.

"What's inshallah?"

"If it's God's will, we will swim."

I shook my head. "That's not how it works," I said. "You have to meet God halfway." It was like trying to push a very large rock up a very large water slide.

Actually, I found these guys more amusing than frustrating. Especially when we ran into each other after hours at a local bar. I'd be nursing a beer with a buddy when a couple of them would saunter in. They'd be wearing silk shirts and gold chains and have a girl on each arm. Not pretty girls, mind you, but girls nonetheless. The looks on their faces said, "Hey, hey, look at us playboys with these girls. It's time to disco!" The vibe was very "Two Wild and Crazy Guys." These dudes were having the time of their life. I didn't have the heart to tell them it wasn't the seventies anymore.

This wasn't quite how I'd pictured spending my first weeks in Pensacola, but I guess we did some good. By the time we handed the Saudis off to their next instructors, they were in much better physical shape and could even manage a few laps in the pool. Who knows, maybe they even passed their fitness and swimming tests. Inshallah.

A Final a Day

Early in 1994, I entered Aviation Indoctrination (AI) in Pensacola. This involved classroom study of aerodynamics, navigation, weather, engines, and rules and regulations—not to mention more physical fitness training and running of obstacle courses (the Marines always make you run obstacle courses). After three months of AI, I was sent to Naval Station Corpus Christi, Texas, to begin Primary Flight Training. In other words, finally, flight school.

I knew there'd be tests at flight school, but I had no idea they'd be almost daily. It reminded me of my finals weeks in college. Those were the worst. I spent too many late nights cramming a semester's worth of knowledge into a brain that was still recovering from last weekend's party. It was always a lot of pressure.

At flight school, every time you flew the T-34, a prop plane that served as our training aircraft, it was like a final exam—and you flew four or five times a week. A typical day started with going up with an instructor and being tested on whatever that day's subject was, such as flying in formation. You landed, you debriefed with the instructor (hopefully you passed the exam), you filled out paperwork on the flight and his comments, you filled out paperwork for the plane's maintenance. You stopped for a burger on the way home. As soon as you got to your apartment, you hit the books to study for the next day's flight and test. Rinse. Repeat.

Have I mentioned that I wasn't always the most dedicated student? Some nights, my mind wandered. Some nights, I found myself watching reruns of *The Real World* on MTV instead of studying. (A stand-up comedian named David was getting kicked off the show. This was must-see TV—it would have been irresponsible to miss it!)

My roommate, Mike Kaminski, was a great dude—professional and serious about his career, yet with a sense of humor. He was also highly disciplined, which is probably why he eventually qualified for the prestigious duty of flying the HMX-1 Marine helicopter for presidents George W. Bush and Barack Obama. Mike became a little concerned about me. I'd be lying on the couch, staring into space, wondering what my girlfriend in Houston was doing. He'd say, "Hey, man, you gonna read tonight? You're going to do your reading, right?"

"Yeah, yeah, don't worry," I'd say. "I got it."

Some nights, that was true.

Dilbert Dunkers

The Dilbert Dunker was named after an old Navy cartoon figure who couldn't do anything right. It was a device invented to train pilots how to properly escape from a submerged plane. They had one for training to escape a helicopter too. For the helicopter version, you and a crew strapped into a mockup of a helo fuselage that dangled on steel cables above a pool. At the start of the test, the fuselage dropped rapidly into the pool. It slammed into the water and rolled to one side or the other, turning you upside down. As water poured into the fuselage, you had to take a deep breath, get reoriented, release your seat belt, locate your exit, and swim to the surface—all within twelve or so seconds, because those helos were heavy and sank quickly. Sounds fun, right? At flight school, we had to successfully complete eight dunk tests, four for each version of the dunker. It was hard enough doing it with your eyes open, but half of the tests had to be performed while wearing blackout goggles, to train for a night crash.

I don't mind admitting it—the dunkers sucked. The experience was unnerving. I was confident as a pilot in the air, but this was about how you performed under pressure while underwater, a panic and swim test. In the moment, you had to remain calm. You couldn't rush things. But you also had to move with purpose because there wasn't much time.

At least I'd grown up around water. I'd learned to water ski on the Lake of the Ozarks at the age of five. Our family was out swimming in the lake all the time in the summer. I was practically a bottom-dwelling bluegill. A lot of guys at flight school didn't have that kind of background.

I remember one dude, Wilson, who had the thickest neck of anyone I'd ever seen. He looked like a bull. He was older, maybe twenty-eight, and a crusty SOB. In the gym, he crushed it. He was strong, incredibly fit, and cocky. But get him near the pool, and it was a different story.

On the day of one of our helo dunker tests, we had a contingent of ten. Besides the two pilots in front, Wilson and I were strapped in facing each other in the back of the fuselage along with another six crew members. I noticed right away that Wilson was off his game. He bit his lip and his eyes kept darting to the open doorway. He looked like a hooker who'd just been caught stealing an old man's Rolex.

We splashed down and flipped over. The fuselage rolled in Wilson's direction, which meant he'd drawn the short straw—his side was going underwater immediately, while I had a couple of extra seconds to take a deep breath. I watched his face contort into a combination of fear and fury. He managed to say "Motherf—" before water drowned out the rest.

I filled my lungs with air before I was submerged. Our procedure was to wait for the helo to stop rolling before releasing seat belts and exiting the aircraft, and to wait for those closest to the exit to go first. Wilson didn't wait for either. He just wanted out of there. Before we'd stopped rolling, he shot toward the exit, arms and legs flailing. I started taking body blows from this wild man.

For the love of God, quit kicking me! I thought. *Get out of the helicopter or die already!*

I had my arms up to protect my body, but for the coup de grâce, just before he exited, Wilson kicked me in the head, twisting my helmet.

You asshole—calm down!

Finally that maniac was clear of the fuselage, so the rest of us were able to exit in an orderly fashion. On the surface, Wilson was bug-eyed and gulping air. Meanwhile, with my helmet covering half my face and my own eyes bulging, I probably looked like *Young Frankenstein*'s Igor in flight gear. I'm sure the poolside instructors wondered what I'd been doing down there. Fortunately, we also had instructors in scuba gear beneath us who'd watched every move. They knew the real story.

I was thrilled that I passed all eight of my dunker tests. I did not want to do that more than absolutely necessary. One kick in the head while underwater, upside down, holding my breath, trying to escape a sinking tomb and a raging bull was enough for me.

Uh, Captain? The Cable Broke

The T-34 has two cockpits, one in front and one right behind it. As the student, I always sat in front, with the instructor behind me. During flights, instructors liked to throw fake emergencies at you to see if you'd been reading your manual. It was like taking a test and having a pop quiz in the middle of it.

One day during a lesson, the instructor in the cockpit behind me barked over the intercom, "All right, Riggle, you've got simulated fumes in the cockpit."

Okay, I thought. *That means I need to put on my oxygen mask so the fumes don't disorient me.* I put it on. Check.

Fumes in the cockpit—I need to land, but I can't activate my landing gear electronically 'cause it could spark a fire. I've got to engage the landing gear manually.

I reached for the landing gear hand crank on my lower right, which wasn't easy to operate because everything was jammed so tight in the cockpit. I pulled out the metal crank and started turning it in a circle. I felt the tension in the crank as the landing gear slowly extended. Everything was going fine, until . . .

Snap.

Uh-oh. That's not supposed to happen.

"Uh, Captain?" I said. "The cable broke."

"What the fuck are you talking about?"

"Sir, the cable broke. I'm cranking it and nothing's happening. The landing gear isn't all the way out."

My instructor mumbled something unintelligible that probably wasn't appropriate for young children. He had me try the electronic switch to lower the landing gear, but for some reason that didn't work either.

"All right," the instructor said. "I'm taking the plane now. I have control."

"You have control."

"I have control."

(Pilots don't talk that way because they enjoy repeating themselves. It's because it's important there needs to be absolute clarity on who's flying the plane.)

We dropped to two thousand feet and circled the naval base airfield. The captain radioed another instructor in the air and asked him to look at our landing gear. "Yeah, your gear is out about forty-five degrees," was his answer. That was not going to work for a landing.

Our next move was to call the tower and get an engineer on the radio. I imagined him pulling out the big emergency manual and flipping pages. "All right, here's what you need to do," the engineer said after a few minutes. He described three circuit breakers that had to be located, pulled out, and pushed back in. Since the circuit breaker panel was in the front cockpit, this was my job. There were about a hundred breakers, low in the cockpit and hard to see, so I found them more by feel. I counted rows until I'd pulled and pushed the right ones.

"Okay," the engineer said after I'd finished. "Anything happen?"

"Nope," the captain replied.

"Well, shit," the engineer said. "Okay, give me a minute."

We tried another round of circuit breakers, then another. The result was the same. *If we don't figure this out,* I thought, *we're going to have to try a belly landing. Is he going to land on the infield grass or the pavement runway? Shit, I'm in front—I don't want propeller shrapnel flying into the canopy. This is not great. Still, the instructor's calm. He knows what he's doing. There's not much I can do about it. At this point, I'm just along for the ride.*

"All right," the engineer said in an exasperated voice. "Try this." As he described another group of circuit breakers to disconnect, I had the feeling we were down to our last attempt.

Zzzzzzt.

I smiled at the sound of our landing gear extending. *It worked!* A pilot confirmed that our gear was in position. I breathed a sigh of relief. Crisis resolved—we landed without incident.

Did the cable-snap caper shake my confidence in flying or flight school? Not at all. I knew we had good maintenance crews and great instructors. I remained sure of my own ability to handle an emergency. It was just one of those things that can happen when you're up there.

Even so, I couldn't quite picture Tom Cruise leaning over in his cockpit, blindly fingering rows of circuit breakers, and unplugging them like a 1940s switchboard operator. Was this really what being a Marine pilot was all about?

The truth was that I was starting to feel uncertain about flight school and my future as a pilot, but it had nothing to do with circuit breakers, the pressure, or any lack of glamour. As the weeks went on, I noticed my mind wandering when instructors explained a new lesson on aerodynamics. I watched Kaminski and other friends enthusiastically describe the details of their flights that day, using their hands as planes as they demonstrated each tricky maneuver in the sky. I never used my hands to talk about my day—they stayed in my pockets. I didn't seem to be feeling it the way the other guys did.

I was doing all right. I was passing my flight tests. My classroom grades were okay. But something was off.

What is wrong with me? I thought. *How come I'm not as excited about flying as the rest of these guys?*

Deep down, I already knew the answer. I blame it all on a fraternity brother, good friend, and obscenely optimistic bundle of energy named Kevin "Kus" Kuster.

PART TWO

. . . I MEAN, COMEDIAN

EIGHT

F U, Fear!

Kevin Kuster and I met at the Fiji house at KU. He was a year older than me and always the most passionate guy in the room, a natural salesman. He could show me an ordinary pencil and say, "Riggle, have you seen these pencils? Oh my God, the quality of these pencils is amazing. And they're so light—I can barely hold this thing down! If you don't go out and get some of these pencils right now, you are the dumbest person on earth. These things are the best." Next thing I know, I'm ordering a hundred fucking pencils and I didn't even want one.

Kus also had a taste for outlandish humor that I appreciated. For instance, he once organized a group of guys to lift, pull, and roll a Toyota Corolla owned by, yes, Diamond Dave the Love Slave (Dave, wherever you are, I hope you're doing well!) up the front steps of the fraternity house, through the entrance and foyer, and into the back of our piano room. The finely tuned operation involved planks, pulleys, and levers—Kus had been planning this for a while. After the guys were done, they put each piece of furniture back in its proper place, as if nothing had happened. When Slave returned from class, I was there to enjoy the stupefied look on his face—for once, he was speechless. The whole incident was actually an impressive demonstration of Kuster's energy and comedic creativity.

A Chicago native, Kus returned to his hometown after graduation to pursue a career in photography and graphic design. But he also carved out time for something else. One night soon after I'd arrived in Corpus Christi, the phone in our apartment rang. It was Kus.

It didn't take long for us to get to it. "Riggle, I'm taking these comedy classes at The Second City," he said.

"Oh, yeah?" That piqued my interest. I hadn't heard much about Second City, but I did know John Belushi, Dan Aykroyd, and Bill Murray had all honed their chops there. "Tell me more!"

Kaminski, my roommate, had been studying at the kitchen table. I guess I'd gotten a little loud. He shot me a some-of-us-are-trying-to-become-pilots-here look, picked up his books, and headed for his bedroom.

"Man, you wouldn't believe it," Kus said. "It's hilarious. They're doing all the fuck-around stuff we did in college, only it has a name—it's improv!"

"Seriously?" I said. "What's improv?" I knew the term, but I'd always seen it associated with a club or with stand-up or sketch comedy. Kevin explained that this was something entirely different—longform improv, where people onstage make up scenes or even an entire comedy show, all on the fly. Part of what made it so amazing and hilarious to watch was that no one knew where a scene might go—one minute a guy would be interviewing for an office job, and the next minute he'd be having sex with a copy machine. The possibilities for creative fun were endless.

"You gotta come do this, man," Kus said. "I'm going to these classes and watching people onstage at these shows—you're better at this than they are! I'm telling you, you'd be amazing up here. You could do this—you absolutely could do this. You need to get up to Chicago!"

At first, I thought Kus was just buttering me up to ask a favor. Maybe he'd gotten crossways with the Chicago mob and needed me to speak to his bookie. But I soon realized he was sincere. *He thinks I could be a successful improv comedian!* "Well, shit, man," I said. "I'm kind of committed to this flight thing. I signed a contract!"

Kus didn't back down. He did more than plant a seed with that phone call. He watered it and made sure it took root.

Over the next several weeks, when I should have been focused on the aerodynamic properties of density and velocity, I found myself revisiting Kuster's words.

Kus thinks I'm funny—am I? Could I really make it in comedy? Do I want *to? How would I do it? Where would I start? What about flight school and the Marines? What about the commitments I've made? Everybody will think I'm crazy!* I had many questions and no answers.

One Friday night, Kaminski and I and another flight school buddy, Gabe Valdez, made the rounds in Corpus Christi. We hit the Executive Surf Club, a downtown bar where all the professionals went after work. Then we stopped at Booter's country bar, which was always filled with pretty Texas girls who wanted to dance. Gabe and I had bought cowboy hats specifically for our appearances at Booter's. We finished our tour of Corpus Christi hot spots—still just the three of us—at a Whataburger while lamenting our lack of female companionship for the evening. Like three old and frustrated Florida fishermen, we told tall tales to each other about the big ones that got away.

It was well after midnight by the time Mike and I got back to our apartment. Mike crashed. I, naturally, settled on the couch to watch TV and make a pig of myself with another Whataburger. At first, I had no idea what I was watching, since the room was spinning. I was definitely feeling the effects of a night of line dancing and two-for-one Budweisers.

Gradually, the TV screen came into focus. I realized I was seeing a Tony Robbins infomercial. "Are you tired of being poor?" Tony was saying. "Do you want to have good relationships with women? Are you tired of being a fat piece of garbage?" (Those might not have been Tony's exact words, but that's what I heard.)

I did a quick self-examination. I was drunk and sprawled on my couch. I had grease and mustard stains all over my T-shirt—I looked like Belushi in *Animal House*. I was a disgusting mess. Tony Robbins, meanwhile, was looking like Tony Robbins. *I gotta get my shit together*, I thought. *This is ridiculous.*

"Yeah," I said out loud. "Yeah! Fuck yeah, Tony, I *am* tired of it!"

The next day, I ordered Tony's book *Unlimited Power* (my bank account wasn't big enough to cover his cassette tape series—that would have to wait). I devoured the book in a few days. Then I read *Awakening the Giant Within*, a thicker book that took a little longer. Tony's words resonated with me. Affirmations like "You can do it. You can do anything," "You have the power within you," and "Somebody's going to do it. Why not you?" might sound trite, but they can also be true. At the time, they felt like exactly what I needed to hear—and like another kick in the ass toward a potential career in comedy.

It got to the point where I thought about it all the time. I just wasn't sure what to do. Becoming a military pilot had been Granddad's dream—I felt like if I gave that up, I'd be letting him down. How could I do that to Granddad after he'd paid for my pilot's license? I'd given my parents all these reasons for why the Marines made sense to me. What would they think? What would my friends say?

It didn't help that I believed I couldn't talk to anybody about what was going on in my mind. I didn't think my parents would understand. I didn't think my girlfriend in Houston, who was starting her own career, would understand. My flight school buddies were all so gung-ho about flying. If I said, "Yeah, I'm not sure that aviation is for me after all," they'd take it as a personal assault on their career choice. These guys were fully committed. They knew why they were here, whether it was patriotism, a passion for flying, a sense of adventure or purpose, or some combination of all that. Nobody else was going through an existential crisis. I was the only one. The guys just wouldn't understand it. Shit, *I* didn't understand it!

In *The Hunt for Red October*, Sean Connery's character, the Soviet submarine commander, pulls a "crazy Ivan"—he makes a sudden, radical turn to find out if anyone is following him. If I left the Marines for comedy, it would be me pulling a crazy Ivan. The world of Wayne and Garth and "Party on!" was about as far from the military as you could get.

I felt completely alone, like a best man after his toast to the bride and groom when he joked about how hot the stripper was at the bachelor party, only to have the entire room audibly gasp in horror instead of roar with laughter. The questions and the stress kept building. I fell behind on my flight school reading—not that I was in danger of failing, but it was enough that I wasn't on top of things. Kaminski started acting like a worried older brother. "Hey, man, you got a flight tomorrow," he'd say. "Did you look at the syllabus? Are you ready?" He could tell I was distracted.

That August, I completed Primary Flight Training and started the intermediate stage. I also learned that I'd be flying helicopters when I finished intermediates. Most of the class got helicopter assignments—only about 20 percent, the guys with the highest flight test scores, got the jets. I was disappointed but not at all surprised. If I'd applied myself more, could I have qualified for jets? That's a question for the ages. All my jet pilot buddies would have said no way. Personally, I like to think I could have done it. But I was okay with how it turned out. The helicopter guys were more fun anyway.

After I learned my assignment, I started doing the math. I was twenty-four years old, five months away from completing flight school and getting my wings. At that point, I would have been committed to another eight years with the Marines, and after that I'd be only ten years away from retirement, so I'd probably end up serving another decade. It would be important work, an honorable way to serve my country, a great career in so many ways—but was it what I truly wanted? I had my whole life laid out in front of me and wasn't sure I liked what I saw. Comedy and acting sounded *fun*, something I could be passionate about and look forward to every day. I truly loved comedy and movies. Yet I didn't know a soul in the business. I had no professional "in," no one to help me get a foot in the door or offer advice.

I remember driving home from flight school one evening, parking my car, and staring into my rearview mirror at eyes that looked like glazed-over dogshit.

"I think . . . I think I want to quit flight school," I said to the distressed dude in the mirror. "I think I want to try being a comedian and actor. But . . . that's just crazy!"

It was that time—time for my inner drill sergeant to pay me another visit.

INNER DRILL SERGEANT: *Good evening, Lieutenant Riggle! What seems to be the problem now? You look a little stressed out, like someone took away your* Playgirl *magazine.*

ROB: *I don't know what to do! I'm actually considering quitting flight school to go into show business. But if I do, holy shit, my parents will lose their minds, my girlfriend will freak out, Granddad will be disappointed in me, and all my friends will think I'm insane! I've been talking nonstop about the Marines and about flying for the last four years, and now I'm just gonna walk away? For what? A chance to bus tables somewhere and pursue a dream that probably won't go further than a bad audition for a crummy play that no one's ever heard of? I guess Kuster thinks I can do it. I've always enjoyed making people laugh. I like the idea of acting. But I don't know anything about the actual business of comedy and acting. I don't know what to do. I don't know what to do!* I don't know what to do!!!!!

IDS: *Calm down, Bambi. Breathe. You're gonna be fine. Let's start using your brain and think.*

ROB: *Okay.* (Gulp of air) *Okay. This is good.*

IDS: *Now, listen up—you need to get perspective here. You're not talking about jumping off a cliff into a volcano. You're not jumping on a grenade. It's your life. It doesn't matter what your family or anyone else thinks. So, take a deep breath, and let's figure this out.*

ROB: *Yeah, okay, I guess I can do that.*

IDS: *Damn right you can do it!*

ROB: *It's just that I've been set on becoming a Marine pilot for years. This would mean walking away without ever finding out if I could do it. It would mean quitting. I've never quit anything in my life!*

IDS: *Again, dummy, perspective! So many guys never even made it to flight school. They got the boot 'cause they were colorblind or their eyes weren't sharp enough or they were too short or too tall. You've been training. You've been putting in the work. You could be a pilot; you're just thinking of making a different life choice. Hell, if you want to be a comedian and don't go after it, you're quitting on yourself!*

ROB: *I guess that makes sense. But . . . I'm still not sure . . .*

IDS: *Holy fuck, Riggle, just make up your mind! You're more indecisive than newlyweds at Bed Bath & Beyond! If you believe you should be a comedian, be a comedian! Shit or get off the pot! But if you go for it, commit yourself. There, see how easy that was? We're done. My God, you're dramatic.*

That SOB in my head helped. He calmed me down and got me to step back a little as I wrestled with all the questions jumping around in my mind like fleas in a circus. But it was actually another resource that made the biggest difference.

Not everyone knows this about me, but I'm a Christian. I believe in God and Jesus and like to think I have a strong faith. I'm far from perfect. I make mistakes, and I sin. Like a lot of people, when I struggle, I tend to think, *Hey, God, I could use a little help here!* But when life is easy and I'm in the zone, I often feel like I'm handling things just fine, and I start to drift away from that relationship. It's taken me a while, but I'm gradually figuring out that I do better and have more peace when I keep focused on God—who would've guessed?

I've always prayed, though. I think it began in junior high after I started going to meetings of Fellowship of Christian Athletes and Young Life. Back then, I mainly prayed about not getting my ass kicked and not embarrassing myself, and that someday God would bless me with puberty. I guess God meets us where we are, because all those prayers were eventually answered.

After that fateful call from Kus, I started praying even more. Our apartment in Corpus Christi was located near an unusually pungent onion field, so when I started a run, I'd push the pace to get past that smell and pray, *God, I'm trying to figure out if I should go for this comedy and acting thing. Could you give me some guidance? Some clarity? I just want to know what to do, you know?* (I still associate talking to God about important life decisions with the smell of onions.)

As I ran, I wasn't expecting a dove to land on my shoulder or anything biblical like that. I was just asking for something that would give me a clear sense of direction.

The thing is, I *was* getting an answer to my questions. I had a feeling in my gut that wouldn't go away. It kept saying, *You gotta go for it.* But I wasn't trusting it. I was denying it because I didn't believe in it. I didn't believe enough in myself. I was too worried about what people would think.

On a September Saturday a few weeks later, I drove my Second Lieutenant Mobile—it seemed like every guy who became a Marine officer acquired a new car, in my case a Ford Explorer—right onto the beach at Corpus Christi. I parked on the sand about fifty yards from the Gulf of Mexico/America (TBD), with the back end facing the water, popped the hatchback door, and sat down, my legs dangling over the rear bumper. The waves, sunshine, light breeze, and lazily circling seagulls gave me a welcome sense of calm. I needed it. It was time to make a decision.

Yes, I loved entertaining people and making them laugh. There was nothing quite as rewarding as cracking people up and seeing their faces light up with joy. I'd always had the itch to try acting and comedy. The idea seemed nuts . . . but Kuster made it sound actually *possible.*

Still, it would mean quitting—and as I told my drill sergeant, I didn't see myself as a quitter. I mean, I guess you could say I quit playing the bass guitar when I was twelve. However, the only reason I started taking lessons was because a bunch of guys in the neighborhood had formed a band, and I thought I could join and become a rock star. As thought every boy in the early eighties. But I had no musical talent and no passion for learning how to play an instrument. That's a problem. Also, I had a *terrible* music teacher. He hated me because I wasn't familiar with the Beatles song "Let It Be." When I told him I didn't know the melody, he gave me the silent treatment. Seriously, he stopped talking to me. We would just sit in his little studio in the basement of a music store in Prairie Village, Kansas, and he wouldn't talk to me. Three "lessons" later, I quit. Wherever that teacher is today, I hope that every time he tries to play in public, all his guitar strings break and he gets booed off the stage.

This was different. This would mean quitting something I'd invested in. The Marines have a saying for facing adversity (the Marines have a saying for everything): "Improvise. Adapt. Overcome." Nothing there about quitting. In the Marine Corps, you're taught to find a way, to believe that if you persevere, nothing can stop you. If I quit flight school, would I be rejecting everything I'd learned?

On the other hand, leaving flight school didn't necessarily mean I was done with my military career. Since the Gulf War with Iraq was over and the Marines were downsizing, they would probably let me out of the two and a half years remaining on my contract if I dropped out of flight school. But that didn't feel quite right. Up to now, I'd been training and going to school, but I hadn't really *done* anything yet. *I'm still a patriot*, I thought. *I still feel called to serve. I want to be out in the fleet! Maybe there's a way I wouldn't have to be a quitter after all.*

I'd brought my Tony Robbins *Unlimited Power* book with me to the beach. I picked it up. Tony had written that thinking was a matter of asking questions of yourself, then answering them. The better the questions, the better and more useful the answers. According to Tony, if I was willing to work for it, I could achieve whatever I wanted for my life. The obvious question—the one I kept asking myself—was, *What do I actually want?*

I realized I knew the answer. *I want to be a comedian and actor.*

The next questions were the real ball busters: *So why do I keep hesitating? What's with all the excuses? Why don't I just pull the trigger already?*

That's when it hit me. *I am afraid.*

I was afraid of failure. I was afraid of throwing a meaningful career away on a huge gamble. I was scared that my family and friends would think I was an irresponsible flake. Let's be honest: I was afraid I was fucking up.

Fear is a funny thing. Today, I understand that it's the great obstacle to just about anything worthwhile that we want to accomplish. It can be a sign that we're close to what we really want most. When we finally confront our fears, that's when the good stuff happens. I didn't understand any of that at the age of twenty-four, but I had learned from the Marines that if I faced down my fear and persevered, I could achieve what at first seemed impossible.

Fuck you, fear! I thought. *I have to live with the choice I make right now. If I don't go after comedy and acting, will I regret it? Yes—it will haunt me for the rest of my life!*

That was no bueno. *I can live with leaving flight school. It might suck at times, but I can live with what people will say about me, with the judgment. But I don't think I can live with not knowing what could have been.*

I fingered the spine of *Unlimited Power* and thought about what could happen if I truly committed to a career in the arts. I flipped to the back of the book and wrote on the inside cover, "If I quit, what I will accomplish?" I underlined that a few times.

The next words my pen scribbled were "I'm going to get on *Saturday Night Live*."

Wow. Talk about shooting for the moon. But crazy or not, there it was, in writing—a goal big enough to inspire me and to scare the shit out of me. This was what I really wanted.

I read the words aloud. It was a lesson my mom had taught me, to use all my senses to retain important information. This was about as important as it got.

Something about that moment, about writing out my goal and seeing and hearing it in plain English (even if it did mean defacing my book), made it seem possible. Tony Robbins said I could do it. Kuster thought I could do it. My inner drill sergeant believed I could do it. Maybe I was ready to start believing it myself. *C'mon, man, you're a Marine!* I thought. *You can do anything you put your mind to!*

The Marines were all about making a good plan, executing the plan, and then evaluating that plan to make sure it was working—and if it wasn't, revising the plan until it *was* working. Now I had a plan. I was going to serve my country by fulfilling my commitment to the Marines, then pursue a life in the arts as a comedian and actor.

Decision made. Finally. A huge sense of relief and peace washed over me—which lasted for about ten seconds.

What the fuck have I done?

NINE

How to Make a Good Impression

I stood on the deck of the USS *Ponce de Leon*, an amphibious transport ship, and watched the green North Carolina shoreline gradually shrink as we powered farther into the Atlantic Ocean. *Well, Riggle*, I thought, *no turning back now.*

Not that I wanted to turn back. I was an officer on my first Marine Corps deployment, and I was as excited as hell.

It was late May 1996, a year and a half since my decision to quit flight school and my discovery that I'd grossly underestimated all my relationships. My parents handled my new career intentions beautifully. "Wow, okay," my dad said when I told him that I wanted to go into show business. "What brought that on? Tell me your plans." My mom bought me books on acting and improv. It was her way of saying "We're with you. Good luck." My other family and friends were just as gracious—no judgment. Of course, I got sideways looks from a few guys in my flight class that I didn't know well, but that didn't bother me. Then there was the commodore in charge of all the flight squadrons. When I explained that I was leaving flight school to pursue a career in comedy and acting, he said, "That's amazing. I wish you luck. But don't tell anyone what you just told me." We both laughed. He was right—most people in the military just didn't get it.

I did decide to fulfill my Marines contract, which meant I needed a new assignment. I reported to the Marine Corps administration office at the base in Corpus Christi to talk about it with the admin chief. "We need a supply officer in Okinawa," he said.

Oh, shit, I thought. *That sounds about as exciting as being a supply officer in Okinawa.*

"Are there other options?" I asked, trying not to sound desperate.

The chief pulled out my file and looked it over for a minute. "Looks like you did a lot of radio and television in college. What about public affairs?" He explained that it involved writing and speaking, dealing with the media, and other public relations work.

That's more like it, I thought. *That would be an interesting challenge, plus I'd learn skills that would translate to the real world.* "That's what I want!"

From Corpus Christi, I was sent to Defense Information School at Fort Benjamin Harrison in Indianapolis, the military's version of journalism school, and then assigned as a public affairs officer to the 2nd Marine Aircraft Wing headquartered in Cherry Point, North Carolina. My post-Marines plan was to move to Chicago in another year, hook up with Kuster, and join either Second City or another comedy troupe, ImprovOlympic, to get my career started. If I was as good at improv as Kus seemed to think, I figured I had a decent chance.

For now, though, I was laser-focused on the Marines. Nearly six years after my first dressing down by a drill instructor at Quantico, I was finally on a real operation. In the West African nation of Liberia, heavy fighting had broken out between two opposing factions, particularly in Monrovia, the capital city and home of the US embassy. Historically, America and Liberia had close ties. The violence threatened the few thousand Americans and allies who lived there. The US ambassador in Monrovia reported taking their phone calls: "You would hear the Americans actually screaming over the phones, begging for help. You could hear over the phones of people breaking in . . . using sledgehammers to smash down the doors."

Not a good situation, obviously. A Marine Expeditionary Unit (MEU) had already been dispatched to secure the embassy from the warring factions. Now I was one of more than seven hundred Marines whose orders were to evacuate our embassy staff, other Americans, and various allies before somebody killed them first.

I learned just how nasty the situation could be during an intel briefing in the ship's chow hall. I sat with about twenty-five other officers to see a video from a few years earlier of one of the current rebel leaders, Roosevelt Johnson, in the office of Liberia's then president, Samuel Doe. Johnson was leaning back in his chair, his boots on the president's desk, drinking a Budweiser, while the president was tied up on the floor, begging for his life. One of the rebels proceeded to cut the ears off the president. It was hard to watch.

Okay, I thought. *These are hardcore, ruthless folks. I've never hated anybody enough to want to torture or kill them. I guess I've also never been oppressed by a virtual dictator like these guys have, so maybe I shouldn't judge them. But that's ruthless.*

It was sobering to see what these guys were capable of. But if all went well, we wouldn't be interacting with them. This was a noncombatant evacuation operation (NEO). Our rules of engagement were clear. We couldn't point weapons at anyone unless they did it first, and we couldn't shoot unless someone shot at us first. It was a "Leave us alone, we'll leave you alone" scenario.

Maybe it sounds strange, but as I sat and watched that video, I wasn't worried about my personal safety. If anything, I felt proud and happy to be part of a mission that mattered. America was at peace, and there wasn't a whole lot popping in the world—except in Liberia. *I'm finally getting a chance to serve my country in a real-world operation,* I thought. *We're the tip of the spear.*

I was confident that our task force would handle things when we got there. Any butterflies I had were more about wanting to do my job well and make a good impression. Colonel Tony Corwin was the commanding officer (CO) of Special Purpose Marine Air-Ground Task Force Liberia. He was also my boss. As the public affairs officer assigned to the mission, I was a one-man shop reporting directly to the CO. My primary tasks in Liberia would be to convey our progress to external and internal media and document what we were doing through stories, photos, and record-keeping. I would also be responsible for dealing with any on-site media—but since the embassy sat on the edge of a war zone, I wasn't expecting too many reporters to be dropping in for tea.

Colonel Corwin was a big man, six-foot-four, muscular, with a square jaw—imagine every Marine Corps recruiting poster from the beginning of time. Someone told me he'd played football for the University of Oklahoma. I could picture him as a linebacker, pulverizing another team's running back. When I met him for the first time at Camp Lejeune in North Carolina, a couple of weeks before our departure, I learned he wasn't going to be a micromanager. "Lieutenant Riggle, public affairs is your domain," he said. "I expect you to know what to do, how to do it, and when to do it. As long as you've got it under control, I'm not going to bother you. Just keep the fucking media away from me."

I was intimidated by him but also pleased that he would trust me to carry out my duties. I had the feeling that as long as the "fucking media" didn't interrupt his work, we were going to get along fine.

I also wanted to set a good example for the enlisted men. Even though I wouldn't be in charge of any Marines in Liberia, I would be working around and among them. As young and inexperienced as I was at twenty-six, I still had more maturity (hey, stop laughing!) and training as a Marine than most of the enlisted guys, who were almost all under the age of twenty-one. These guys were new to the game.

In many ways, I am a teacher at heart. I still remember those magical moments when a junior high or high school teacher or mentor would present a lesson I'd heard a hundred times before and never really understood, but this time, the way they said it made sense to me. The light bulb finally clicked on. It was like every sappy song on the radio in the eighties about losing love (I'm talking to you, Michael Bolton)—you'd hear one, roll your eyes, and think, *That is so pathetic.* But then your girlfriend dumps you and you hear "How Am I Supposed to Live Without You," and as the tears well up, you think, *Oh my God, now I get it.*

In Liberia, with no one working for me, I wouldn't be passing on pearls of wisdom (or singing weepy love songs) to my staff. But I could at least try to model what a Marine officer looked like by doing my job well and keeping to a strict daily regimen. Oorah!

Two weeks after leaving North Carolina, we reached the coastline of Liberia. The embassy sat at the edge of Mamba Point, a cliff overlooking the Atlantic. There was no dock. We had to helicopter into the embassy. When my turn came, I watched a compound with green trees, a few open spaces, and more than twenty mostly one-story buildings come into view. This would be home for the next couple of months.

We landed on the small helipad near the edge of the cliff, behind the main buildings. I disembarked and got my first look at the place where I'd be working. It wasn't much to see—a two-story office building, the off-white paint peeling in spots. The inside wasn't any better. Fluorescent lights, old tile, and the smell of mold reminded me of a seventies-style DMV. I wouldn't have an official office, but since most of the embassy staff had already been evacuated, I had my pick of several empty spaces to do my work.

Since the arrival of the MEU, the rebels had mostly left the embassy alone. One day soon after I got there, however, some of them decided to see what they could get away with. From beyond the walls of the compound, rebels started firing with AK-47s on our guys. Our Marines returned fire. No one inside the embassy was seriously hurt, but at least two rebels were killed. I was inside the embassy at the time, so I missed all the action.

Once the word got out that we were ready to evacuate them, Americans living in Liberia, personnel from other nations' embassies, and other American allies showed up regularly at our gate requesting transport. Once they had a departure date scheduled, they came back to the embassy to fly out. Our orders were to stay behind the embassy walls, so I'm sure it was dangerous for some of these people to get to us. The rebels weren't actively fighting the Americans, but some of these "warriors" were just teenagers. They'd shoot at a puddle in the street just to see the water splash. Not exactly a stable environment.

It wasn't my job to stand at the gate with a clipboard and check the evacuees in, so I didn't interact with them. I did often step outside to observe their departures, however. They had to go out the same way we came in, by helicopter, which took them to neighboring Sierra Leone. I didn't expect trouble from the rebels during the evacuations, but you never knew for sure. If something did happen, I thought it would be useful to see it firsthand (plus it was just nice to get out of those drab offices for a few minutes). When I heard the familiar *thwop-thwop* of a CH-46, I'd step into the courtyard and from a distance of about fifty yards, watch the bird nestle down. I was always careful to turn my face away and down—the prop wash (air turbulence created by propellers) from those things was extreme. The last thing I needed was a chunk of Liberia real estate in my eye.

The helicopter crew would unload pallets of water and MREs, then start taking on about a dozen evacuees. Whoever it was—Americans, Belgians, Japanese, you name it—I could tell they were grateful to be getting out of there. There was no hesitation, and they were all smiles. We had helicopters flying in and out all the time, sometimes carrying Marines and supplies, and sometimes carrying civilians. These piecemeal evacuations went on for weeks.

This is so cool, I thought. *We're doing what Marines do—fulfilling our mission, securing an embassy, evacuating people whose lives are in danger.* It might sound corny to some, but in those moments, I was proud to be a Marine and proud to be an American.

I soon developed a daily routine. Most of our Marine force rotated back and forth between the ship and the embassy, but since I was among the dozen or so members of the command staff reporting directly to Colonel Corwin, I stayed at the embassy and slept on a cot in a small exterior building with seven other guys. I'd get up at 0600, check in with the night watch to see if potential evacuees had come to the embassy overnight or if anyone had shot at us, attend a morning briefing led by Colonel Corwin, work out in the embassy gym, do some paperwork or whatever else was on my plate that day, have lunch, do more office work, walk the embassy grounds, and attend an evening briefing.

The later evenings were my chance to relax—no more colonels or enlisted men to impress. Most nights were filled with watching the Olympics on TV, another workout in the gym, a game of poker, or watching a video of something like *Dumb and Dumber.* Taking in a comedy with the guys and quoting lines to each other was always fun. Hearing "According to the map, we've only gone four inches!" seems to mean more when you're on a deployment.

My daily routine was occasionally interrupted, however. One of the more pleasant interruptions was a fellow first lieutenant from Seattle named Terry Thomas. The majority of Marines walk around with a brooding "Fuck you" expression on their face. You don't find out their personality until you get to know them better. It's their way of displaying military toughness, I guess. Terry was the opposite of that. He was more like a happy puppy, a skinny little fast talker with white-blond hair and a big smile.

Terry was in charge of our sig-intel, so I didn't see him a lot during the day. But in the evenings or wherever I bumped into him, he'd have a story to tell about one of the Marines working for him or something going on at the embassy. One day, Terry stuck his head in the door of the office where I was working and said, "Hey, Riggle, did you hear the good news? We both got promoted to captain."

"No shit?" I said. "When did the list come out?"

"Just yesterday." He showed me a printout with the promotion details.

I read the list and frowned. "Oh, man," I said. "You're getting promoted as soon as we get back—I don't get promoted till November! Shit, that means I gotta salute you."

Terry laughed, obviously enjoying my (mostly) mock indignation. Of course, I actually loved knowing I'd be promoted. It meant I'd be in charge of other officers for the first time. It was another level of responsibility and a sign of respect, not to mention a bump in pay. It also meant that there would be no more excuses. Because they're young and inexperienced, lieutenants screw up often. Once you make captain, the Marines expect you to have your shit together.

Another entertaining distraction was a guy I call the Invisible Man. Every few days, this dude—possibly inspired by an afternoon of chewing khat, the local stimulant of choice—would take off his clothes and paint his whole body with an unknown white substance. Then he would sneak toward the embassy. By "sneak," I mean he would hunch over and creep ever-so-slowly onto United Nations Drive, the street that ran along the wall at the front of the embassy. According to our intel, he believed that if he was painted white and he moved slowly, he was invisible.

Yep.

He wasn't carrying a weapon—which was obvious, since he was naked—so he didn't pose a threat. When the Invisible Man made an appearance, the Marines on watch at the top of the wall would elbow each other and say, "Here he comes! Get ready for the show." Apparently, this sort of thing wasn't that unusual in Monrovia, because the traffic simply weaved around naked painted-white guy as he gradually made his way across the street.

Once he reached the sidewalk on the embassy side of the street, he was only ten or twelve yards away from the wall. Our guys would yell down to him: "Hey! That's far enough! We see you!"

The Invisible Man would freeze for a moment. Then he'd take a couple more tentative steps toward the wall.

"Halt!" would come another shout. "We see you, dummy!"

The guy never spoke or acknowledged the Marines watching him. He just slowly turned around and crept back across the street as carefully as before.

I'd given our guys strict instructions to call me whenever Invisible Man showed up. I wanted to see what this was all about. To my great frustration, however, he was always on his way back across the street by the time I got there. I'd arrive at the top of the wall just in time to see him finish crossing United Nations Drive, then take off running down a cross street.

I've always wondered what the Invisible Man would have done if he'd made it to the embassy wall. Since he already believed he was invisible, did he think he also had special climbing powers? Or that he could just walk through the wall into the embassy compound? Was he planning to steal all our Popsicles? I'll never know. It's one of life's mysteries that I'll never solve.

Between April and mid-June, Operation Assured Response evacuated nearly five hundred Americans and almost two thousand citizens of other countries from Liberia. We'd moved quickly to resolve what could have been a disaster for our people and our allies. I'd been part of an important mission to help get people out of harm's way. For me, it underlined why it's so important to have a force like the Marines and why I wanted to be part of it.

We continued to provide security for the embassy until the first week of August, but then our mission was done. I was quite pleased with myself. I'd conducted my business like a professional. Colonel Corwin seemed happy with my work (since no media had showed up at the embassy, it wasn't hard to keep them the fuck away). I felt that I'd done my job and completed any task asked of me. I'd even been promoted. I considered my first deployment a success.

We staggered our departure, taking turns flying out by helicopter, so the rebels wouldn't realize we were leaving town. Soon it was my turn to go. I carried all my gear, a hundred pounds of it—my sleeping bag, pistol, sea bag, and ALICE pack (that's All-Purpose Lightweight Individual Carrying Equipment for you non-Marines—basically a large rucksack with huge pockets).

I also had several oversized three-ring binders full of papers. Remember, this was 1996. The Marines were not fully electronic yet, so keeping track of paperwork was another important part of my duties. The binders contained a few hundred pages of information about Liberia and the warring factions that I'd brought with me, as well as documents on what a public affairs officer was supposed to do and what forms I had to fill out to record what I'd done (for some reason, I don't recall my recruiter saying a word about the joys of filling out military forms). I'd managed to stuff most of the binders into my sea bag—all but one that just wouldn't fit. I had to carry that one loose.

A commander announced, "Okay, time to go!" The dozen of us who were leaving ran into position, twenty-five yards from the helipad, and hunkered down. To make it harder for any bad guys to shoot down the CH-46 transport with a rocket-propelled grenade (RPG), the pilots flew low over the ocean, then swooped up beside the cliff to make a fast and always dramatic landing. The idea was for us to make a quick exit. With the engines still running, the ramp at the back of the helicopter would lower, we'd run onboard, and we'd be off.

The problem was that when the helicopter suddenly appeared and landed, we were so close that the prop wash blasted us with terrific force. The three-ring binder in my hands was no match for the burst of hurricane winds. The binder flew open. Sheets of paper, hundreds of them, ripped out of the binder and flew into the air. The sky filled with swirling white sheets—it was like being inside a snow globe. All the guys around me started laughing. I was mortified. Classic lieutenant shit! Soon, Marines were scrambling around the landing zone, grabbing papers out of the air or off the ground and handing the crumpled remains to me with grins on their faces, clearly enjoying my embarrassment.

"Who the fuck did that?" a grizzled gunnery sergeant shouted. As I stuffed what was left of the mutilated documents into my bag, someone pointed to me.

"Oh, it was a fucking lieutenant," my commanding officer said to the gunny. "Don't worry about it." Apparently, I wasn't the first Marine lieutenant to look like an idiot at a landing zone. Still, I had the sinking feeling that all those weeks of showing the enlisted guys how a professional Marine officer conducts his business had just been irretrievably forgotten, replaced by the image of me standing like a hapless dickhead in the midst of a blizzard of paperwork.

A couple weeks later, the boot was on the other foot. With our mission complete, we'd sailed to Spain's Canary Islands for four days of liberty. I need to point out that liberty is not the same as leave. Leave would have meant "See you later, report back in four days." Instead, we'd be released at 0945 each morning and had to return to the ship no later than 0200 early the next morning. Our leadership understood that the Canaries are the Bahamas of Europe. We're talking bars, beaches, and beautiful women. We're also talking about young American males, mostly Midwestern, corn-fed boys, who'd been on a boat for three months lifting weights and who hadn't seen a girl in all that time. The testosterone was off the charts. Colonel Corwin was smart enough to realize *I'm not going to just turn several hundred Marines loose on this poor little island for four days.*

To lessen the chances of losing a Marine during the mayhem of shore leave, everybody had a liberty buddy. You looked out for each other and were responsible for each other. If you returned to the ship without your liberty buddy, you were in big trouble. My buddy was Terry. Like practically every other Marine, as soon as we got off the ship, Terry and I headed for the beach. We quickly located a little cantina right on the sand—a shack with fishing nets and lanterns—grabbed a table, and started drinking cerveza. We weren't the only ones with that idea. The cantina quickly filled with Marines. It was hot enough that some wore T-shirts and some did not. We were a strange sight—fifty guys in shorts and every shirtless white guy, me included, sporting an absurd tan. Our forearms and faces were a deep brown, but the rest of our bodies were a bright, ghostly white, as if a supernatural light was emanating from inside. It was spooky and ridiculous at the same time.

We just sat there enjoying our freedom, our beer, and the views. It was Europe's holiday season, so every minute or two a group of beautiful women from Belgium, the Netherlands, France, Germany, or Austria would walk by. In bikinis. Or not. Apparently, Europeans didn't mind going topless when they were on holiday. I knew I didn't mind.

Our peaceful reverie was interrupted when a wild-eyed Marine burst into the cantina, pointed in the direction he'd come from, and shouted, "Nude beach!"

I never saw any group of Marines move faster. Chairs and tables were overturned as nearly everyone in the place rushed out of there. They peeled off shirts and shoes as they sprinted away. It was like Iwo Jima all over again, the Marines storming that beach with an intensity and focus that must have scared the hell out of any civilians nearby.

Since we were so much older and wiser, Terry and I just stayed in our chairs and laughed. These guys were picturing a coastal version of Mount Olympus, goddesses with perfect naked bodies sashaying about on the sand. I knew it wasn't going to be that. I'd been to a nude beach before and was still trying to erase the images from my mind. It was mostly a bunch of overweight senior citizens. They were exhibitionists who wanted to be seen, whether you wanted to see them or not, or they were just so old they didn't care anymore.

Despite my helicopter-binder disaster, I still felt some responsibility to set an example for the junior enlisted guys. I made sure to get back to the ship by 0100 hours, just to be safe. I didn't go to my stateroom, however. Instead, I joined a couple hundred other Marines and sailors lined up along the flight deck, quarterdeck, and bow of the ship, about four stories above the pier. A show was about to start.

A few minutes before 0200, the pier suddenly became a madhouse. It was like the evacuation of Saigon down there. Taxicabs roared up to the pier and screeched to a halt, as well as bicycle cabs, pickup trucks, and other modes of transport. Out of each emerged some of the sorriest-looking military men I've ever had the privilege to witness. Guys were wearing grass skirts and coconut bras. Some were doing their best to pull away from clinging or kissing female companions. Others were completely passed out and being carried or dragged by fellow Marines. One was totally white in front and lobster-red from head to toe in back—he'd obviously fallen asleep on the beach. Another semi-comatose sucker arrived strapped to a pedicab. All of them were drunk, stumbling around and crashing into each other as they raced to the gangplank to beat the 0200 deadline. If they were late by even a second, their liberty would be canceled for the next day.

Those of us already onboard shouted down encouragement between howls of laughter. "Three minutes left!" Then, "Two minutes! You can do it!" I felt a little sorry for the guys who weren't quite going to make it—and was thankful to not be one of them.

Colonel Corwin had a somewhat sadistic side. At 0700 the next morning, several hundred Marines in green T-shirts and shorts stood in formation on the concrete pier. Remember, after three "pure" months, everyone had just spent an entire day eating tacos and getting hammered. The smell reminded me of being in a brewery, only much worse—the aroma was a mixture of alcohol, body odor, and the scent of tacos coming through people's pores. I glanced at the young lance corporal next to me. He did not look well. His eyes were only half open. His lips were a pasty white. Even though he was supposed to be standing at attention, his shoulders slumped.

This guy, I thought, *is in for a long morning.*

"Good morning, Marines!" the colonel shouted with an evil grin. "Let's get some PT! Right face! Forward march! Double time!"

We ran down the pier and onto a road, led by staff sergeants singing a cadence: "I used to drive a Cadillac! Now all I do is hump a pack! I used to drive a Bonneville! Now all I do is charge a hill!" I noticed many of the voices around me sounded weak.

Don't get me wrong, I was feeling it some myself. But I'd only had a few beers. My discomfort was nothing compared to what most of these guys were going through. As we ran through the streets, our singing was drowned out by the sounds of heaving, retching, and splashing vomit. I don't mean polite, Hollywood-style movie vomit, where a guy puts his head down for a moment and drops a few chunks of soup. This was horizontal, projectile, Monty Python vomit—mass quantities of it. It was all around me. I had to dodge heaping puddles of puke as I ran.

Holy shit, I thought, *this is so disgusting and so hilarious. No one is going to believe it.*

I had to give those Marines credit, though. As far as I could see, no one dropped out of formation or stopped running. They knew the rules—if they weren't well enough for PT, they weren't well enough for liberty. These were Marines committed to paying the price. Improvise. Adapt. Overcome.

We went through the same routine for each of the next three days—PT in the morning, followed by onboard showers and liberty, followed by a comical late-night rush back to the ship. I did notice, however, that the ranks of the last-minute party Marines got just a little bit smaller each evening.

A couple of weeks later, our task force returned to America. Terry Thomas got his promotion to captain, and I reported to Colonel Corwin at Camp Lejeune to go over his written evaluation of my performance in Liberia. I looked forward to it. I felt I'd done my job well and believed he was pleased with me.

"Riggle, come on in and have a seat," he said when I arrived at his office. "As you know, you're here for a debrief and evaluation.

You did a good job out there. I think you're a good leader. Congratulations, I know you got selected for promotion. I think you're going to be a fine captain. Here's your fitness report." He handed me some papers. "Give this a read and let me know if you have any comments or questions."

I scanned through the report and saw several high ratings. *Nice!* I thought. *Colonel Corwin loves me! This will be great to have in my file for future promotions.*

I flipped to the last page, which contained a comments section. I felt my chest puffing out a little more with each word—until I reached the last line.

> Lieutenant Riggle showed strong leadership ability and capabilities. He demonstrated proficiency in his military occupational specialty as a public affairs officer and successfully fulfilled his duties during the deployment. Lieutenant Riggle should be considered for promotion. Lieutenant Riggle has a semi-athletic build.

Wait—what? A semi-athletic build? What the hell does that mean?

You have to understand, I'd been working out every single day in Liberia, sometimes twice a day. I was a big, burly Marine, walking tall and looking good. I was *jacked.*

What, I have to have a thirty-inch neck and be a body builder to impress you? You might as well have written, "Lieutenant Riggle is a fat body." Semi-athletic build—what the fuck are you talking about?

I didn't say a word about his comment. I just smiled, said "Thank you, sir, for the opportunity to serve," did a crisp about face, and got out of there as fast as I could.

TEN

"Hold on Loosely..."

Planning is a good thing. Preparation is a good thing. But as 38 Special (a great rock band from the eighties) might say, you still have to hold on loosely to those plans, because nothing ever goes quite the way you expect. From my earliest days at Officer Candidates School, when a three-mile run scheduled for 0400 might turn into a weapons inspection instead, I learned that the Marines mindset was "Change in plans. We're going to succeed anyway." No time for excuses or pouting. Flexibility was the name of the game.

I did not love the constant changes during my first years in the Marines, but I soon became thankful for all the practice I got at adapting, because the changes kept coming. I learned to handle each one with a cool head and a positive attitude. Okay, not really—I sometimes bitched and moaned as much as the next guy. But then I got back on track and into the Marine mindset.

For example . . .

Playing Tetris in New York City

In the spring of 1997, my time with the Marines was nearing its end. My contract would expire in August. I was thrilled with my military experience and proud to have served. I'd been on a deployment, risen to the rank of captain, and developed a new confidence in myself and appreciation for what I could accomplish. I was in prime physical shape (regardless of what Colonel Corwin thought). But now I was ready to pursue my true dream: comedy and acting. It was go time! I was a little nervous about the financial part—I'd gotten used to that paycheck on the first and fifteenth of every month. But I figured I'd get a day job as a bartender or waiter and take comedy and acting classes at night. I'd already moved some of my stuff into a storage unit in Chicago. Kevin Kuster knew I was coming. I was set. Chicago, here I come!

Remember what I just said about plans?

I was serving at Marine Corps Air Station Cherry Point in North Carolina. One day in May, the 2nd Air Wing chief of staff, a colonel, called me into his office. "Riggle," he said, "I understand your contract's almost up and you're not trying to extend. What's going on?"

Based on my past experience with trying to explain my comedy and acting dreams, I kept it vague. I said I had some opportunities in Chicago and knew the Marines didn't have a base or an office there.

The colonel leaned back in his chair. "If you could go where there were Marine offices, where might you possibly consider?"

I was certain the colonel was just being kind, letting me feel a little bit wanted by the Marines as a parting gift. Even so, I needed to give him an answer. *Well, what are the prime cities for launching a career in show business?* "I suppose, sir," I said, "that if I had orders for New York City or Los Angeles, then I would probably extend." But even as I said it, I thought, *Yeah, that'll be the day. The Marine Corps doesn't take requests. They give orders.* I figured I'd just given the colonel a polite brush-off.

At that point, the colonel dropped it and wished me luck. I didn't give it another thought—until the next morning, when I got to my office and found paperwork ordering me to report to New York City to become deputy director of public affairs there.

Wow—I guess the colonel wasn't kidding! Apparently, after investing this many years in training an officer, the Marines weren't going to give up on me so easily.

Now what do I do?

As I thought about it, the idea grew on me. New York was obviously a great place for comedy, not to mention the home of *Saturday Night Live*, Broadway, and huge subway rats! I needed a day job anyway, and a captain's salary in the Marines was better pay and far more secure than work as a bartender. It even included a housing allowance. I didn't know a soul there, but maybe the Big Apple was my destiny. It was like what Marine General Oliver Smith, at the Battle of Chosin Reservoir during the Korean War, famously said while leading a withdrawal: "Retreat, hell! We're not retreating, we're just advancing in a different direction."

The result was that on a steamy August afternoon, I drove a U-Haul to Manhattan and the second-floor studio apartment I'd rented sight unseen. I unloaded my stuff that night—which didn't take long, because all I had was a bed, a futon, a TV, and a little coffee table. When I opened the door of my apartment for the first time, I did not find my new dream home. The space was only 350 square feet. Once I moved my belongings inside, each piece of furniture touched another piece. If I wanted to get from the futon to the kitchenette, I had to move stuff around—it was like playing a game of Tetris. Which was fine. It wasn't like I was going to be hosting Martha Stewart parties anytime soon.

I would soon learn about the apartment's unique heating and cooling system. It had a pre–World War II radiator controlled from a central location. Management turned it on every October 15 and left it on till April 15. The only way I could regulate the heat was by opening the window. Since my bed was jammed next to the window—there was no other place to put it—and I had to sleep with the window open in winter, I'd lie under a blanket, trying to drift off with snowflakes falling on me from the sky and shouts from the Eurotrash bar on the corner wafting up from the street.

Small, shitty apartment, big dreams, I thought. *At least the plan is underway and I'm finally here in Chicago.*

Uh, make that New York.

Rob Riggle, Tackling Dummy

Most of the time, when plans change, it's because of some external factor—you're out hiking and the sunny day turns into a monsoon; your boss wakes up in a cranky mood and fires everybody on the staff. Sometimes, though, the shift is self-inflicted. Like my little detour into a sport the English invented one afternoon in the 1800s while trying to figure out a cool way to beat up on each other.

The day after I moved into my Manhattan apartment, I explored the neighborhood and discovered a grocery store, video store, and laundromat, along with the closest subway stop. Now I knew I could survive. More important, I located the local sports bar, Ship of Fools. Now I had a place to drink!

It turned out that Ship of Fools was the home bar for the New York Rugby Club, the oldest rugby club in America. That's right, I'm talking about rugged, big-man, smash-'em-up, holy-shit-that-hurts *rugby.* The no-holds-barred sport that gave us that wonderful word *scrum* (when players from each team bind together and push against each other to compete for possession of the ball). I'd never played, but I'd always been fascinated by what looked like a mash-up of soccer and American football. I thought it would be fun to try, so when my new friends at Ship of Fools invited me to tag along for a practice one weekend, I said, "I'm in."

It wasn't long before I was on one of their teams, regularly playing in matches across the region. I became a second-row forward, which meant one of my responsibilities was . . . *hm*, how to describe this . . . during a scrum, I'd stick my head between the two beefy thighs of the front-row player ahead of me, jam my shoulder against his butt, and put my arm around his crotch or whatever I could grab hold of, in order to lock the line as we pushed forward. You can imagine the smell . . . although you probably don't want to. Second-row forwards were known for their "cauliflower ears," which came from the constant rubbing against another guy's thighs. I know this sounds painful and ridiculous, and to a certain degree it was. However, it was also a blast and a great challenge. I loved it.

More important than me getting acquainted with my teammates' private parts was that I was making friends, including one I stay in touch with to this day, a behemoth of a man who was always easy with a smile, Tom "T-Bone" McMahan. I even dated a rugby player (yes, a girl—the NYRC has women's rugby teams too . . . and they're great). Was I good at rugby? No, not really. But I was having a great time.

Until one Saturday in December, that is. The NYRC hosted a huge "sevens" tournament (as in seven players to a side instead of the usual fifteen) every year on Roosevelt Island, beneath the Triborough Bridge. During a game against a team from Boston, I was running with the ball near midfield. A stocky, fast guy on the other team converged on me in a hurry.

Uh oh, I thought. *This guy's out to nail me.*

I tried a feint to my left, but this bowling ball of a man didn't go for it. He dove for my middle and took me down with a legal but *I'm-gonna-feel-this-in-the-morning* tackle.

That wasn't the worst part. As I lay on the grass and rolled the ball toward a teammate, another opponent running my way stepped on my face. It was an accident. This shit happens. But rugby cleats are long and metal, and they're attached to strong legs. I felt like I'd been squashed by a rhino wearing ice skates.

I got some kind of injury almost every time I played rugby. In previous matches, I'd injured a shoulder, pinched a nerve, and hyperextended an elbow. But this was my face! I had a pretty healthy scrape on my cheek. It wasn't enough to put me out of the game, but it sure hurt like hell.

After our match, I walked over to a different field to watch another team from our club finish its match. During play, two players collided. Next thing I knew, one of our guys was walking toward the sideline holding his face. There was lots of blood—for good reason. His nose was broken and his face permanently changed.

Well, shit, I thought, *that could easily have been me.*

I was still thinking about it when I got into a teammate's car for the ride back to Ship of Fools. *What am I doing out here? That guy is a rugby veteran who knows what he's doing, and he still just got his face rearranged. I* don't *know what I'm doing. I mostly run around with my head on a swivel, trying to keep myself alive. How long before something really bad happens to me?*

Which is when it occurred to me that I'd been in New York for four months and hadn't taken a single step toward achieving my show business dreams. *Oh, man, what did I come here for? I came here to do comedy and I haven't done* anything! *What is wrong with me?* The truth that I didn't want to admit to myself was that I didn't know how to start and I was scared of being a bust.

It was at this point that my inner drill sergeant piled on the guilt faster than a Jewish grandmother.

INNER DRILL SERGEANT: *Good Lord, Riggle! Did you come to New York to be a tackling dummy or to be a comedian? What the fuck are you doing?!*

ROB: *I'm just getting my bearings. I mean, come on . . . it's New York! I've been dating and making friends. It's like Winnie-the-Pooh always says, "A day without a friend is like a pot without a single drop of honey left inside."*

IDS: (sputtering) *What . . . the fuck . . . did you just say? Did you just quote me a line from Winnie-the-fucking-Pooh?? Do you even* hear *yourself?*

ROB: (more timidly) *But . . . even a comedian needs friends, right?*

IDS: *Oh? I'm sorry, I didn't realize you were already a comedian! I should have known by all the hard work you've done on comedy. Oh wait, that wasn't you—that was some other guy. You're the guy who's drinking every night, playing rugby, and getting your face stepped on! Listen up, fat boy! If you expect to make it in show business, you have to actually work on show business, not on filling out your social calendar. You're already twenty-seven—you're behind the curve, dickhead! Plus, if you keep playing rugby, you're going to end up uglier than you already are.*

ROB: *That seems a little harsh. But . . . I hear you. You have a point. My face does look like someone ran over it with a tractor.*

IDS: *You gotta do more than hear me, wizard—you need to get off your ass and get working! You gave up flight school for this, remember?*

ROB: *Yeah, yeah, okay, you're right again. I need to get started.* Saturday Night Live, *here I come—let's go!*

I'd learned enough about improv to know that longform improv, with extended scenes and stories, was what I was most interested in. But I didn't think anyone could make a career out of longform improv. Plus, as far as I knew, there was no longform improv in New York. I'd also read that most comedians started by doing stand-up, so I figured I needed to start that way too. Every time I walked from my apartment to the Ship of Fools, I passed the oldest stand-up comedy club in New York, Comic Strip Live on Second Avenue. People like Jerry Seinfeld and Robin Williams had performed there, not to mention my old heroes Eddie Murphy, George Carlin, and Rodney Dangerfield. In the window of the club was a sign advertising stand-up comedy classes.

Okay, I thought. *That's what I'm going to do. It starts there.* I would stop playing rugby and start focusing on comedy. I went into the comedy club and put down three hundred bucks for five weeks of classes.

I had a plan. Again.

Hello, Is This Thing On?

"And now, for his Comic Strip Live debut, please put your hands together for the man from Kansas, Mr. Rob Riggle!"

I remember the moment so well. I'd been calm—serene, even—as I sat at a table in the back of the club and sipped a beer, waiting for my turn to launch my career as a stand-up comedian. I'd memorized my five-minute act. I knew just when I would make a dramatic pause. I knew when I would ironically tilt my head, when I would make a humorously exasperated face. I wore what I thought was the perfect combination of classy and casual—button-down shirt, jeans, sneakers. I was *ready*.

But when the emcee introduced me and I strolled through the crowd toward that famous faux-brick stage, I realized I was *soooo* not ready. The adrenaline began flowing faster than a DeLorean trying to time travel. Even as I stepped up to the mic to face the bright lights and the few members of the ninety-plus audience members I could actually see, I felt and heard the *lub-dub, lub-dub* of my racing pulse. Every instinct in me shouted, "No, no, no, I've changed my mind!"

You know that scene on the beach in *Jaws* where the camera zooms in for a close-up of Roy Scheider while the background recedes, creating a shocking and frightening perspective distortion? That's what it felt like! Yes, I was a Marine who'd served overseas and had flown barrel rolls, stalls, and spins on solo flights over the Gulf of Mexico/America (still TBD). And yes, I was terrified.

I'd been going to classes at the club for five weeks. The house comedian and class instructor was a grizzled dude named D. H. Sweeney. D. H. looked like a much shorter, disheveled version of Art Garfunkel—he had an afro but was balding and wore an untucked shirt and old khakis. He had clearly been in the game a long time. D. H. sighed a lot, never smiled, and always seemed to wish he were somewhere else. His general vibe was, "Let's get this over with."

At my first class with about a dozen other students, D. H. mustered the energy to stand up and address us. "All right," he grumbled, "here's the deal. We do three jokes per minute here. Setup, punch line. Setup, punch line. Setup, punch line. That's how it works. At the end of the classes, you'll go up and do five minutes onstage here at the club. You'll bring at least two friends, and there's a two-drink minimum."

I was already mentally rebelling. First of all, no way would I invite friends to the club. The only people I knew in NYC at the time were my rugby buddies, and as nice and fun as they were, they were still New Yorkers. They would not tolerate bad comedy. They would give it to me straight—and I was not ready to receive that level of honesty. So, fuck that, D. H.

But more important, I didn't want to tell jokes, I wanted to tell *stories*. Seeing Eddie Murphy in his stand-up special *Delirious* had been a life-transforming moment for me. I'd thought, *Yeah,* that's *what I want to do. I want to get onstage and tell stories that are so fun, so full of hilarious characters, so surprising and amazing, that the crowd can't get enough.*

I didn't know shit, however, and I was too self-conscious to share my ideas, so I tried to do it D. H.'s way. It didn't help that I attempted to come up with generic jokes out of the clear blue sky—as in, "This is my first time onstage and I'll be honest, I'm a little uncomfortable. I don't know if it's the stage or the mashed potatoes in my underwear." (Yes, they were that bad.)

What I needed was a teacher telling me "What makes you unique? You're a Marine? Perfect! That's a great source of comedy material." What I had instead was a not-so-interested teacher who was sick of dealing with idiots . . . aka beginners. (Drawing on my Marines experience had occurred to me, but for the life of me I couldn't think of anything humorous that met the "setup, punch line" criteria.)

I came up with a series of one-liners for my five-minute routine. It wasn't my style, and the jokes weren't great. Nevertheless, I somehow ended up on that stage, facing a merciless New York audience. *Shouldn't a professional be doing this instead of me?* I thought. I stared at the people at the table in the front row. They stared back with an expression that said *Okay, dude, dazzle me*. My mind tried to find a gear. *What's my first joke again?* In those final seconds before I opened my mouth, fear didn't just move into my neighborhood; it curled up on the futon in my apartment and asked for the remote.

Finally, my brain engaged enough for me to mumble my opening line. It got a few laughs. I kept saying more words. Dramatic gestures? Pausing for the audience to react to my jokes? No, that was all out the window. This was a race to the finish. It's like I was on autopilot. My mouth kept saying lines, but at the same time I thought, *I've just gotta get through this. I don't care about the audience. I just have to keep talking and get through five minutes.*

At one point, I actually *did* notice that I'd made a joke and no one had laughed. I tapped the mic. "Helloooo, is this thing on?" I said in classic hack fashion. More silence.

I realized later that I just wasn't prepared. In the Marines, you train and drill until the correct response to a situation is second nature. At Comic Strip Live, I'd had no idea what I was stepping into. D. H. had said bupkis about nerves. There was no "You're going to be scared, you're going to be nervous. You've got to plan for that. You might try some deep breathing, you might try some walking around, move your body, get some physiology going, to get that nervous energy out." He didn't tell us shit! I was petrified wood up there. I looked like an Old West bank robber who'd been shot up and put on display in front of the saloon.

Somehow, though, I made it through the full five minutes. After my last joke and a "Hey, that's my time, I'm outta here!" I hurried off the stage in the direction of the club bar, where I stayed just long enough to down a beer in one pull. Then I walked out and hurried as fast as I could toward my apartment.

What just happened back there? Oh my God, I ate shit—they hated me!

I felt like I'd been in a car accident—I was in shock. I wasn't certain, but it seemed like I'd just perpetrated a crime and now I was on the lam, hoping no one would identify me from the disaster I'd left behind.

I bounded up the stairs to my apartment, slammed the door behind me, and breathed a sigh of relief. I was safe. The adrenaline finally started to wear off. On my way out of the club, someone had handed me a videocassette recording of my performance.

The idea of watching that tape sounded about as fun as a donkey kick to the balls, but I figured I'd better find out just how badly I'd done. I popped the video into my machine.

To my surprise, it wasn't as terrible as I thought it was. *People are actually laughing! Well hell, Riggle, you gotta slow down and give them time to enjoy the humor . . . Okay, that last joke wasn't too hot, but the next one went over all right.*

The problem was that even as I calmed down and saw that it hadn't been as bad as I thought, I realized I still hated the whole experience. I didn't see myself getting any better or feeling any less panicked. I believed that I was funny, that I could tell a good story, that I could play different characters. But if the expectation in the comedy world was that stardom began with telling only one-liners, I didn't think I would ever truly succeed.

What I hated most, though, was the feeling of vulnerability. I was a macho, successful Marine, a guy used to operating in the masculine zone. What was I doing, getting up in front of a crowd, trying to tell jokes? I'd felt so . . . exposed. I was showing myself, what *I* thought was funny and clever, and it seemed that not everyone agreed with me. It was a mighty lonely feeling.

That was not the plan—I hated that! I never want to do that again! Have I thrown away my chance to be a Marine pilot for nothing?

It was just so sad. I didn't know what to do.

And yet . . . as I lay on my bed a few nights later, mentally reliving my personal Nightmare on Second Avenue, a sliver of the self-confidence I'd gained from the Marines seeped back into my addled brain.

What the hell did you expect, Riggle? You're a beginner! Every master starts out as a beginner. Sure, some of it was terrible, but not all *your jokes bombed—some got genuine chuckles. You know what to expect now, so it's bound to be better the next time. Maybe stand-up wasn't quite what you expected, but is that a reason to abandon the plan already? Does a Marine give up every time a plan doesn't work out the way he wants? No fucking way!*

I pulled my blanket tighter under my chin as snowflakes began to drop through my open window. I was here in New York. This was where comedy magic happened. Maybe it really could happen to me.

Grit, spit, and never quit. Somehow, I would find a way.

Above left: Two years old…not much to report. I guess Mom had some time on her hands? *(All photos courtesy of the author)*

Above right: Six years old, second grade school picture. I had been crying all morning because my parents made me wear that awful suit! The teacher felt so bad for me that she called my dad, who came to school and took me out for lunch and then back home so I could change into my Fran Tarkenton jersey and return to school with dignity.

Below: Sophomore in high school, age fifteen. I had just gotten my braces off and was starting to "feel the flow." Puberty was just days away!

Non-school senior year picture my mom arranged, age seventeen. I can't remember if it was done at the mall or not . . . I'm gonna say it was.

ABOVE: Interview with local Monrovian officials inside the US embassy in Liberia, summer 1996.

BELOW: On the flight deck of the USS *Ponce de Leon*, getting ready to fly into the US embassy in Liberia, summer 1996.

Above: First Lieutenant Terry Thomas and me at the LZ in the US embassy in Liberia, summer 1996.

Below: Breaking down the language barrier at the refugee camp in Albania with some youngsters, summer 1999.

Opposite: Kosovo fighting hole, summer 1999.

KFOR

Opposite: Standing with some of the weapons we confiscated from the Kosovo Liberation Army.

Above: Working out of the public affairs tent in Kosovo, summer 1999.

Below left: On stage at the UCB Theatre with the original UCB members, my teachers and mentors.

Below right: Respecto Montalban, one of the best improv troupes in the world! I loved every moment on stage with these talented people—and still do to this day.

Opposite and Above: Working in and around Ground Zero in New York City days after the 9/11 attacks.

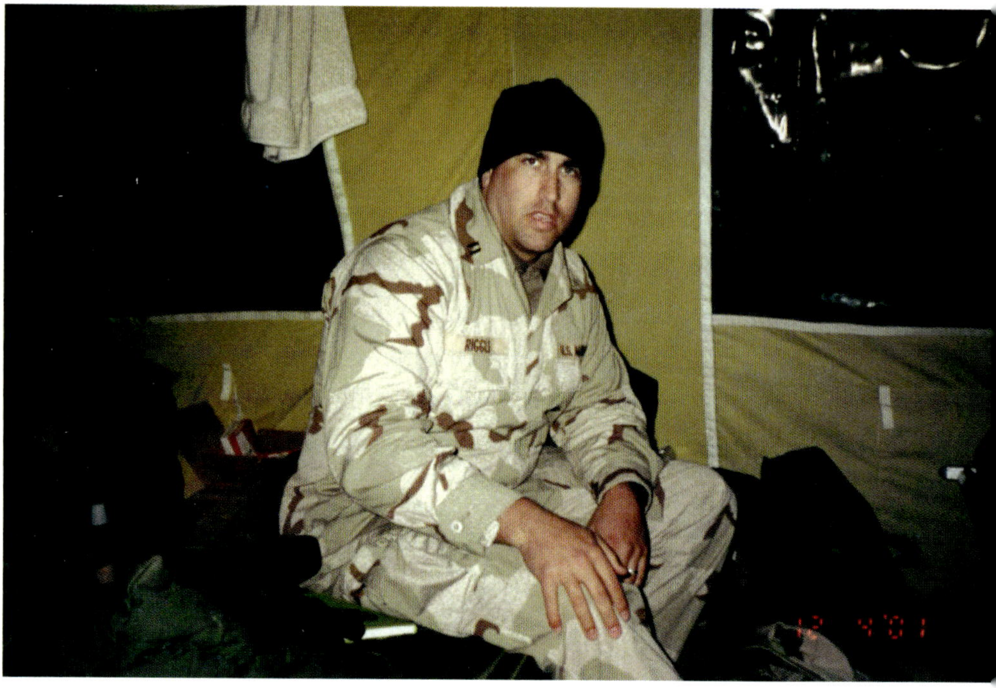

ABOVE: First night in Uzbekistan on my way to Afghanistan, November 2001.

BELOW: Outside tent 81 at K2 in Uzbekistan, waiting for a flight into Afghanistan, November/December 2001.

Above: Here I am receiving a haircut with hand clippers from one of our new Northern Alliance allies in December 2001. Talk about trust!

Below: Surrounded by children in Mazar-i-Sharif while meeting with local officials, December 2001.

Above: Explaining how to take a picture to a young Afghani girl at a new school that had just opened, December 2001.

Left: Me and my interpreter, Salim, in Mazar-i-Sharif in December 2001.

Opposite above: Gunny Lynch and me standing outside the bombed-out Taliban headquarters in Mazar-i-Sharif, January 2002.

Opposite below: Me and Gunny Lynch about to talk with the newly arrived French contingent at the airport in Mazar-i-Sharif, February 2002.

Opposite above: High in the mountains of Afghanistan, summer 2002.

Opposite below: Desert extraction in Afghanistan, summer 2002.

Above: General Franks and me at the coining ceremony upon my return from Afghanistan, late February 2002.

Coffee makes things better after a long night
on (mechanized) patrol in Kosovo, 1999.

ELEVEN

There's No *T* in Team!

I've been part of teams for as long as I can remember. It probably started for me with fifth grade football. I've always loved the sense of camaraderie and collaboration that comes from joining forces with other people to work toward a common goal. Sometimes that means shared success. Other times, it's about shared misery—like the end of my first week of two-a-day football practices during my sophomore year of high school.

This was in August, during a blistering afternoon of hundred-degree heat with 100 percent humidity. Our coach made us do bear crawls—walking on our hands and feet—for a hundred yards, followed by wind sprints up a hill, followed by another hundred yards of bear crawls back to where we started. It was intentional torture, not unlike my later experience with the Marines—our coach also wanted to weed out the physically and mentally weak. In between bear crawls, Coach marched us down to the water fountains near the practice field, lectured us on the need for mental toughness during games, and marched us away again without letting us drink. People get fired for that kind of stuff today, but this was the eighties, when if you lost a few students during football practice, it was no big deal.

Of course, all of us were on the brink of collapse, and some guys did drop in their tracks and quit the team. I felt ready to drop myself. But then I snuck looks at my buddies who were also still awkwardly bear-crawling toward the finish line—Jeff Robbins and Bill Konen. Bill gave me an exhausted yet encouraging grin. *Those guys haven't given up*, I thought. *If they can do it, I guess I can too. I just need to make it to the end of this practice.* A little later, I heard a shout from Terry Mohajir, a running back and the best player in our class: "You're doing it, Riggle! Keep it up!" It was another shot of motivation.

I did get through practice and ended up playing football all through high school. Going through the joys of winning and the heartache of losing—not to mention the trauma of endless bear crawls—with your teammates creates an amazing bond. It must be why I'm still friends with all those guys today, because I can't think of any other reason why they still put up with me. All I know is that we have a special connection and that I learned being part of a team was important to me.

Speaking of connections . . . after my Comic Strip Live disaster, I was lamenting to an old high school friend about my experience. "I quit flight school and came to New York to do comedy," I said, "but it sucks. It's not what I thought it would be."

My friend happened to know a guy named Dave Koechner. I knew that Dave was one of the exceptional few—I'd seen him recently as a cast member on *Saturday Night Live*. I soon learned that he was well respected in the comedy community for his improv and character skills.

My friend suggested I talk to Dave about comedy and what I was trying to accomplish. When I called, he was kind and gracious and offered to meet me for coffee. A few days later, I showed up early for our appointment. As I waited, I took a deep breath and thought, *Be cool, Riggle*. I tried to ignore the part of my brain that was freaking out and saying, *Holy shit! This guy has been on* Saturday Night Live*!*

After Dave arrived and we got a table, he asked about my comedy experience so far. I told him about my class, my frustrations at Comic Strip Live, and the kind of storytelling comedy I dreamed of doing.

"It sounds to me like you want to do longform improv," he said.

"I know!" I said. "I should have gone to Chicago. They do longform there, but they only do stand-up here in New York."

Dave leaned forward. "That's not true. Some friends of mine moved out here from Chicago a little over a year ago. They're starting an improv comedy theater. They call themselves the Upright Citizens Brigade. They're great. They're some of the best comedians and improvisers in the country."

"Really!" I said. "Who are they?"

"Amy Poehler, Matt Walsh, Matt Besser, and Ian Roberts."

"Okay. I don't know who any of these people are, but it sounds awesome."

"Every Sunday night, they do a longform improv show. You need to check out the show. If you like what you see, go up to Matt Walsh, tell him I sent you, and sign up for their classes."

The next Sunday, I took a cab to 17th Street and walked into a building that should have been condemned. You could see through some of the steps on the staircase, so I chose to ride the elevator to the theater on the fifth floor. The elevator made so many creaks and groans on the way up that I wondered if I'd survive the trip. The tiny black box theater wasn't in much better shape—but the energy in that room was palpable. The place was packed with more than a hundred people. It was standing room only, so I bought my ticket and squeezed into the back.

What I saw that night blew me away. Amy, Matt, Matt, and Ian walked onto that stage and were in complete control. The typical start of an improv scene has all the players lined up against the back wall. The show host asks the audience for a random suggestion to get things rolling, such as a place, and picks someone out of the crowd. That person says something like "bowling alley." Then one or two of the performers step forward and start the scene. Maybe one is a newcomer to bowling, just walking into an alley for the first time. The other player quickly establishes that he's a longtime employee and part-time inventor, and the scene develops from there. More players step off the wall, introducing new characters to the scene. Before you know it, the employee has everyone lined up in a triangle like human bowling pins and he's trying to knock them over with his newest invention, a five-foot-tall bowling ball.

At the show, once the four UCB players got started, it was nonstop laughter for me and the rest of the audience. They bounced ideas off each other like Ping-Pong players, adopting hilarious characters and producing escalating silliness that fit together perfectly. The connection and collaboration between them were amazing. It was as if they'd been rehearing these scenes for years. I couldn't believe they were writing all this in their heads, creating it right in front of me. For me, it was an epiphany, like the moment in *The Blues Brothers* where John Belushi is in the Triple Rock Baptist Church, gets hit by a beam from heaven, and shouts, "I have seen the light!" This was my beam from heaven. This was what I wanted to do. This was where I belonged.

After the final bows, I waited until most of the crowd had filed out. Matt Walsh was still onstage, so I introduced myself and explained Dave's recommendation.

"Oh, yeah!" Matt said. "Koechner said you might come. What'd you think?"

I was so pumped up that I didn't even answer Matt's question. I couldn't contain it any longer—I just had to get the words out:

"I want to sign up. I want to take classes. I want to learn from you guys." Matt just laughed at my eagerness.

I registered for my first class that night. I think it was three hundred bucks for eight weeks (in those days, anything related to comedy cost three hundred bucks). The classes would be held at Dick Shea's on 14th Street, an old dance studio where the UCB was renting a room. I couldn't wait. I'd been so dejected after my stand-up attempt, but now I had seen improv magic. I felt reborn. *Okay,* I thought, *maybe I didn't totally screw up my life. I've got a second chance here. This is a better comedy fit. I'm gonna learn. Something good is going to happen.*

In the Marines, if you're five minutes early, you're late. So, on the night of my first improv class, I took a cab from my apartment to make sure I was on time. I ended up arriving about forty-five minutes before the 7 p.m. class.

This was a mistake.

Yes, I was still excited, but you have to understand my mindset at the time. Now that I was actually on the verge of putting my dream into action, I was nervous—again. It had only been a few weeks since my stand-up debut. Memories of D. H. Sweeney and my five-minute fear fest were still fresh. The last thing I wanted was to revisit that sense of out-of-control terror. Instead of walking into Dick Shea's, I paced on the sidewalk in front of the studio. I double- and triple-checked the address. I walked around the block. I started to imagine all the awful things that could happen if I walked through that door. *What if I suck? What if I don't understand how to do this? What if I can't get past my stage fright? How do you improvise? Holy shit! I don't know anything!!!*

They say that panic attacks are just little reminders that every decision you've ever made was wrong. I don't want to say I had a panic attack in front of Dick Shea's Dance Studio, but it was panic attack–adjacent. *This is bullshit*, I thought. *What am I doing here? I'm not ready for this.*

Before I even realized what was happening, I had hailed another cab, ridden back to 75th Street, and stepped onto the sidewalk in front of my apartment. By now, you've probably decided that I'm the biggest wuss on the planet. I can't even go to a comedy class? But I bet there's something that scares the piss out of you too. Snakes? I've got no problem with snakes. Spiders? Those teeny little guys don't bother me. Tiny, tight spaces? Box me up and mail me to Jamaica, I don't care. Stop judging me for being scared to get up onstage in front of people to try to make them laugh. You've got your issues too—so suck it.

I stood on that sidewalk, ready to escape to my apartment, only minutes before my first improv comedy class was supposed to start. I was not happy with myself. That was when my inner drill sergeant again stepped in to save me. He was not about to put up with my shit.

INNER DRILL SERGEANT: *All right, Riggle, what seems to be the problem now? Why are you running back to that crappy little closet you call an apartment?*

ROB: *Well, uh . . . see . . . I guess I'm just not comfortable at the moment. This comedy class doesn't feel right to me.*

IDS: (in a mocking tone) *Oh, is the little baby uncomfortable? Is he having a hard day? What the hell, Marine! Since when is comfort part of the equation? What is your malfunction, numbnuts?*

ROB: *I don't know. I just . . . I just don't want to go into that classroom. I can't do it!*

IDS: *Give it to me straight, Riggle—what is going on here?*

ROB: (channeling my inner Rocky Balboa) *I'm afraid! All right? You want to hear me say it? You want to break me down? All right, I'll say it:* I'm afraid!

IDS: *Finally. At least now we're getting somewhere. What exactly are you afraid of? Just what do you think is going to happen if you go to that class?*

ROB: *Well, since you asked . . . If I go to class and they make me get up onstage and I try to be funny and I'm not . . . they'll judge me. They'll hate me. They'll laugh at me. They'll boo and hiss and spit on me. I'll hate me. I'll realize that I'm not at all funny and that leaving flight school and coming here was a terrible mistake. I'll finally see that I'm a total failure and I'll binge on burgers and beer and I'll gain three hundred pounds. I'll start snorting talcum powder and I'll lose my job and my friends, and my parents will shun me. I'll never find love. I'll die miserable and alone and be remembered as a fat quitter loser and my tombstone will read "He tried to be funny and wasn't." That's if I don't have a panic attack during the class and die right there onstage.*

IDS: *Wow. That's quite a list. It's also 100 percent bullshit.*

ROB: *Huh?*

IDS: *You're just making excuses. This is what you came here for, dipshit. Stop being a pussy and get your ass into that class! So, what if no one laughs and no one asks for your autograph on the first day? Did you expect this to be easy?*

ROB: *(long pause) Well . . . no.*

IDS: *This is your dream! Stop fucking around and* go to class!!!

That mental kick in the ass was what I needed. I flagged down another taxi (if nothing else, I was doing my part to support the families of New York cab drivers), arrived at the studio at seven, and ran inside and into the classroom just in time.

The instructor was Ian Roberts, truly one of the best improvisers and writers I've ever met. Ian would go on to act in numerous movies and TV series, as well as write and direct for the Emmy-winning television show *Key & Peele*. I looked at him like he was an NFL Hall of Fame quarterback—I could hardly believe I was breathing the same air as him.

I sat in the back of the room and planned to just soak in wisdom for that first class. Ian started out with a talk about the basic rules of improv. Then he had us do warm-up games like Zip Zap Zop (you stand in a circle, someone starts by saying "Zip" and pointing to another person, that person says "Zap" and points to another person, and around it goes) and Crazy Eights (everyone shakes out their limbs—right arm, left arm, etc.—for eight counts while making eye contact with the rest of the group). Just like war-mups in my college theater classes, it felt pretty silly to me, especially now that I was an active-duty Marine Corps captain. But I knew that if this was going to work, I had to get out of my own way and embrace it, silly or not.

Then Ian announced, "Everybody's going to do a scene today." Inwardly, I groaned long and loud. I did not want to perform.

Ian had people come up in pairs and improvise a five-minute scene, then he made comments. Some of the scenes were decent, and some, not surprisingly, were pretty rough. I watched each with the intense stare of a hungry buzzard circling over a napping camper. *What kind of character is she creating? What is he saying? How is she reacting as his partner?* I noticed right away that the confident performers drew me in, while the nervous ones made me uncomfortable. *Okay,* I thought, *try to project confidence.* One pair did not listen to each other or play off each other at all. He was selling bananas and she was looking at an X-ray. *Got it*, I thought. *Listen to your scene partner!*

We had about twenty people in the class, so the scenes took some time. Class ended at 10 p.m. I watched the minutes tick by and crossed my fingers. *Maybe,* I thought, *I'll be able to skate by this time without getting up there.*

Near 10 o'clock, just when I thought Ian was going to dismiss the class, he instead said, "Has everybody gone?" He scanned the room and locked eyes with me. "You," he said. "You haven't gone." *Oh, shit,* I thought. *Here we go.* He found another victim, a woman named Dannah Feinglass, who I think was also hoping to just watch. Ian summoned the two of us to the front of the class.

The adrenaline rush wasn't as bad as Comic Strip Live—only mild terror instead of I'm-probably-going-to-die-right-now terror. I reminded myself that this was a class and that some of the other scenes hadn't been that great. We were here to learn—it was okay to look clueless.

Someone made a suggestion for our scene—I think I was supposed to be a real estate agent trying to sell a home to a prospective buyer—and we were off. Obviously, Dannah and I were both green as St. Patrick's Day leprechauns, but we had just enough comedic instincts to play off each other. Soon we were creating a scene where all the neighborhood kids were camping in tents—uninvited—in the backyard of the house for sale, and I tried to convince a skeptical Dannah that this didn't happen every weekend.

It sounds ridiculous, but it worked. I felt it. Dannah felt it. People in the class laughed. Most important, when we were done, Ian said, "Good job."

Little did I know that Dannah, a lovely and talented woman, would become a good friend who I would perform with for years. We were among the first UCB students, and she was the first person in our group to score a big break—in 2000 she landed a role on *Mad TV,* the sketch comedy TV show.

All I cared about as Dannah and I walked down the stairs together after that first class was that we'd nailed our first improv scene. "I loved it when you made that incredulous face!" I said.

"I loved when you tried to sell me on all the advantages of being the neighborhood mom," she said. "That was great!"

That little burst of initial success was the highlight of my week and made it so much easier to come back the next time. The fact that I got to share it with Dannah is part of what I love about improv. The stand-up comedy world is so competitive. When you step onto that stage, all you've got is yourself. The attitude tends to be "I need the spotlight on me. Everybody else? You're the enemy."

Improv is a completely different animal. Like on a football team, it's collaborative. You have to depend on and trust each other. Improv's most important rule is "yes, and"—when a castmate throws out an idea, your job is to embrace the idea, no matter how outlandish it is, and then build on it. No rejections or redirections allowed. If a player says you're hiking up an erupting volcano, you don't kill the scene by saying the eruption has stopped. Instead, you both jump into the collapsable canoe that was in your backpack and paddle down the mountain in a river of lava! "Yes, and" is more than a rule. It's a philosophy, a mindset, that builds trust and teamwork.

In improv, teamwork is everything. When one person in your group is on their game and creates a character that the audience loves, it raises the success level for everyone. Likewise, if someone is struggling, you don't celebrate. You try to pick them up. It's like what I learned in the Marines. When you go into combat, you are trusting the guys around you with your life. I loved it when I saw guys excelling. It raised my comfort level and trust in them. You *want* your squad mates to be the best Marines they can be. People aren't too worried about individual credit or about who's the one to actually complete the final piece of an objective. We all know that it takes a team to get it done and that we need each other.

It reminds me of when I was in The Basic School in Virginia, after I'd been commissioned as a second lieutenant. Sometimes they'd spring a march on us without notice. You didn't know if the march would be three miles or ten; you just knew you had to pack up all your gear and be ready to move in a few minutes. Well, some guys did not drink enough water beforehand. We'd be eight miles into a march on a hot summer day, and these guys would get lightheaded and start slowing down. Nobody wants to see a fellow platoon member collapse from heat exhaustion. Plus, if we were on a deployment in the jungle somewhere, we wouldn't be leaving a Marine or his weapon behind. So, you lightened his load. On more than one occasion, when I noticed a guy nearing his limit, I had to say to someone next to me, "Hey, you take his helmet and I'll carry his rifle" or "Hey, you grab one side of his ALICE pack and I'll grab the other." You did what was needed to get everybody through it. If *I* were dehydrated or sick, I knew these guys would be there for me in the same way. We were a team.

I didn't expect any of my classmates to collapse onstage from heat exhaustion, but I knew we'd still need to find ways to lift each other up. Now that I was an improv comedian—or at least trying to be one—I hoped I'd be a worthy teammate.

TWELVE

Be All In or Get All Out

Once I started that first class with Ian Roberts at the UCB, I was fully committed. I immersed myself in the world of comedy. I took all three levels of the classes offered, then took them all again—not because I'm a slow learner, but because I was so excited to have finally figured out what I wanted to do. There's a saying I like, based on a poker expression: Be all in or get all out. There is no halfway. Whether it's a big pot or a big dream, you can't win if you aren't willing to risk everything—your money, your time, your energy, your reputation, your dignity (see my stand-up debut at Comic Strip Live). I've seen it over and over in my life.

Which reminds me of a recent poker game. Let me tell you the story . . .

Thick clouds of cigar smoke hung in the air as I peeked again at my cards. I took a quick glance at the seven celebrities joining me at the poker table. Most studied the cards in their hands or on the table, intense expressions on their faces—all except Paul Rudd, who was stuffing his face with potato chips.

Two pair, I thought. *Black aces and black eights. The infamous Dead Man's Hand held by Wild Bill Hickock when he was murdered in a saloon. Stay cool, Riggle. These guys have been fleecing you all night. This is your chance to get 'em back. Don't give it away!*

For sixteen years now, I've cohosted an annual charity event for Kansas City's Children's Mercy Hospital called the Big Slick. It started with a poker tournament and has grown into a massive weekend event that attracts celebrities from across the country for activities like a celebrity softball game, a Royals baseball game, a variety show/concert, an auction, and more. Still, a bunch of us always end up in a hotel suite for a late night of Texas Hold 'Em poker. I'm in those games mainly to "donate" money to the real players—I'm not that good. But I always have a blast listening to the stories.

On this night, though, I finally had a chance at making a killing. I had a pretty decent hand. I knew, though, that three of a kind or better would beat me—and if I lost, these guys would ride me into the dirt. I'd never hear the end of it. But hey, that's poker and life, right? To feel good about yourself, sometimes you have to trust your instincts, take a chance, and go for it.

It was the last round of betting. I pushed all my chips into the middle of the table and tried to project confidence as I locked eyes with the other players and said, "I'm all in."

The table erupted.

"Riggle, you're full of shit!" Sam Levine said.

"I thought you were already out of chips!" Kevin Rahm added.

Even so, players who obviously had squat began throwing down cards and folding. Kevin Pollack stared at me. "I've got you with two pair, which beats my one pair. I'm out."

How does he know? I thought. *Oh, right. According to these guys, I have about thirty tells. Everybody can read me like an open comic book.*

In moments, everyone at the table was out—everyone except me and Andrea Savage. She eyed me coolly. "At best," she said, "you're sitting on a pair of jacks." She pushed in her own pile of chips. "I call."

I think I've got this, I thought. *I think I'm gonna win!*

The dealer flipped over the last card, known as the river, which either of us could use in our hand. It was a seven of hearts. I was feeling good.

I put my cards down. "Aces and eights—Dead Man's Hand," I said.

Andrea's face twitched ever so slightly before it broken into a grin. She laid down her cards—two sevens. With the river, that made three of 'em.

"Nooooo!" I shouted.

"You know what?" Andrea said as she scooped up all the chips on the table. "This is an easy game."

Yeah, I got smoked that night. But I don't regret it at all. I love poker and I love hanging out with good people. And I'd at least given myself a chance at a big score (relatively speaking—if I'd won, it might have paid for dessert at the Cheesecake Factory). Like I said: Be all in or get all out.

That was my attitude when I took all those classes back in 1998 at the UCB. Because each member of what was known as the UCB Four had a unique style and perspective, I wanted to absorb as much knowledge as I could from all of them. Something was always happening at the UCB theater, so I literally was there seven nights a week. If I wasn't in class or performing, I volunteered as a tech assistant, operating the stage lights or sound cues for other people's shows. Or a bunch of us would pool our money and hire a more experienced classmate to teach us that night. Or I'd get together with other classmates to write sketches or even an entire show based on improv scenes we'd created. If nothing else was going on, I simply sat in the audience and watched whoever was performing that evening, taking mental notes on what worked and what didn't. I learned something new every night. I was basically getting a master's degree in improv comedy.

When I "graduated" from that first level 3 class, I started joining what the UCB called house teams, made up of advanced classmates. I was in groups called Remedial Zen and Cowbot before joining up with an especially talented crew in 1999. You probably know some of the names—besides Dannah Feinglass, there was Owen Burke, Chad Carter, Jackie Clarke, Rob Huebel, Paul Scheer, and Danielle Schneider. Owen, who was a pun machine, came up with a name we all liked: Respecto Montalban, a twist on the name of actor Ricardo Montalban. We performed regularly as a group for the next six years.

What was it like playing and performing with these guys? I'll tell you. We rented a rehearsal space in the Village in lower Manhattan. We practiced in the evenings. Since I went to an office as a Marine every day and was the only one with a full-time job, I'd always be the last to arrive for practice. Even that first evening, as soon as I opened the door to the rehearsal space, work briefcase in my hand, I was in the middle of a scene, with everybody talking to me at once.

Dannah ran up to me, shouting, "Dad, Dad, you're home! Guess what, I got an A on my geometry test!"

Paul Scheer and Owen Burke hurried forward and ran circles around me.

"Dad, I hit a home run at baseball practice!"

"Dad, I got hit in the eye by a grounder!"

Jackie, playing my wife, had an imaginary drink in her hand and a slur in her speech indicating it wasn't her first tipple of the day. "Oh, look who decided to come home," she said. "I suppose you want dinner? I hope you brought one with you!"

Meanwhile, Rob Huebel was barking like a dog, nonstop, at the top of his lungs, and running around the room, jumping onto and off the furniture like—well, like a dog. The scene went on for a full ten minutes, with me immediately stepping into the role of Dad, trying to listen to my kids, trying to get my wife to stop drinking, and yelling, "Would somebody please shut that dog up!"

I had such a blast with these guys. They became not just partners in comedy but cherished friends. I still perform with many of them today.

The center of my comedy universe, though, remained the UCB Four: Amy, Matt, Matt, and Ian. They showed me what being all in was all about, not only through their dedication to their craft, but through their commitment to helping us novices become real comedians. They weren't just amazing, talented performers; they were genuinely nice people—how does that happen? They were who I wanted to grow up to be (even though we were all pretty close in age).

I've already talked about Ian. Let me tell you a little more about the rest of these guys. I had just one class with Amy. For some reason, I always got nervous around Amy, which didn't make sense because she couldn't have been kinder to me. In one of my first classes with her, my character had to take his pants off—maybe I was supposed to be a superhero named Captain Marvelous and I was changing into my costume. Mind you, at an improv show, you don't *actually* take your pants off—you just pretend. You pantomime. But I was so green that I didn't know this at the time. I was focused and in-the-moment, so I whipped my belt off, for real.

"Hold on, time out," Amy said, while giving me a patient smile (no doubt thinking at the same time, *Oy, what I have to put up with*). "Rob, if you have an actual belt in your hand, the audience is going to expect you to use it. But if you start flailing that thing around, someone could get hurt. Just make the motions and *act* like you're taking it off—everyone will get the idea."

Since I always felt tongue-tied around Amy, I didn't say anything. I just thought, *Ugh, this is embarrassing. But right, I get it. Make it an air belt. This is object work.*

I think I was nervous around Amy because she was just so talented. Her comedic mind and character work were fantastic—she could play anything from an oil tycoon to a spastic nine-year-old. In later years, I wasn't surprised at all by her success on *Saturday Night Live*, on the TV show *Parks and Recreation*, and in other shows and movies. It was obvious she was that good. At the time of the UCB classes, I just did not want to look dumb or fail in front of her. I wanted her approval.

Which is what made one moment particularly gratifying. I was playing an improv scene at the UCB theater with the Matts, Ian, and Amy (more in a bit on how that came to be). I don't recall the details of the scene, though it must have had something to do with food. I just know that when I entered the scene, I introduced myself as Bob Gravy. It was funny enough that it made Amy break character—she started laughing. You're not supposed to do that when you're onstage. It reminds the audience that you're playing a role. Once in a while, though, if something really cracks you up, you can't help it. You lose your composure and start laughing. I got Amy to laugh during a scene, which made me feel like a million bucks. Honestly, it was one of the highlights of my years at the UCB.

Matt Besser is an outstanding comedian, writer, and actor who would later appear in movies like *Walk Hard* and *Junebug* and on sitcoms such as *How I Met Your Mother, New Girl*, and *Community*. He thinks three steps ahead, a guy who's almost too hip for the room because he's just brighter than everybody else. He was also the toughest teacher at the UCB. If the UCB had a drill sergeant, it would be Matt. He wasn't interested in debate. If a student resisted his teaching and started explaining with a "Here's why I did that," Matt might answer, "I don't care why you did it. You did it wrong." Or if we were in his class doing a bit that started going nowhere, Matt might get mad and stop the scene. I remember one time when he cut off a scene we were performing and confronted one of the other players. "What the hell are you doing? What is the game of this scene?"

"Uh, I dunno," the student said. "I'm trying to sell a car."

"No, that's what you're *doing*," Matt snapped. "What is the game?"

Meanwhile, I thought, *That's what* I *would have answered. I better get my shit together and figure out what the game is myself.* I soon learned that the game is whatever is unique and/or unusual about a scene. It's that first, unexpected twist that drives everything that follows. During takeoff, for instance, a copilot in the cockpit might mention to his captain that he got drunk at a recent party. The game starts when the captain then says to the copilot, "That's nothing. I'm actually drunk *right now*." The players in the scene have no choice but to build on a statement that surprising.

I think Matt has softened some today, but he had an edge back then. I didn't always enjoy the intensity that came with being in his class, but I learned a lot. It kept me from getting complacent. He made me realize there was always another higher level to aspire to.

Then there was Matt Walsh. Little did I know that he would one day earn Emmy nominations for his role as the press secretary in *Veep*, or that he and I would both appear in the movie *The Hangover*. In 1999, I didn't have an agent, but I heard through a friend about a casting call for a TV miniseries being produced by Tom Hanks and Steven Spielberg. It was *Band of Brothers*, depicting the story of the 101st Airborne Division's Easy Company during World War II, a show that would go on to win a gazillion awards. It wasn't comedy, but I was interested in dramatic roles too. More important, I was open to anything that actually paid and got me time onstage or in front of a camera.

I auditioned for *Band of Brothers* and got a callback for a second audition. At that point, I decided I needed some help. Even though I was nervous about asking, I went to Matt Walsh's office.

"Hey, Matt," I said. "I've got this big audition coming up, and I don't know what I'm doing. If you have any time, I'd love to get your opinion on some stuff."

"Absolutely, man," he said. "When are you free? Come swing by my office and we'll do it."

So, I did. Matt was incredibly gracious. He was in the middle of writing sketches for his own TV show, yet he spent nearly two hours with me. We talked about the three scenes I had to prepare, talked about the bigger picture, and read through my scenes. Matt gave me his thoughts on how he would approach the scenes and how to make them better. We ran each scene a few times. After each pass he offered a few things for me to think about—suggestions of how to find specific moments that weren't so obvious. I left his office feeling grateful and confident that I'd be ready for the audition. The producer I met with did like my audition . . . but I didn't get the part, which was probably a blessing. There was no way the Marines would give me months off to shoot a TV miniseries in England. What was great, however, was that Matt took the time to help me do my best and get more experience with auditions.

With me fully committed to learning my new trade and surrounded by so many talented and successful people, you might think I was in a constant state of inspiration, ready to take on the world, fully confident that my big break was about to hit me on the head. You would be wrong.

In April 1998, I turned twenty-eight years old. That made me six or seven years older than most of my UCB classmates. They were just starting out in life and making ends meet by waiting tables and serving drinks. I had a regular, full-time day job and felt like I was already in mid-career. To put it another way: I felt old. Because of that, I was impatient. I believed that unlike the students around me, my time was running out. I would meet with established actors and comedians and lament that I wasn't getting enough work to attract an agent. It was my not-so-subtle way of asking them to introduce me to their agent. Instead of doing that, though, they'd always tell me to keep putting in stage time. "Keep learning and growing," they'd say, "and the agents will come to you."

I'd think, *I don't have time for that. I need to make it* now *or it's never going to happen.*

It didn't help that all my friends were getting on with their lives. My high school and college buddies were being promoted to management positions or starting their own business, getting married, and buying houses. My Marine buddies were advancing through the ranks, flying F-18s and Cobra helicopters. Everybody I knew was moving ahead while I stayed up till 1 a.m. making up silly characters in front of tiny audiences who had nothing better to do. I'd go home to Kansas for holidays, and friends would ask, "Hey, are you still trying to do that comedy thing? What's up with that? Have you done anything I might have seen?" I heard judgment in their questions and started hating myself. I had to keep reminding myself that if other people were making it in show business, I could too. I had to just keep at it so I'd be in a position to grab my opportunity when it arrived.

And then, to my surprise, it *did* arrive.

I was in my tiny studio apartment, polishing off my standard dinner—beans, rice, and sour cream takeout in a pie tin. I was not happy that night. I'd been burning the candle at both ends, with little to show for it other than gaining forty pounds—I was beginning to resemble Jabba the Hutt. As I licked up the remains of my meal, it occurred to me that my eating habits might have something to do with my expanding belly. I was frustrated, even angry. *Maybe,* I thought, *this is all a waste of time.*

My phone rang. It was Amy Poehler.

"Hi, Rob," she said. "How you doing?"

I wiped off the sour cream that was dribbling from my chin. "Great!" I said.

"Hey, are you free this weekend? Would you like to come down and play with us?"

I realized immediately what she was asking. The UCB Four had a TV show at the time, a half-hour sketch comedy series on Comedy Central. Before filming sketches, they would test them and work out the kinks in front of a live audience. Each sketch was scripted, but they also left room to improvise if someone got inspired. Sometimes a student would get asked to play supporting characters for these rehearsals. Even better, after finishing the sketch work and taking a break in the greenroom, the group would come out and do another hour of improv comedy—the UCB Four plus one lucky student.

In other words, I'd just been invited to do a show with four of the best improvisers on the planet.

This was the call every minor leaguer wants to get. *That's it!* I thought. *I'm going to the big leagues! I'm going to the Show!* I was Nuke LaLoosh in *Bull Durham*, about to trade in my scuzzy flip-flops. If I'd had a meeting with the president scheduled that Sunday, I would've canceled it. This was my dream turning into reality.

On the phone with Amy, I tried to sound more composed than I felt. "Yeah, I'm free," I said. "I'll be there."

"Okay, great, thank you," Amy said.

"Thank *you*!"

Little did I know what I was getting into.

When I arrived at the theater that night, I learned that my scripted sketch scene required me to wear a full-body blue dolphin outfit. I'm a fairly large guy—six-foot-two and about 250 pounds at the time—so this was a big dolphin. In addition to being huge, the costume was made of heavy foam. Once I put it on, I started sweating—it was hot under all that padding. Even worse, the thing smelled like . . . well . . . foam that had been soaked in body odor . . . in a dumpster . . . in August (it's probably best that I never found out who wore it before me). The whipped cream on the sundae was that no one had cut eyeholes into the costume—I couldn't see a thing. I was pretty much helpless in my dolphin getup.

One of the Matts then explained that my dolphin character would be the centerpiece of an onstage ménage à trois. This was just a few minutes before we went on.

"Oh, yeah?" I said. "Um, okay, sure."

Getting gang-banged as a dolphin wasn't quite what I'd imagined for my debut with the UCB Four. But this was what improv and sketch comedy was all about, trusting the people around you and going all in on whatever the scene called for. I wasn't about to throw away my chance at performing with these guys because the audience wouldn't see my best features (or any features, in this case).

Once I heard my cue, I shuffled onto the stage, making high-pitched *me-me-me-me* dolphin sounds. I don't remember many details of my scene, but suffice to say, it didn't take long for the rest of the group to take advantage of the hapless marine (no pun intended) animal onstage. The character played by one of the Matts tricked the dolphin into giving him a blow job. While my larger-than-life-size dolphin was bobbing up and down in the throes of passion, the other Matt watching this got "excited," so he started ramming the dolphin from the rear. It was a sausage sandwich, with me in the middle (at least I'm pretty sure that's what was going on, since I couldn't see a thing). Apparently, it fit the scene perfectly. When the Matts started doing their thing, the audience absolutely roared with laughter.

Today, I sometimes hear aspiring actors and improvisers complain about some of the roles they get asked to play. I guess they want to be politically correct or control their image or something. I just think, *Shut up. You don't even know. I started out as a double-teamed dolphin.* It's what we do for comedy. I didn't feel abused or humiliated. The whole thing was so absurd and ridiculous that the audience loved it and so did I.

And then came the payoff. As promised, I was invited to join the group for the improv part of the show. There was just one problem—I was paralyzed. While our host asked for suggestions from the audience on how to start our scene, we all stood onstage against the back wall of the theater in front of everyone. As soon as someone had an idea, they stepped forward and started the action.

I wasn't worried about the audience, but I *was* nervous about my castmates. These people were my heroes. I did not want to screw up in front of them. For the first half of the improv show, as the superstars around me stepped into scene after scene with clever and hilarious characters, I stood frozen and mute. I did not partake in a single scene. I was stuck to the wall like chewing gum to a grade-schooler's desk.

After a half hour, we took a short break. In the greenroom, Ian Roberts immediately approached me. "Hey, Rob," he said, "you gotta get off the wall, man."

"I know," I said, shaking my head. "I know."

"Don't even think. Just step out and it will take care of itself. We'll help you. You're here for a reason. Just step out and say or do something. Whatever it takes, get off that wall."

That was Ian, so encouraging and gracious. After the break, Ian stepped out and started a scene where he was looking for something. I was still frozen on the wall. I looked at the rest of the group—they weren't moving either. They'd heard Ian talking to me in the greenroom. They were waiting on me.

I knew I couldn't leave Ian out there by himself. *Oh, hell, here we go,* I thought. I took a deep breath and stepped out. I didn't have a single idea in my head. *I'll guess I'll figure it out as we go, just like they do.* I was scared shitless, but I also knew Ian was great.

He could make anything work. I played along with Ian, and pretty soon we were a pair of clueless archaeologists digging in the dirt for bones. I don't really recall the details of the scene, but I remember making choices and statements. Some of those statements even got laughs. I was "yes, and-ing." I was listening, I was playing the game of the scene. It was happening—slowly but surely, I was improvising with the best players in the world, and I was loving it!

Getting off the wall and playing that scene was like being at the pool and inching out onto the high dive for the first time. Everybody's telling you you're gonna be fine. Your dad's in the water, waving you on, shouting up, "You'll be okay, son, you can do it!" And you know they're *probably* right. But it still takes a leap of faith—in this case, literally. If you jump off that board, you really are all in. You want it, though. So, you take a deep breath, close your eyes, and go for it—and it's great! Once you hit the water and pop back up, you can't wait to get out of the pool and do it again.

That's how I felt after stepping off the wall and performing that scene with Ian. *Hey, I didn't die. We got some laughs. I made a few good choices there. Yeah, okay, maybe I* can *do this.*

All right, what's the next scene? Let's go!

THIRTEEN

Tomorrow Is Promised to No One

I first met the woman who would become my wife when a friend introduced us at a Kansas City bar. This was in the summer of 1997, during a visit just before my move to New York. I liked Tiffany right away. She was attractive and funny and probably most important, she thought *I* was funny. The bantering started immediately.

TIFFANY: *What's your last name again?*
ME: *Riggle.*
TIFFANY: *Hahahaha! That's not a real name. That's made up, right?*

We started a mostly long-distance relationship until a year after my move to New York, when she moved into my tiny, Tetris-game apartment with me. She brought two suitcases and nothing else—there wasn't room for more.

We were both in love and feeling like marriage was the next step. By the end of that year, I was ready to propose. I'd gotten to know Jules Roinnel, a manager of the Windows on the World restaurant at the top of the World Trade Center, during a Marine

Corps event there. On the big night, I took Tiffany to Windows on the World, and Jules made sure we got the best table in the house. Then we went to *Les Misérables* on Broadway. After that, we walked to Times Square. I forgot nearly every word of the little speech I'd prepared, but I remembered enough to say something, get down on one knee, and pop the question. She said yes.

Our plan was to get married in Kansas City during the second half of October. But God and the Marines Corps make their own plans. It was 1630 hours on a Friday, April 9, 1999. The end of the week was just a half hour away. I'd already dismissed the rest of the staff for the weekend. I looked at the clock again: 1635. *Ah, I'm out of here. Nothing's gonna happen in the next twenty-five minutes.* I grabbed my briefcase, walked to the office door, flipped off the lights, and opened the door.

The main office phone rang.

A word of advice: Never answer the phone twenty-five minutes before five o'clock on a Friday afternoon. You'll get screwed every time. I did not take my own advice. It *was* still office hours, and I was a responsible young captain. I walked back to my desk and picked up the phone: "Good afternoon, Marine Corps Public Affairs office, Captain Riggle speaking, how can I help you?"

"Captain Riggle?" the major on the other end of the line said. "Just the man I'm looking for. How does the phrase 'Leaving on a jet plane' sound to you?"

This is the thing about being in the military—you know that you can be called at any moment and expected to drop everything to respond to a crisis. It's a reality that you accept the minute you join. Before I went to Liberia, I was supposed to have been a groomsman in my friend Jim Davis's wedding, but my deployment erased that plan. So, it's not shocking to get a sudden deployment call—but it still kicks off an adrenaline surge.

I knew that NATO had recently initiated a bombing campaign against the Serbian army to try to stop aggression and abuses against ethnic Albanians in Kosovo. On the phone, the major informed me that I'd been tapped to join NATO's international effort to resolve the humanitarian crisis caused by the fighting and displacement of thousands of civilians. I was to leave for Germany, Albania, and Kosovo—ASAP.

When I asked about my return date, the major said he had no idea. I explained my October wedding plans. The major didn't care (I decided not to fill him in on our floral arrangements). He said I had until Tuesday to draw my gear and catch a flight to Frankfurt. I had no vote on the matter.

Oh my God, I thought, *Tuesday? What do I need to do to get ready? What do I need to pack? What about my improv classes?*

What about the wedding?

Tiffany was not happy to hear that the October wedding was off. But she also understood that I was a Marine and this was my duty. It was frustrating to disappoint her, but there was nothing I could do.

Over the weekend, I started thinking about the risks on a deployment. Soldiers, sailors, airmen, Marines—they died all the time in training. They died on operations even when they weren't in combat. You could, for example, accidentally roll a Humvee on a muddy road. To be honest, I wasn't too worried about my survival. The odds were definitely in my favor for this deployment—I wouldn't be kicking in doors, and I wasn't a trigger puller. Still, I'd be in a combat zone. *It's unlikely,* I thought, *but it's certainly possible that something bad could happen.*

I knew that if something *did* happen to me, Tiffany—as my fiancé but not wife—would get no information or benefits from the military. I did not want to leave her in the lurch if the worst occurred. *I've already been planning to marry her in October,* I thought. *Why not get married now?* When I talked to Tiffany about it, she thought it made sense too. That Monday, the day before I had to fly out, we went to city hall to file for a marriage license.

Normally, you had to wait twenty-four hours to get married after you filed. I waited in line for my turn to file and to explain my unique situation. The clerk was a woman behind a wall-to-wall wooden counter that reminded me of something you'd see in a 1930s police station. Come to think of it, this woman looked like *she'd* been there since the 1930s. She was on the plump side (imagine a female version of John Goodman before he lost weight), with gray hair, black glasses on a chain around her neck, and a two-pack-a-day smoker's rasp.

When I finally got my chance to speak, I patiently explained how I was a Marine being deployed and how we couldn't wait twenty-four hours to get married—we needed to get married now!

The woman's expression did not change as I spoke. I'm not even sure if she heard me. "Twenty-four hours," she growled when I was done. "You apply today, get married tomorrow."

I had not gotten through to this woman. "I am getting *deployed*," I said more loudly and slowly, like an obnoxious American tourist. "Tomorrow's too late!"

"Twenty-four hours," she said. "Next!"

You know how in *Beetlejuice*, the people who commit suicide have to be civil servants in the afterlife? I think this lady was one of those.

As this uncivil servant and I argued, a man in a suit walked by. He stopped, turned back, and asked what the problem was. I explained our predicament again.

"Tell you what," he said with a hint of a smile. "I was a Marine in Vietnam and I'm a judge. Come back after lunch and I'll marry you."

That's exactly what we did. After splitting a footlong at a Subway sandwich shop across the street, Tiffany and I walked back to city hall, and the judge performed the ceremony. I wore jeans and a flannel shirt, and she wore an Ann Taylor sweater. Three of my officemates brought flowers for Tiffany to hold and served as witnesses. My parents and Tiffany's mom listened to us exchange vows over our flip phones. It sure wasn't anybody's dream wedding, but we got it done before my flight in the morning. Thank God for Marines!

Just a few days later, I found myself in cammies on the tarmac at Tirana International Airport in Albania. The American-led contribution to NATO's efforts was named Joint Task Force Shining Hope, or the catchy acronym JTFSH. (The military loves acronyms. Advanced Short Range Air-to-Air Missile becomes ASRAAM, for example, while Man-Portable Air-Defense Systems are MANPADS—and no, I'm not making these up.) In Albania, forces from America and other nations had gathered to provide food, water, and shelter for people displaced by the fighting between Serbs and Albanians. When we got to Kosovo, we would be in charge of keeping the peace in our assigned sector. This meant making patrols, providing security, and collecting weapons from everybody we came across. Basically, we would try to restore peace between two groups of people that didn't like each other very much.

As in Liberia, my job was public affairs officer, which meant helping handle the media for my superiors, writing stories about what was happening for the media and military newspapers, and escorting camera crews and reporters as they shot footage or conducted interviews. It was easy to tell the experienced war correspondents from the newbies. The old-timers traveled light and were always ready to go. The rookies carried loads of shit wherever they went and wore gear with the price tags still on, as if they'd just stopped off at REI. They were usually disorganized and hungry. I would help them get their bearings and often provided them MREs so they didn't starve.

You could also tell which reporters were just looking for headlines and which were trying to dig deeper. Some would ask me questions like, "Has anybody been shot? How many injuries have you had? When was the last firefight?" It was the old newspaper saying: If it bleeds, it leads. But when I escorted Ted Koppel of ABC's *Nightline* or Christiane Amanpour of CNN around our sector in Kosovo, the questions were "What are you seeing here? What effect has the military's presence here had?" They were pros.

In Tirana, Joint Task Force Shining Hope and my public affairs tent—my work station—were on one end of the massive airport, while the Air Force, the chow hall, and the tent that served as my living quarters were on the other end, two miles away. Scattered throughout were smaller contingents representing countries such as England, the United Arab Emirates, and the Netherlands. One of my bosses was US Air Force Lieutenant Colonel Tom Dolney. We usually didn't have vehicles at our disposal, and he didn't like us wasting time walking between the chow hall and the public affairs tent every day, so he ordered mountain bikes for us to ride (the Air Force always seemed to get what they wanted, and on time—I loved working with the Air Force). To do my work and get my meals in, I rode my bike at least ten miles a day. At least I was getting back in shape.

One night during the first week of May, I'd just finished evening chow and was about to launch into my next Lance Armstrong impersonation and ride back to the public affairs tent. It was dusk, the end of a beautiful day. I was on the "ramp," the huge concrete area where they parked planes and helicopters, when another of my bosses, Navy Lieutenant Commander Jeff Breslau, nudged me.

"Hey," he said, "something's going on."

I looked to my right. One hundred fifty yards away, a large contingent of US Army 82nd Airborne troops were in formation, slowly approaching a C-130 aircraft parked on the "hold short line," the last position before a plane taxis onto the runway.

I realized immediately what was happening. I'd heard that an Apache helicopter had crashed during a training run in Albania and that both pilots had been killed. They were the first NATO casualties of the operation. This had to be the service for those pilots. Their squadron mates and comrades were saying goodbye.

Three years before, I'd been in a nighttime training exercise at Camp Lejeune when two Marine Corps helicopters collided, killing fourteen people. I hadn't seen the crash and didn't know the pilots, but it had been another reminder that I was in a hazardous profession. Now, though, I was seeing the coffins after a fatal accident for the first time.

Those poor families, I thought. *Someone back home has just found out that the person they love most in the world is coming home in a box.* It broke my heart. I was also upset that these men had died serving their country, and it was likely that no one outside of their families, friends, and fellow soldiers even knew about it. *Maybe* they'd be briefly mentioned in their hometown newspaper or on the local news of the base they were from. These guys had paid the ultimate sacrifice, what Abraham Lincoln called the "last full measure of devotion." I just hoped—and still do today—that people in America understood that even in peacetime, there's a huge price to pay for the freedoms and security we enjoy.

The commander and I, along with just about everyone else in the area, walked closer until we were about twenty yards from the procession. We didn't want to interfere, of course, but we wanted to show our respect.

I heard the mournful tones of a trumpet playing "Taps." A handful of soldiers carried two flag-draped coffins. They were led by a color guard displaying a US flag and the flag of the 82nd Airborne. Surrounding these groups were nearly one hundred soldiers standing at attention and saluting. Like everyone else around me, I straightened and saluted as the somber procession passed before me.

Even when we're doing supposedly routine shit, I thought, *this is still a dangerous environment. Things can and do go wrong. And God forbid, what happens if things heat up with the Serbs and we get into a ground fight? What if we start going toe to toe? This could all get nasty real fast.*

As the uniformed pallbearers stepped toward the C-130, which waited with its cargo bay open and ramp extended, I felt grateful—grateful to be alive, thankful for my wife and parents, grateful for *all* the people in my life that I cared about. I didn't want to take any of them for granted. I was twenty-nine. That Apache crew was about the same age . . . and just like that, their time was up. They weren't getting any more chances at anything.

Tomorrow is promised to no one. I can't change the past, and I can only try to plan for the future. The present, right now, is all I really have. I don't want to waste my life worrying about if I'm going to be the perfect husband or Marine or if I'm going to make it in comedy. I gotta just keep going after my dreams! I gotta show the people I care about how much I love 'em! When my time comes, I want to be able to say that I gave everything I had.

Nothing *ever* happens when you or I say "No." However, we never know what amazing things are gonna happen when we say "*Yes!*" Life has to be lived. Experiences must be had. Fear must be faced. Otherwise, what the fuck are we doing here? Paying taxes and counting our toenail clippings??

The soldiers carried the two coffins up the C-130's ramp and disappeared from sight. Moments later, the pallbearers reappeared and exited, the ramp closed, and the C-130 roared down the runway and lifted into the sky.

No regrets. That's how I want to live. No regrets.

That evening at the Tirana airport wasn't my last reminder of the risks of service. The NATO bombing campaign ended in June when the Serbs withdrew their forces from Kosovo. I then learned I'd been attached to a force of about 250 Marines from the 26th Marine Expeditionary Unit, which was headed for Kosovo to fill the power vacuum and keep the peace. I met them in Greece for the move north through Macedonia into Kosovo, riding in Humvees and an amtrac, an assault amphibious vehicle that stunk of diesel fuel and left me covered with black soot (after three hours in that hunk of metal, I looked like a coal miner). Our MEU was assigned to establish law and order in a sector in the north of the country.

I joined the MEU's small public affairs team, made up of another captain, a staff sergeant, a corporal, and me. As a public affairs officer, I needed to have situational awareness—to know the names of the towns and villages, what they looked like, where the trouble spots were, where the borders were. The guys going on patrols knew this. They'd often say, "Hey, Captain, we're going out and we've got an extra seat. You want to come with us?" I usually went. That way, when reporters quizzed me on what was happening in our sector, I could give them intelligent answers.

One day I rode on a patrol that had three Humvees and a Light Armored Vehicle (LAV). We traveled on a twisty two-lane highway through rolling green hills. Our vehicles took up both lanes—this was a narrow road built for little Yugos, not big-ass Humvees. At one point the officer in the lead Humvee stopped us so he could talk to a farmer, possibly hoping for some local intel. Our drivers spaced our vehicles across about three hundred yards of highway, parking them at angles so we looked like a fishbone—it spread out our defense, making us a more difficult target, and created a natural perimeter. Along with several other Marines, I got out to do a 360-degree security check and stretch my legs. About five hundred yards ahead of us on the highway, higher on a hill, was a village. From this distance, it looked like a one-street small town from 1950s America that had been abandoned, with a few run-down buildings that might once have been grocery stores, gas stations, and diners.

As I glanced around, I heard a hissing noise overhead, accompanied by a small *pop-pop-pop*.

What's that? I thought.

"Take cover!" someone barked.

Holy shit, someone's shooting at us! I couldn't quite believe it—but I believed it enough to crouch, scuttle back to the Humvee, and flatten myself against its frame.

This was my first experience with getting shot at. *Okay,* I thought. *So that's what it sounds like.* I was pleased that my racing pulse was already returning to a relatively normal rate. I actually started to feel calm. I also noticed that my attention to the moment had increased by a factor of about a million. Apparently, nothing gooses your ability to focus quite like someone trying to put a bullet in your brain.

"Where's it coming from?" I asked as we crouched.

"That village ahead," a Marine answered.

We weren't being pinned down by a hail of gunfire, so this was likely a lone sniper. We jumped back into our vehicles. The shooting stopped. We rolled into town along the main street, every eye alert. The adrenaline returned. *Okay, we're closing on whoever did this. What's this guy going to do? Is he going to flee or is he going to dig in to make a last stand like in* Butch Cassidy and the Sundance Kid? Either way, since all I had was my 9-millimeter Beretta sidearm, I probably wouldn't be contributing a lot if we engaged.

I scanned the buildings from my seat in a Humvee as we drove in and parked. A couple of the gray structures were two stories high. I watched the windows above us but didn't see movement.

Four Marines carrying automatic rifles got out of the lead Humvee and started checking the buildings, which seemed deserted. I stayed put. Apparently, whoever had taken a dislike to our presence didn't feel up to battling a fully armed Marine patrol. We couldn't find the sniper, so we continued with our patrol. Just another afternoon in Kosovo.

A patrol a few weeks later also got my attention. As we returned to our Forward Operating Base (FOB), we came to the small village at the base of the hill leading up to the FOB. A sentry flagged down our lead vehicle and spoke to the officer in charge. "Hey, sir," he said, "I've got something I think you should take a look at."

We emerged from our vehicles and did a security check, then accompanied the sentry about fifty yards up the road. One of the guys with us happened to be a Navy Explosive Ordinance Disposal (EOD) specialist. "How," the Navy guy said, "did *that* get *there*?"

He was staring at a silver canister about the size of a beer can. It was just sitting in the middle of the road.

"Some kid from the village brought it over," the sentry said. "I didn't like the way it looked, so I told him to set it down and just get away from it."

The Navy guy's face had turned white as a sheet. "Dude," he said quietly, "that's unexploded ordinance. It's got to be part of a cluster bomb that didn't explode. It could go off at any second."

No one was touching this thing. We had to quickly clear the area. The EOD guy put a detonation charge next to the bomb, piled a pyramid of sandbags around and over it, and then blew it in place. Fortunately, no one was killed or injured.

It gave me a new sense of confidence in the competence of the American military personnel I was working with. They recognized a dangerous situation and knew exactly what to do about it. Still, it had been a close call for that kid and anyone near him. *What if he'd dropped the bomb or put it down too hard? He'd have been vaporized.*

Some threats are more serious than others. On my first night in our Kosovo sector, a group of Marines and I came across an abandoned chicken processing factory on top of a hill. It was a hard structure with a roof, and since it was pouring rain, those of us who didn't relish sleeping in a Humvee decided to crash there for the night. The place was breaking down, but it was a shelter. I found a spot on the floor, zipped myself up snug in my sleeping bag, and nodded off.

In the middle of the night, I was having one of my usual bizarre dreams. I was a heavily muscled pork chop, like you would see in a cartoon. My head on a pork chop body. No big deal. Only in this dream, I was also being devoured by something with sharp teeth. It was nibbling on me for a snack.

I began to wake up. I was still groggy, but I gradually realized—to my horror—that something *was* sniffing or quietly chewing on the back of my head. My arms were pinned inside my sleeping bag—I could barely move. So, I slowly twisted my neck. An inch away, staring malevolently into my face, were the beady eyes of the hugest, ugliest rat in all the recorded history of rats. From my angle on the floor, at point blank range, it looked roughly the size of a Shetland pony. This was the Queen Mother of All Rodents, a rat so enormous that it had to bend down to reach me—and it was about to take my head off.

As you might imagine, I handled this crisis well. *"Holy fuck holy fuck holy fuck!!!"* I shouted in a tone five octaves higher than normal. I somehow jumped to my feet, but I was still trapped inside my sleeping bag. I wriggled and twisted like I was the giant worm monster from *Tremors* having a seizure—I frantically tried to get free of my sleeping bag so I could defend myself against the monster pony-rat. Frightened by either my girlish screams or my other-worldly dance moves, the rat scurried away, ran up a pipe along the wall, and disappeared into a hole in the ceiling.

The commotion woke up all the Marines around me. Fortunately for my reputation, they saw the massive rat too. "Sir," one said, "did it bite you?"

I felt the back of my head. To my surprise, my cranium seemed intact and wasn't gushing buckets of blood. "I guess not," I said. "I seem to be okay. But I think it was about to bite my head off."

A corporal who'd been on watch popped his head into the doorway of the chicken factory. "Sir, what was that high-pitched squeal?"

"Uh," I said, thinking fast, "I think someone stepped on a pig somewhere?"

"But . . . I heard the squeals saying words," the corporal said.

"Never mind, Corporal," I snapped. "Just get back to your watch." I noticed the Marines on the floor with me in the chicken factory were suddenly avoiding eye contact.

The corporal left. The rest of us tried to settle down, but no one could relax now that we knew a predator was in the house.

"Well, I can't sleep," one Marine finally said. "Let's get that rat."

That sounded great to me. "I'll give anyone ten bucks," I said, "if you put him out of action."

"Fuck yeah!" another Marine said. Those two got up and prepared to hunt. I snuggled back into my bag and fell into a contented sleep, secure in the knowledge that some of the military's finest were on the job. I learned later that the rat did indeed meet his demise . . . that's what they told me, anyway.

On another night at the chicken factory, my sleep was suddenly interrupted by the unmistakable sound of one of our M240 machine guns: *Da-da-da-da-da! Da-da-da-da-da!* When those bad boys go off, everybody starts moving. It means that someone is trying to get through the perimeter and we're under attack. Instantly, I and the rest of the Marines around me were up and running toward our battle stations, some of us yanking on boots and grabbing ammo as we ran. I thought, *This had to be a mistake. Who the fuck would attack us on this hilltop?* But then I thought, *That's why they're called surprise attacks!* I didn't question further. I just hauled ass to my fighting hole.

The firing went on for a full minute, maybe two—which is a lot of lead being thrown. Then it stopped. We quickly got a grasp on what had happened. Rather than a full-bore assault by the Serb army, the "attacker" was actually a lone cow that had apparently wandered off someone's farm, slipped through some fences, and made it to our perimeter. We had a series of defenses designed to discourage would-be attackers and alert us if someone was approaching: barbed wire, wire with cans tied to it, trip flares. The unfortunate cow had set off a trip flare. I guess the Marine on duty figured it was the start of World War III.

The good news, though, is that everyone else did what they were supposed to do that evening. Our guys got to their battle stations, no one panicked and started firing indiscriminately, and we quickly figured out what was going on. It made for an interesting night for us—and a bad night for one unfortunate bovine.

I hope that cow lived a full and meaningful life . . . whatever is meaningful to a cow, that is. Because whether you're a cow or a human, you never know when you're going to accidentally wander into the wrong place and find your world ending faster than you can say, "Oh, shit, did that sign say 'Trespassers Will Be Shot'?"

FOURTEEN

Focusing on the Mission

When I meet people these days, the question I hear more than any other is "Dude, how do you go from Marines to comedy?" I understand the curiosity. A Marine's mentality is vastly different than a comedian's mentality. The Marine Corps mission is clear and direct: "To locate, close with, and destroy the enemy by fire and maneuver." That takes a certain mindset. As a comedian, my mission is to make people laugh (slightly different outcome). That takes a very different mindset. Respect authority, question authority—many would say the worlds of the Marines and comedy are polar opposites. (Though if you think about some of the hilarious shit I've seen as a Marine—I'm remembering the drunk dudes in coconut bras trying to get back to the ship in the Canaries—maybe those worlds aren't so far apart.)

For me, it's all about the lane I'm in at the time. I'm fortunate. I've always been pretty good at transitions—at making the shift from one activity or mindset or character or lifestyle to another. I seem to have a gift for moving between lanes effectively and, once I'm there, putting all my attention onto that lane. When I have on my Marine hat, I'm very much a mission-focused Marine. When

I have on my comedy hat, I'm very much a freewheeling comedian who might say some really obnoxious shit about anything and everything, up to and including most sacred cows. (This does not mean I've turned on the military, that I want to take down the government, or that I hate this or that group. I just think we gotta be able to laugh at ourselves.) When I'm off duty and offstage, hanging out with family or friends, I'm focused on being present and enjoying time with them. Staying in the moment and keeping mission-focused is what allows good things to happen.

Back in 1999, I was mission-focused during my deployment in Kosovo. But when the fighting in Kosovo died down in June and our task force started wrapping up operations a couple months later, I knew it would soon be time for me to shift my focus. One day late that summer, I got my new orders. I had to be off to Germany to catch a commercial flight home the next morning. (Turns out that Tiffany and I could have waited till October for the wedding after all—oh well!)

My orders home happened so fast that I didn't have a chance to let my new wife know I was coming—which gave me a somewhat devious idea. I decided it would be fun to surprise her. I landed at JFK International Airport near midnight, then took a cab to our apartment, arriving in the wee hours of the morning, anticipating the joyous look on Tiffany's face when I arrived unannounced. I got up to our apartment with all my gear, attempted to put my key in the door, and discovered it no longer fit. I looked around in confusion. *Am I at the right door? Do I have the right key? Am I in the right building? I've only been gone four months.* I took a second look around. *Okay, I* do *have the right building, apartment, and key. Then what the hell is going on?*

In order to keep to my surprise plan, I decided to pound loud and fast on the door, like I was part of a SWAT team ready to break in. I heard stirring inside. To add to the surprise, I covered up the peephole in the door so she couldn't see who was there.

This'll be great.

Speaking of transitions . . . it's probably best to give people a warning before you start pounding on their door in the middle of the night. Otherwise, you will scare the shit out of them—as I discovered that night.

I heard Tiffany reach the door and try to look through the peephole. "Who is it?!" came the half-angry, half-terrified voice from inside the apartment. "Move your hand right now or I'm calling the cops!"

I moved my hand. "Honey, it's me!" I said. Fortunately, the relief of finding out I wasn't a gangster or some drunk from the Eurotrash bar on the corner overcame her temporary terror long enough for her to let me in. (Turned out she'd accidentally locked herself out of the apartment a couple days before and had to get the locks changed.)

I'm aware some folks have trouble making the shift from a deployment back to stateside living, but it just wasn't a big issue for me. I immediately jumped back into working at my Marine Corps office on Third Avenue by day and refining my comedy skills at the UCB at night.

Late in the summer of 2000, I began to see evidence that my mission-focused philosophy was actually paying off. Another benefit of being involved at the UCB was that casting directors and producers sometimes hung around, looking for new talent. One of those was Cecilia Pleva, a producer for *Late Night with Conan O'Brien*. She called one day and invited me to play a bit character on the show. It would be my first appearance on television. I was thrilled—someone in the industry had noticed me! The show in question had a back-to-school theme, so I was to play a bully who would give another UCB "graduate" that I knew—Andy Daly, one of the funniest comedic actors and improvisers around—a swirlie in a toilet (ironic, considering my past experience with bullies). Besides being hilarious, Andy was a lot smaller than me, so he was the perfect choice for the part.

What I didn't know at the time was that when they called Andy, they said, "We can't do it today because we're trying to find a prop toilet. We'll let you know when we're ready." A couple days later, they called me and Andy and said to come down to Rockefeller Center to film the bit. We proceeded to a bathroom on the sixth floor, where the crew was ready to shoot. Andy's face transformed from amused to horrified as he realized there was no prop toilet—I was going to dunk his head into a real toilet.

A cleaning crew had just finished doing its best to clean the area. The whole room reeked of ammonia. "I'm so sorry about this, man," I said to Andy as we stood together in the stall while cameras were set up. "I'll try not to push you down too far. Whatever I can do to help."

Andy shook his head. "Just keep a good hold on me," he said, "so I don't actually swallow anything."

Picture this scene—Andy and I were in the bathroom, both dressed like high school students in jeans and T-shirts. My line was "Hey, freshman, how about a swirlie?" Then the camera would show Andy upside down, me holding him by the torso and stirring his head in the toilet.

We took our positions for the shot. You have to understand my dilemma—this was my first TV appearance! I wanted to be the best student-dunking, swirlie-stirring high school bully in the history of televised bullies! I had a powerful urge to stuff Andy down there until only his ankles showed. Yet I also felt sorry for Andy. I didn't necessarily want to drown him in a cesspool. That might leave

Conan and the producers with a bad first impression of me. On the other hand, maybe it would make for great TV and this could turn into a recurring character—Rob Riggle as the Serial Swirler!

With my hands firmly around Andy's ankles and his head turning a shade of purple as blood rushed to his brain, I mentally debated what I should do—play it straight or condemn Andy to the bowels of the Rockefeller Center sewer system? Andy's hygienic life was literally in my hands.

At the last moment, common decency—or maybe it was common sense—kicked in. I managed to keep Andy above the surface. Fortunately for him, we shot the whole thing in one take.

My big television debut ended up taking only about ten seconds of screen time. I emailed a handful of friends who stayed up that night to watch it. They emailed me comments like, "Rob, I saw it, you were great!" Andy was less excited about it. In fact, in an interview with Conan years later, Andy identified our bit as his least favorite *Late Night* sketch—for obvious reasons.

Andy might not have enjoyed the moment, but I was thrilled. This was my first taste of working on TV. It was a chance to start building a reputation and a highlight reel that I could show to producers. It was evidence that I was on the right track, that there really was a chance I might be able to make it in this business.

I never did get a call to bring back the Serial Swirler, though. If you're reading this, Conan, I'm ready!

The *Conan* appearance wasn't my only comedy breakthrough at the time. I must have done a decent enough job with my dolphin sex scene back before my deployment, because the UCB Four invited me to perform in more rehearsals and shows with them. That led to an even bigger opportunity: *ASSSSCAT*. What is *ASSSSCAT*, you ask? Don't try to figure out the acronym, because the explanation takes too long. Some say it has something to do with a sprinkler system. Others say that one night when the UCB Four and others were onstage back in Chicago, the performance was going south. It devolved into all the players leaving the stage and shouting nonsense words at each other from the wings. One of those words was *ASSSSCAT*, which eventually became the name for the UCB's two-part, longform improv show. Ian, Amy, Matt, and Matt did two *ASSSSCAT* shows every Sunday night and often invited one or two students to join them. Starting near the end of 2000, I was lucky enough to be one of them.

This was a big deal. *ASSSSCAT* had become one of the most popular comedy shows in New York City. People would wait all afternoon in a line that snaked around the building to get in. The shows were always standing room only. *ASSSSCAT* also attracted some of the most talented people in New York to perform. Cast members and writers from *Saturday Night Live*, *Late Night with Conan O'Brien*, *The Daily Show*, *Late Night with David Letterman*, Comedy Central, and The State started showing up and would get invited to play onstage. Producers and directors from those shows, as well as casting directors for TV shows and commercials, made up part of the audience.

Apparently, I was improving at this comedy thing because I became an *ASSSSCAT* regular. Years later, when I guest starred in an episode of *The Office*, John Krasinski came up to me and said, "You don't know me [of course, I did], but I remember you from an *ASSSSCAT* show in New York where you said the funniest thing I ever heard." John went on to describe the whole scene. I didn't remember a thing about it, but the fact that John remembered it and thought enough of it to say so meant a lot to me.

I was staying mission-focused and gradually gaining confidence in my comedic skills. But just when you think you've got life by the balls, it has a way of turning on you and kicking you there. You've heard the song "The Night the Lights Went Out in Georgia"? Let me tell you about the night they turned the lights off on us in Minnesota.

At the time I was doing the *ASSSSCAT* shows, a group of eight of us, including Paul Scheer, Owen Burke, and Andy Daly, performed a longform improv show every Saturday night at the UCB theater. It was a parody of the MTV reality show *The Real World*, which featured a bunch of people living together in the same house. We called it "The Real Real World," and we each played characters we had created ourselves. It became very popular and started selling out.

Somebody in our group heard about an improv festival in Minneapolis, so we sent in a video of us doing "The Real Real World" and got accepted. It sounded like a fun trip and a chance to take our show to a new audience. We were excited.

We shouldn't have been.

The "improv" festival was held at a comedy club on the fourth floor in the Mall of America called Knuckleheads. In hindsight, the name of the club should have been our first clue that we might be headed for trouble. When we arrived for our first performance, we noticed that all the acts preceding us were stand-up comedians. No ensembles. No improv.

I took a closer look at the crowd filling the tables. They seemed older than the student types we attracted to shows in New York. These were working-class and white-collar folks who'd just gotten off their jobs. This was the middle of winter, and all two hundred of them were cold, tired, and thirsty. They were ready to drink and ready to be entertained.

Our turn arrived. We stepped into the bright lights focused on the foot-high stage. Our narrator, Paul Scheer, addressed the audience and asked for suggestions for a city, for what was in our house, and for what was going on in the world that day. Once that was established, he got us started: "And now, from New York, please enjoy 'The Real Real World.'"

We began improvising a scene. I looked out at the audience. Blank faces. Lots of them. I had the sudden fear that none of these people had heard of *The Real World*. Or improv comedy. Or New York.

We continued playing our characters, improvising lines as always . . . but no one in the crowd seemed to understand. Confusion turned—and I mean almost instantly—to anger. I heard someone say, "What the fuck are they doing?" These people didn't know what to make of a slow-building scene. They were used to stand-up comedy. That's what they'd come to see. They wanted dick jokes, and they wanted 'em (pardon the pun) hard and fast.

The angry murmurs intensified. I think I realized a little bit more quickly than the rest of my castmates that this was a pack of wolves that needed meat. So while everybody else onstage tried to stay in character—and God bless 'em for being true to the show we brought—I started cussing. That drew a few chuckles from the audience, but not for long. Five minutes into the scene, the crowd was all over us—heckling, catcalls, boos. I'd never seen an audience turn ugly that quickly.

I'll never forget this one guy at a high-top table in the front row. He was a total Scandinavian—huge, red-faced, blond hair, flat-top haircut, wearing a white dress shirt with his tie loosened. The look on his face, which in those first five minutes changed from red to various shades of purple, communicated rage. He was only a few feet away, so you could actually see the veins on his neck bulging. I think he felt we were pulling a prank on him personally. He looked like a modern-day Viking who wanted to drive an axe through each one of us.

Finally, this guy couldn't take it anymore. "Fucking hell," he roared, "what is this? Kill yourself!" He repeated the phrase whenever someone new uttered a line: "Kill yourself!" It seemed as if everyone else in the audience was yelling too. It was so bad that we could barely hear each other over the angry shouts from the crowd.

That's when the lights went out.

This was no power failure. This was a mercy killing by the club owner. He'd seen enough.

The crowd cheered.

The eight of us onstage froze. We exchanged glances in the shadows. Someone said, "I guess we're done." Our hour-long show was over after ten minutes. We slinked off to the wings. One of the girls in our group began to cry. We were all in a state of shock. It was a disaster unlike anything I'd ever experienced.

You know what I said about being mission-focused? I realized that my mission had just changed. Maybe I got it more quickly because I was older than my castmates—I was thirty and they were in their early or mid-twenties. Maybe it was because during all the interviews of famous comedians I'd watched, they always said at some point, "You're gonna bomb one day. It happens to everybody. If you go into comedy, sooner or later you're going to bomb, and it's going to feel horrible."

They were right. It was ugly. I hated it. I wanted to hide in shame. It sucked! But I also had enough life experience to have some perspective on what had just happened. *Okay,* I thought, *that was awful. But we're all still here. None of us are hurt. We're all still breathing. There's no imminent threat of death and dismemberment. Life can get a whole lot worse than this.*

Then I remembered the advice I'd gotten about bombing.

Hey, it happened! We bombed! Okay, now I know what it feels like. We got it out of the way. I don't ever want to feel like this again, but now I know I can survive it.

Which is why I started laughing. My mission was no longer to entertain a bunch of Minnesota meatheads who didn't have the first clue about longform improv comedy. It was to put what we'd just suffered into perspective—and to help my castmates see the absurdity of it all.

As I laughed, everyone looked at me in confusion, including the tear-soaked gal.

"Please don't cry," I said. "Can you see the humor in this? All we were trying to do was make them laugh, and they *hated* us. It was *so* out of proportion. If you think about it, it's hysterical!"

Everyone was too stunned to fully embrace my message, but I did see several nods. I think it helped ease the pain a little.

We gathered in the greenroom behind the stage. None of us wanted to go back into the club. No way were we going to face that angry mob. "Let's just grab our coats and go," someone said. "Let's get the hell out of here."

A door at the back of the greenroom opened into the mall, so we made a beeline to the bar in a Planet Hollywood. Since I was the only person with a real job, I bought the first round of drinks for everybody, and we talked about what had just happened.

As our adrenaline wound down and our alcohol content went up, the group started to relax. "We aren't bad performers," Paul said. "We've been doing sold-out shows, getting great reviews, for two years in New York. We've been killing it!"

"Right!" I said. "It's just that we're an improv group that got stuck in the middle of a comedy festival for stand-ups. Even so . . . that crowd was beyond obnoxious. They were so terrible, it was fucking hilarious."

Don't get me wrong: I wasn't happy about our little nightmare. Bombing in front of an audience and battling with "fight or flight" feelings is nobody's idea of a good time. You want to die. But I'd learned a lesson—when the hatred meter for a *comedy show* gets turned up that high, you really have no choice but to laugh and focus on the next mission.

I also learned it's a good idea to stay away from bars named Knuckleheads.

PART THREE

TERROR, SPERM BANKS, AND BLESSINGS

FIFTEEN

Send Me

Then I heard the Lord's voice, saying, "Whom can I send? Who will go for us?" So I said, "Here I am. Send me!" —Isaiah 6:8

It was a beautiful New York day in the fall of 2001. A year earlier, I'd completed my active-duty commitment to the Marines, though I'd stayed in as a Marine Corps Reserve. I still wanted to serve, and it required only a couple of meetings a month, some drill sessions, and two weeks of active duty per year. It meant I was available if they needed me. I'd recently started a midlevel corporate office job in Midtown Manhattan, and I continued to hone my comedy skills at night. I'd been married for more than two years. I was making progress on my comedy dream. Life was good.

On this particular morning, I sat at my desk at work, playing catch-up after returning from a wonderful vacation with my wife, my parents, and my sister's family at Lake of the Ozarks in Missouri. I'd started the day with a phone call to my mom. It was her birthday: Tuesday, September 11.

One of the office assistants, Stephanie, popped her head into my office. Her face was pale. "Hey," she said, "a plane just flew into one of the Twin Towers."

I glanced up. "What?" I said. "That's terrible." *Talk about a tragic accident.* But I was preoccupied—I had so much work in front of me. I went back to reading the document on my desk.

Then Stephanie's words began to sink in. *A plane hit one of the Twin Towers?* I looked outside. Still nothing but blue sky. *There's no way a plane would accidentally fly into a building on a day like this.*

I glanced at a clock: 8:55 a.m. I got up and found Stephanie talking to some of the other assistants. "Hey," I asked, "was it a small plane or a big plane?" Stephanie said she wasn't sure but that our boss, Mike, had a television on in his office. I moved to Mike's office, saw smoke belching out of the North Tower on TV, and was shocked to learn that it was a commercial plane.

A few minutes later, my cell phone rang. It was my wife. "Are you seeing this?" Tiffany asked. She was on a high floor in a building farther downtown, close to the towers, and was watching the whole thing through her office window.

Suddenly, horrific screams exploded out of my phone. These were awful, primal sounds, full of fear and shock. They terrified me. "What just happened?" I shouted. *"What the fuck is going on?"*

"Another plane," Tiffany said in a strained voice. "Another plane just flew into the other tower."

I knew it then. These weren't accidents. We were under attack.

I told Tiffany to stay put. I was coming to get her.

When I hit the street, it was surreal. The weather remained perfect. But something was off. I couldn't put my finger on it for a couple of blocks as I ran on the sidewalk. Then it hit me. It was too still, too quiet. No horns were honking. No one was shouting. Because public transportation had been halted, the streets were full of people, yet there was hardly any sound. The crowd just stood there, staring downtown toward the World Trade Center. It was like a science fiction movie.

I found Tiffany and told her everything would be all right, though I'm not sure I believed it. We walked home. The Marine in me made certain we picked up food, water, and batteries along the way. At home, we didn't budge from our couch—we watched the news along with the rest of the nation as that horrific day unfolded.

I was shocked and angry. How could this have happened? Who was responsible? How many innocent people had just been killed? Were any of my friends who worked near the Twin Towers still alive? Was Jules Roinnel working at Windows on the World that morning? (I eventually learned he wasn't and that he'd lived.)

Late on that Tuesday afternoon as we sat on the couch, Tiffany turned toward me, thinking about my position as a Marine reserve, and asked, "What does this mean for you?"

"I'm not sure," I said, "but we'll probably hear something soon."

A couple of hours later, the phone rang. Our unit had been activated. We were to report in our fatigues to One Police Plaza, right next to Ground Zero, at 0800 the next morning.

"Aye-aye, sir," I said.

I'll never forget what I saw when I reported for duty the next day. The scene was apocalyptic. Skeletons of buildings. Burned-out fire trucks, police cruisers, and ambulances. Scattered papers and debris. Stacks of twisted metal and steel. Piles of rubble six stories high where the Twin Towers once stood. One skyscraper with a Brooks Brothers store in the lobby looked like Godzilla had slashed a claw through its lower levels. Much of the concrete from the buildings had been pulverized into a fine powder, almost like moon dust. It kicked up with every step of my boots.

This is surreal, I thought. *Total devastation. It's like something out of* Star Wars. *I hope I never forget this.* It wasn't so much that I wanted to remember, but it seemed important to. I was a witness to an epic, historic tragedy.

My group and I walked to the corner of Trinity and Liberty, where rescue teams worked at the southeast corner of what had been 2 World Trade Center. As far as we knew, there might be hundreds or even thousands of people trapped under all those layers of rubble, so the use of heavy machinery was ruled out to avoid the risk of collapse. Instead, our unit joined firefighters, police officers, and ironworkers to form bucket brigades. We were a human chain passing empty buckets up the line to the top of rubble piles and debris-filled buckets back down the line—we looked like lines of ants going up an anthill. Hundreds of us, all doing the same thing.

I was told that when a whistle blew, everybody needed to stop work so rescue workers could listen for survivors. When I did hear that whistle for the first time, I stopped moving and almost stopped breathing. It was so quiet that the only thing you could hear was the wind whispering between the skyscrapers. I stood about halfway up a multistory rubble pile and watched as a team of rescuers at the top lowered a listening device into the rubble. *Maybe they found someone*, I thought. *I hope so! God, please let them find a survivor.*

After a few minutes of silence, though, the whistle blew again—no luck.

We resumed our work. Occasionally, a basket stretcher would be called for, which meant a body—or a body part—had been found and needed to be transferred to a morgue for identification.

During the week I worked at Ground Zero, we never heard anything from inside the rubble piles. As far as I know, no one was pulled out alive.

On my second day on the bucket brigade, an air-raid horn sounded. Everyone around me started running full speed off the piles. It was unnerving. I didn't know if we were under attack again or what—I guess I'd missed the air-raid siren briefing. But I'm no dummy. If everyone else is hauling ass like we're about to die, I'm hauling too. It was like the running of the bulls in Spain—I and hundreds of other rescue workers converged on one narrow street. We rounded a corner and ran smack into a two-wheeled trailer with a generator and huge stadium lights mounted on top. My legs smashed into one of the two metal bars of the hitch that extended from the trailer and connected at a point about seven feet out. I'd hit the bar just below my knees. More workers slammed into me from behind, so I was pinned. *Oh shit,* I thought, *they're gonna break my legs!*

Like a basketball center trying to establish position in the low post, I drove my elbow and backside into whoever was behind me. It created just enough room for me to slip out, but then the guys behind me got pinned against the trailer hitch by the panicked herd, just as I'd been. I climbed onto the metal bars and yelled and pointed at the workers in back who couldn't see: "Stop! There's a trailer hitch here! Back up and go around!"

Once the area was cleared, I continued my run to safety—but safety from what? When we were a couple blocks away, I finally got another rescue worker to tell me what the hell was going on. "The air-horn blows, you run for your life," he said. "It means someone in charge saw something and thinks the surrounding buildings are about to collapse." Eventually they said we could go back to work. Like we weren't already stressed out enough down there.

I spent a week working at Ground Zero. People ask me what I remember most about those days. My answer is the smell—wet, mashed concrete mixed with the odor of burning metal. It was a distinct and awful aroma, one I'd never experienced before and hope to never experience again.

The other thing I'll never forget is that I was surrounded by tough rescue workers, guys who had seen truly terrible situations before, and how often they all cried openly. We were surrounded by devastation and death; sometimes the emotions just became too much. There was no shame in it.

One day after my shift, a coworker dropped me off a few blocks from my apartment. I was in my cammies, covered from head to toe with white dust from the rubble piles. As I walked on the sidewalk, a few people made eye contact—rare in New York before the attack—and said a heartfelt "Thank you." Each time, it stirred up something inside me. Who knew if these people had lost a loved one and were desperately hoping for good news.

As I neared my apartment, I waited at a crosswalk for the signal to change. A clean-shaven man who was probably in his fifties—old enough to have had a daughter or son working in the Twin Towers that day—joined me at the crosswalk. He glanced my way and almost smiled, then cast his eyes down. To me, he seemed both friendly and sad.

"How's it going down there?" he finally asked.

I sighed. "It's slow."

His next words were so quiet I could barely hear them: "God bless you."

The crosswalk signal light changed. The man walked away, but I stood rooted to the sidewalk. Something about that man's demeanor and words pushed me over the edge. I couldn't hold it back—the tears started flowing.

Over the next few days, I tried to process my emotions. I was still in shock. I felt so sorry for the families of people who had suddenly lost loved ones. I'd been standing on rubble piles that were the gravesites for some two thousand people. Every one of these innocent victims was the most important person in somebody's life. They never had a chance to escape or fight back. They didn't deserve to die.

I had so many questions and no answers. *We've just suffered a horrific terrorist attack. Once we figure out who did this, of course we're going to retaliate. Does that mean a global war? Are we looking at World War III? What's America gonna look like? Are we shutting our borders? Will things ever be normal? Will we ever laugh again? Will we ever get over this?*

One thing I knew for sure: The sense of security that so many in America felt a few days before was gone. Things would never be the same again.

I felt more than grief and shock. I was scared, and I was mad as hell. My city and my country had just been attacked. *Whoever these terrorists are, they're a bunch of cowards,* I thought. *Fuck those guys!*

When I learned of the actions of Todd Beamer on United Airlines Flight 93, they moved and inspired me. After Todd and others realized that terrorists had hijacked the plane, they made the courageous decision to storm the cockpit and try to take back control. The result was that the plane crashed in Pennsylvania, killing everyone onboard, but their heroic actions saved who knows how many lives—the reported target of the hijackers on Flight 93 was Washington, DC.

Todd Beamer was thirty-two years old, just a year older than me. Like me, he was newly married. He got on a plane one day and faced a nightmare. *I get on planes all the time. But for the grace of God, that could've been me.* Todd wasn't part of the military. He was just a man trying to do the right thing and trying to get home to his family. But me? I was a Marine Corps captain. I was trained. I'd been deployed. My country had been attacked, and I'd seen the horrible results. This was why I'd joined the Marines—to defend my country from the evil in this world. If ever there was a time to put my skills to use, this was it. Everyone around me was contributing what they could to the surviving victims, the families of victims, and the rescue crews—giving blood, donating clothes and blankets, making sandwiches. I was in a position to do more.

I need to get back on active duty, I thought. *They're going to need people.* There was going to be a response to these attacks, and I had the experience to be part of the solution. I remembered the

Bible verse where Isaiah volunteered to be a messenger for God. I thought, *Here I am, Lord. Send me!*

Before the week was out, I told my commander that if there was a place for me, I wanted to volunteer for active duty again.

I didn't tell anyone about my decision—not my wife or my parents or my friends. When they asked what the 9/11 attack meant for me as a Marine reserve, I said I didn't know—which was true. I didn't know if I'd be called back or not. But I was also withholding information. It probably reflects poorly on me, but I'd made up my mind and didn't want to argue with anyone about it. Of course, they would worry about me. And yes, they had reason to worry. My previous deployments had been a noncombatant evacuation operation, a humanitarian aid operation, a peacekeeping operation. This was different. We wouldn't be going overseas to keep the peace. We were going to kill and destroy terrorists. If I was deployed as a public affairs officer, I might not be on the front lines, but I'd still be in a combat zone. Our enemies were committed to violence against Americans. Even the civilians might be trying to kill us.

I was afraid my wife and parents would try to convince me to not volunteer. Maybe they would have been supportive, but I never gave them that chance. I also didn't want to alarm them unnecessarily. After so much trauma and death, everyone's emotions were raw.

My orders came in on November 10—the Marine Corps birthday: "Captain Robert A. Riggle, you have been recalled to active duty service. Report to Central Command."

By this point, the War on Terror was officially underway. Though nothing had been authorized yet, I understood what my orders probably meant. I was going to Afghanistan.

SIXTEEN

I Love You, Man

There are some conversations you think you're never going to have, but then . . . there you are. Now that I had my orders to report, I had to have the hard what-if talk with Tiffany: "If I'm a vegetable, don't keep me alive. If I die, I want a closed casket with old pictures of me on top. Ask my friends to share stories if they want. If I'm missing for more than two years, I'm not coming back, so you need to move on with your life." We both shed a few tears.

I had a final will and testament made. I also had to consider the possibility that I could get injured in a way that would prohibit my having children (in other words, a bomb could blow my junk off). I hoped to have some little Riggles of my own someday. I believe that's one of the reasons we exist—to pass it on, to have a next generation, to keep the line going. (If someone had warned me how challenging parenting was going to be, I might have decided to let someone else keep the line going, thank you very much. On the other hand, if I'd known back then how much I'd grow to love my kids and how much they would teach me, I might have started earlier and had more little Riggles!)

I decided to visit a fertility clinic—aka sperm bank—to put some sperm on ice, just in case. If you've never been to a sperm bank, it's not at all like a savings and loan and not nearly as sexy as it sounds. Let me break it down for you.

You walk into the waiting room and everyone stares at you. Even if they're not staring . . . they're staring. They know why you're here. You approach the reception window. The nurse at the counter looks like a Mafia girlfriend: heavy makeup, glossy red lipstick, rings, and fingernails so long you can't help but wonder how she does anything. Seriously. Like, how does she open a door? How does she type? How does she wipe? You're not sure if this woman is thirty years old or sixty. She asks—in the loudest voice possible—for your name. You whisper, "Rob Riggle." In a Brooklyn accent, she yells back, "Dat's a funny name! Howdaya spell it?" You're handed a clipboard and you sit down to fill out paperwork. After you turn in the paperwork, you wait. Then you wait some more. You make eye contact with no one. Suddenly, the nurse shouts, "Rawwwwb Riggle!"—making you jump and cringe at the same time—and you follow her down a dingy hallway to your "private room." The Mafia nurse points out the requisite materials for your task—porn magazines, lotion, tissues, and a specimen jar.

After she leaves, you survey the room. The bare walls are a shabby shade of white. There's a little coffee table with the aforementioned materials on top. The magazines are from the seventies and eighties with many of the pages loose from being torn out. There's a faded brown couch with worn cushions. You know that twenty people have already jerked off on that thing today, so no, you're not sitting there. There's also an art deco piece that's all rounded edges and plastic—it's supposed to be a chair, but you don't see any way to actually sit in it without sliding off, so you realize you're going to have to do your business standing up.

You check the lock on the door—three times. It's loose, so flimsy that you doubt it will keep anyone out if they try turning the knob. Now you're paranoid, plus you've seen too many

Dateline-style shows, so you're sure that some sicko at the clinic is secretly recording you. So, you do a twenty-minute search of the room for hidden cameras.

Satisfied you won't be the unwitting star of the next low-budget adult film, you realize it's time to get busy. The sounds of construction work in the office next door don't exactly enhance the mood, however. Someone is beating on a pipe with a wrench, while his partner operates a jackhammer. Despite the obstacles, however, you have a mission to accomplish—plus you just want to get the hell out of this place—so you focus and get to the devil's work.

Once you finish, you take your cup to the "sperm technician." It's another man. The only thing more awkward than handing a cup of your sperm to a woman you've never met is handing it to another man. Then it's back to the waiting room, where you continue to avoid eye contact because everyone knows what you just did, and because they either just did the same thing or they're about to. It's a weird, quiet space full of shame-filled masturbators.

In my case, the one positive result from the whole experience was the doctor's report that I had a good sperm count . . . and good sperm mobility as well (yes, that's a thing). Say what you want about me, but I'll bet on my sperm to get the job done any day of the week. Yeah, baby, that's what's up!!!

Now I was ready to deploy. Overseas, that is.

Actually, that wasn't quite true. I still had to face the heart-wrenching task of saying goodbye to my family.

In mid-November, I drove to the Marine base at Camp Lejeune in North Carolina for a couple days of processing. My parents and Granddad drove over too. We spent those two evenings together, mostly hanging out around their Hampton Inn pool, talking about everything except my imminent departure. I knew my mom and dad were worried. I didn't know what was going to happen either.

Only a few weeks before, I'd stood on the rubble piles at Ground Zero. Now I was leaving to confront the people who were responsible for killing so many innocent people. Would I see my parents again? Statistically speaking, yes, but was there any guarantee? No.

As we sat by the pool, I kept thinking about how lucky I was to have the parents I had. They'd done so much for me and my sister—teaching us, supporting us, encouraging us, challenging us to be better. One day at a time, they'd demonstrated their work ethic and how much they cared about me. Mom taught in a classroom all day, bought groceries, came home to cook dinner, and graded papers all evening, yet she still made time to listen to my problems and help me with my homework. When he wasn't on the road providing for us at his insurance job, Dad came home at the end of the day from his office in town, took off his suit (while reminding me, "Son, you can get a lot of wears out of a suit if you hang it up properly"), changed like Mr. Rogers into his work-around-the-house clothes, and found a fence to fix or a lawn to mow (often recruiting me to be his assistant).

I knew my parents loved me unconditionally and wanted nothing but the best for me. They'd worked so hard to give me and Julie every chance to succeed at life. I would never be able to repay them for all they'd done.

Inevitably, the morning arrived where I had to leave North Carolina and drive to Tampa, Florida, where I would soon catch my flight overseas. We gathered in the Hampton Inn parking lot. I turned to my granddad first. He and I had an understanding—no unnecessary displays of affection. When I was about twelve, he and my grandma were leaving our house after a weekend visit. I gave Grammy a goodbye hug, then stepped toward Granddad to give him a hug, just like I'd done many times before. This time, though, Granddad stiff-armed me like he was Walter Payton and said, "No, no, no, no." He wasn't mad, and it wasn't a rebuke. It was more like a rite of passage. He was saying, "We don't have to do that anymore. You're free of the hugging thing now. We shake hands and wish each other well because you're a young man now." I never hugged Granddad again. That's just how his generation rolled, and I got it.

In the Hampton parking lot, Granddad shook my hand and simply said, "Be strong."

Mom was next. She was the toughest woman I knew, but in that moment, she started crying. I assured her repeatedly that I would be safe (and hoped it was true). We hugged. "I love you," Mom said through tears. "I love you too," I answered.

That left Dad. He walked me over to the car my parents had lent me, an Oldsmobile Bravada SUV (yeah, I'd be stylin' when I drove into Tampa). Dad slipped me a twenty, just as he used to do when I was in high school and going out on a date. Like most men of his generation, Dad also wasn't one to show much emotion, but I knew from his quivering chin that he was holding back some big feelings. "I'm proud of you, Rob," he said. Then we shook hands and said goodbye.

I got into the Bravada and started the engine. Mom, Dad, and Granddad stepped close. The nightmare of 9/11 was again on my mind.

So many people never got the chance for a goodbye like this with the people they cared about, I thought. *They were forced to crash in an airplane or jump off a building—and that was it. You just never know.*

I looked into the concerned-yet-hopeful eyes of my parents and Granddad one more time and took a mental snapshot of each of them. *I want to remember this moment.* Then I waved goodbye and pulled out of the parking lot.

The trip to Tampa was long in more ways than one. I was thankful I'd gotten my chance to say goodbye, but I felt like I'd blown it with my dad. Granddad and I were good, and as always, I'd told my mom I loved her. But I didn't hug my dad and didn't say "I love you." I was so mad at myself. I didn't care what generation Dad was from—*I* wanted to say what I was thinking and feeling.

Not that it was easy for me. Starting with fifth grade tackle football practices, when you got knocked down or hurt and you started to cry, your coach or another player got in your face and said, "Are you *crying*? Are you a football player or a pansy?" You learned right away that boys didn't cry on the football field. You were expected to suck it up and figure it out. Any kind of emotional display was a proclamation to the world that you were weak.

There was a purpose to that. To become men and do the things men are traditionally required to do—provide and protect—boys need to learn how to toughen up and manage their emotions. They need to learn how to be strong when the situation requires it. The Spartans used to send their boys into the wilderness when they turned twelve with nothing but a spear and a blanket. The ones who survived for a month were welcomed back as men and allowed to become full Spartan citizens. We live in a different world today. A world that doesn't require boys to become men under such extreme conditions. Although a little adversity could go a long way toward building more resilient young men . . . just sayin'.

But there needs to be a balance, right? Because so many men my age have been taught to be tough, they mask their feelings. If we want to show appreciation for another guy, it comes out as a punch on the shoulder and a "Fuck you." I envy women in that regard. They can express their emotions for one another openly and honestly. They'll sit on the couch, have a glass of wine, and tell each other how much they love and appreciate each other and talk in great detail about what their friendship means to them. (Three hours later, they might still be on the couch, talking and drinking wine, but at least they know how to communicate their feelings!)

Today's younger generation is also so much better at this than mine. They can say "I love you" and not be ashamed or embarrassed. That's good. We need to say and hear those things!

On that day I left for Tampa, I wanted Dad to know my feelings—that I loved and appreciated him and was so grateful to be his son. I didn't want there to be any doubt, for anything to be left unsaid. As I drove through Georgia on I-95, I made a promise to myself. From that day on, whenever I said goodbye to either of my parents, I would tell them I loved them—whether they wanted to hear it or not.

My chance with Dad came just a couple days later, on the phone from Tampa. I wrapped up the call and said, "All right, Dad. I love you. Bye."

That threw him off. He stammered a bit: "Oh, uh, oh, okay." But then he got there: "I love you too." I've been doing it ever since. It's gotten easier for both of us.

In the years that followed, I started saying the same thing to some of my buddies. I think the first guy I sprung it on was Dan Bakkedahl, who'd been a correspondent with me on *The Daily Show.* Dan is an excellent actor and improv comedian, as well as a "man's man." We were finishing a pretty intense call, talking about our lives, careers, and fears. I closed with "Hey, man, I love you. Hang in there."

"Uh, hey, uh . . . I love you too," Dan answered. I had to chuckle. I don't think he saw that coming. I know it's a little intense for some, but I don't care. I'm thankful for the friends in my life, and I want them to know it. I do keep it fairly nonchalant. I'm not trying to recreate the Paul Rudd–Jason Segel scene from *I Love You, Man*, where my friends and I start saying "I love you, dude." "I love you, bro Montana." "I love you, muchacha." "I love you, Tycho Bro-he." That particular moment of bro magic belongs only to those guys. But I do firmly believe it's important to get it out there.

Today, that applies to my kids too. I've got a daughter and a son. I tell them I love them constantly. I mean, I'm virtually working it into every other sentence: "How was your day? Oh, great. I love you. How was the movie? That's cool! Did you know I love you?" I'm sure they think, *Dad, okay, I get it!*

A while back, I made the mistake of watching an internet clip of some doctor talking about the metabolic and spiritual benefits of an eight-second hug. Now my poor kids have to suffer through an eight-second hug every time we say hello or goodbye. I just lock it in, hold it, and count to eight. I think they're getting used to it.

I'm not trying to be melodramatic. It just gives me peace of mind to know that the people I care about will never have to wonder, *Did Dad really love me? Did Rob appreciate me?*

In fact, gentle reader, I want you to know how much I appreciate *you* for hanging in with me on this book. So let's just go there right now: I love you!

Too much? I don't care. Deal with it!

SEVENTEEN

A Grateful American

In Tampa, I officially learned what I already suspected—I was headed for Afghanistan. I would be part of Operation Enduring Freedom, an effort to rid that country of al-Qaeda and the Taliban, the terrorist groups behind aiding or carrying out the 9/11 attacks. I was to be the media liaison officer for our forces in the northern part of the country. I had a few days, but not many, to gather my gear, get my shots, and attend classes on terrorism, land mines, and biological and chemical warfare. And then, just like that, it was time to go.

On a dark night during the first week of December 2001, I flew on a C-17 transport plane into our base in Uzbekistan, which bordered Afghanistan to the south. I would wait here for a flight into Afghanistan. Joining me on the C-17 was my gunnery sergeant, Andrew Lynch, who would be with me for the rest of my deployment. Gunny spent the first seventeen years of his life in England, then moved to the US and became an American citizen. He joined the Navy but switched to the Marines because he thought Navy folks were "boring and fat." Gunny was a tough Marine—small in stature but solid as a rock, all muscle. He still had his British accent, which he liked because it helped him pick up girls. He hated the

French and loved quality pornography. I was glad he was with me. I knew if we got into a fight with somebody, he'd be a good man to have around.

When we stepped off the plane into Uzbekistan, a freezing gust of wind took my breath away—it was blowing hard and below zero.

Oh my God—it's so cold! I thought. *I can't believe this! How am I going to survive this?* I had winter gear with me, but it wasn't enough for operating in conditions like these. I nearly had a panic attack during my first minute in-country. *This sucks!*

Checking in at a military base in Uzbekistan in the middle of the night is nothing like checking in at a Hilton. No one was holding our reservation. No one was greeting us with a welcoming smile and a brochure explaining where to find the heated pool. Instead, we humped our eighty pounds of gear (each) for five hundred yards over to a small tent with lights, where we found a sleepy Army corporal.

"Where's the joint operations center?" I asked.

"What?"

"Where is the joint operations center?" I repeated, my teeth starting to chatter.

"Oh. It's about a half mile that way. Other end of the runway." The corporal yawned and pointed in the direction I'd just come from.

"Well, shit," Gunny said.

By the time we found the shack we were looking for, Gunny and I were both tired, mad, hungry, and nearly numb. A nineteen-year-old Army specialist sat at a makeshift desk, playing a video game. He grunted and frowned, apparently upset at being interrupted. "What do you guys want?"

Obviously, the specialist had not been trained in the art of hospitality or rank structure. I resisted the urge to take this guy's head off. I also saved the specialist's life by not letting Gunny take the guy's head off. I just wanted a relatively warm bed.

A few minutes later, I had one. Our new temporary home was tent 81, a space about fifty by twenty feet lined with cots. We shared it with nine young guys, a mix of Army and Air Force enlisted. In the morning, while I attempted to catch up on sleep, some of my new tentmates decided it was a good time to listen to music. I'd brought three CDs with me—a Billy Joel, a Blink-182, and a Garth Brooks. Why those three? I knew I only had room for three, so I wanted a diverse selection.

The playlist for my first morning in Uzbekistan, however, was more diverse than I was looking for—it was a punk rock Christmas album. I particularly enjoyed the song dedicated to the lead singer's penis. The song must have been named "Thanks for the Good Times" because they repeated that lyric about a thousand times. I heard the singer wax poetic about the many adventures he'd experienced with his member, the joyous and meaningful moments they had together, all of it screamed at the top of his lungs, all in the name of Christmas. Whether anyone else was involved in these adventures was hard to say.

I did not want to be the grouchy new arrival who shut down everybody's fun, so I gritted my teeth and kept my mouth shut. But I was not feeling thankful for the good times. In fact, that song affected my dreams for the next few days. All I remember now is that it had something to do with me being in Santa's sleigh, without any clothes on. It's probably best I've forgotten the details.

Uzbekistan in December is the coldest place on earth. It's even worse when the wind kicks up, which is often. I got very familiar with this chilling reality because we had to wait for about an hour to get through the chow line—and the line, naturally, was *outside*. I started drinking as much water as I could during the day and none after evening chow. Otherwise, in the middle of the night I had to exit my warm sleeping bag, put on clothes, jacket, and boots, walk two hundred yards through bitter cold to the head, take a piss, and then reverse the whole procedure. A thirty-minute ordeal and a total pain in the ass. I missed home a little more every day.

The plan was to place Gunny and me in Mazar-i-Sharif, the largest city in northern Afghanistan. US forces and Northern Alliance fighters ("our" Afghans) had taken Mazar-i-Sharif from the Taliban only a month before. Executing that plan was another story. Late on December 9, after several false alarms—"Gear up, you're flying into Afghanistan tonight," followed a few hours later by "Sorry, you got bumped, maybe tomorrow"—Gunny and I finally got a seat on a Chinook CH-47 helicopter, which looked like a huge green hot dog with twin rotors on top. We had to share it with four Special Air Service (SAS) guys, the British equivalent to our Navy SEALs, and their vehicle, which reminded me of a jeep out of *Rat Patrol.* We jammed into the Chinook and sat against the fuselage wall on tiny benches made of nylon cargo netting. My knees touched the jeep's fender—it was tight quarters.

Of course, it was a night flight in the middle of a storm. The closer we got to Afghanistan, the more violent our flight became. We flew alongside the massive Hindu Kush mountains, which caused major windshear and turbulence. Snow started pouring in through the door kept open for the Chinook's .50-caliber machine gun. It swirled around in the fuselage like we were in the middle of *The Shining. Heeeere's Johnny!* kept playing in my mind.

As we bounced along, we suddenly dropped ten feet, then surged up twenty. My stomach lurched. That was followed by a loud pounding against the Chinook as the tremendous winds battered us. What was the pounding, you might ask? I had no idea . . . but it wasn't good!

Good God, the fuselage is going to break, I thought. *We're going to crash.*

I glanced at Gunny, sitting to my left, and the SAS guys across from us. They all had their heads down and eyes closed—the international position of prayer. It seemed like a good idea, so I joined in immediately. The beating continued for what felt like an hour.

Somehow, we survived the flight and landed. *We made it!* I thought. *We're in Afghanistan!* I was wrong. The storm was so bad, the pilots had been forced to turn around. We were right back where we started, at the base in Uzbekistan. I didn't care. I was just glad to be on the ground again.

Finally, though, the military made it happen. The next night, Gunny and I boarded a C-130 and we made the gut-twisting corkscrew landing into the desert near Mazar-i-Sharif that I described at the beginning of this book. We pulled our weapons; fanned out around the pallets of food, ammo, and gear that got dumped with us; lay on our bellies; and waited for someone—either US Special Forces or the Taliban—to arrive.

I glanced up. I'd always enjoyed looking at the night sky. Now, with no lights on the ground to dull my vision, every star above me shone in incredibly bright detail. The majestic peaks of the Hindu Kush were clearly outlined by the celestial orbs beyond. The heavens were filled with stars, so many and so beautiful. It was surreal to be here for such terrible reasons yet witness such inspiring beauty.

My musings were interrupted by the sound of vehicles. A minute later, a convoy of white Toyota pickup trucks and vans raced onto the airstrip next to us. *Okay,* I thought, *are these good guys here to escort us to the base or bad guys here to kill us?* I held my breath. It was the moment of truth.

Fortunately, the first guy to show his face was special forces, a Major Mitchell. He smiled. "Hey," he called out, "glad to see you! Welcome to Mazar-i-Sharif!"

Yeah, I was a bit relieved.

The next day, I got my first daylight look at Mazar. The landscape in and around this city of a quarter million people was littered with bombed-out buildings and rusted-out tanks, trucks, and aircraft left behind by the Soviet Union after its failed attempt to conquer the country in the late seventies and eighties. Our combination headquarters and sleeping quarters was an abandoned Turkish high school on the outskirts of town. It was cold and dusty, and the power kept going out. Chow was MREs—not the finest of cuisine—though it was supplemented when local Afghans brought us hot tea in the mornings and rice in the evenings.

Since the school didn't have toilets, it also stunk, no matter where you were in the compound. All we had was a little hole in the floor between some boards that you had to squat over, while hoping your aim was good. Taking a "shower" wasn't much more fun. Every other day I got up at 0500, filled a bucket with ice-cold water, and went to the shower room, which was basically a space with a tile floor and drain. I always brought a flashlight because it was often pitch black since the power kept going out. It was freezing in there—I could see my breath in the flashlight beam—so the last thing I wanted to do was take off the warm clothes I'd slept in. But I stripped down and scrubbed myself with a washrag, an old bar of soap, and cold water, then tried to dry off with a bigger rag that never got fully dry no matter how many days I left it out. Then I threw back on the long underwear and clothes I'd been sleeping in and declared myself "clean." Was it primitive? Was it Spartan? Hell, yeah. So many of my dreams changed from sexual encounters to taking a long, luxurious shower back home. I was horny for some hot food and a hot shower!

On my third day in Mazar, we visited a school and a medical college, which was helpful for me. Now that it was safer for relief workers to come in, I'd be introducing people from the Red Cross and Peace Wins and other nongovernmental organizations to the locals as part of my public affairs and civil affairs work.

I was fascinated by the Afghans. None of the students at the school had ever seen a foreigner. They wanted to practice their

English and talk about everything—where I was from, how harsh the Taliban had been, how long we would stay in Afghanistan. I could tell by their big smiles and eager conversation that they were thrilled we were there. They lived hard lives. Everyone was poor and dirty, and disease was rampant. The men looked fierce. They were all heavily armed and stood on every corner. It was common to see men and boys walking around with AK-47s and RPGs. The women, age thirteen and older, wore burkas, either because of tradition or out of fear of the Taliban.

The kids, thin and shoeless, were curious. They were impressed by my flashlight and wanted me to take their picture, which I did. They were so open and enthusiastic, not serious and wary like the adults—though I certainly understood where the wariness came from.

At a hospital, I met a twenty-year-old Afghan who spoke broken English. He said he loved England and America. He showed me an object he carried, and said proudly, "Look, I have this!" It was a cassette tape of the Backstreet Boys. It might sound crazy to an American, but for him, this had been dangerous contraband. A couple of months earlier, he would have been publicly beaten if the Taliban had caught him with that tape. Near the center of town, adjoining a bazaar and public square, was a stone arch over twenty feet high. I learned that every Friday the Taliban used to round up the locals and force them to watch as they strung up a man and a woman and hung them from the top of the arch. Who knew what infraction, if any, the victims of the week had committed. I don't think it mattered to the Taliban leadership. The point was to demonstrate what would happen if anyone stepped out of line. They ruled through cruelty, intimidation, and fear.

My interpreter, Salim, had a bushy mustache and salt-and-pepper hair. He was a professor at the local university with nine kids at home. One day he was stopped on the street by three Taliban enforcers and asked where he'd been. When he said the market, they yelled at him for not going to the mosque. Then they beat him, hauled him off to a police station, and threw him in a basement cell with no windows and no lights. They kept him there three days—no food, no bathroom, just darkness—while his family wondered what had happened to him. Finally, they released him.

Salim was also very glad we were there. He always showed up for work in a good mood. Sometimes he made up ridiculously silly lyrics to songs and sang them to me, like, "Rob is as fine as wine, he is divine" (no, he wasn't going to be the next Bob Dylan). One day we talked about what the new Afghan flag was going to look like—green, black, and red, he thought, with a circular symbol in the middle of it. He was so excited that his country was getting a chance to change for the better.

It wasn't long before I was interacting with the local population on a daily basis. I rode in a convoy that was to make a three-hour drive to take charge of some al-Qaeda and Taliban prisoners. We were short on vehicles, so we'd purchased a bunch of "gypsy" trucks from Afghans at a price that probably felt like winning the lottery to them. These trucks did not come with factory warranties. The one I rode in this day was an old Soviet delivery vehicle from the seventies or eighties. It had a flatbed in the back with a canvas top, chipping paint, and wheels of different colors and sizes. On the front of all these trucks, the Afghans had put little chain veils that stretched across to each side, which is why we called them gypsy trucks. It was like bedazzling a turd.

My truck broke down (what a shock) before we even got out of Mazar-i-Sharif. I sat in the cab with the driver, a young Army sergeant, as other members of the convoy looked under the hood and tried to get it running again. A crowd of locals began to form. With hand gestures, we indicated for them to keep a distance. I was fine with them as long as they stayed on the curb about ten feet away, but if they got closer, I yelled through my open window for them to step back—not that they understood English, but they knew what I meant. Still, as more people gathered, they kept crowding closer.

At a recent briefing, I'd learned that our enemies had been spotted in town mixing with the civilians. Their intent was to kill Americans via suicide attacks with bombs and small arms. A crowd always increased the pucker factor—you were never quite sure who was Northern Alliance and who was Taliban.

The sergeant and I each scanned the crowd on our side of the truck. "This guy over here has a nasty stare," the sergeant said.

"Which one?"

"The guy in the red, right in the middle of the crowd."

I looked closer. "I don't think he's a threat."

"Why?"

"I think he's blind."

"Oh," the sergeant said with a brief laugh. "Maybe you're right."

The longer the repairs went on, the more uncomfortable I got. Then I noticed a man circling the convoy. He wore layers of black robes and had a long beard. He was probably in his late twenties. It was pretty much the profile for a Taliban fighter. He just acted suspicious. It seemed to me that he was counting vehicles and personnel. I didn't like that I couldn't see his hands. I thought for sure he had a grenade under those layers and was just waiting for the right moment to throw it in our vehicle and run.

"I've got a live one—this guy in the black," I said. "He's up to something."

When the man got to my truck, he quickly stepped forward, stuck his head through my window, and peered inside.

"No, no, no," I said, shaking my head and gesturing for him to back away.

The Afghan removed his head but did not step back. Instead, his eyes locked onto mine. It was the first time I'd seen that look in Afghanistan. His eyes communicated pure hatred. You know it when you see it. It's not the blank look of somebody playing poker and trying to bluff you or somebody who's pretending to be tough and trying to intimidate. This was a "Fuck you" vibe. This guy wanted to kill me.

There was no time to make a plan. The sergeant was busy monitoring his side of the vehicle—dealing with this guy was all on me. I focused on the man's face and movements. If he started praying or sweating, that was a bad sign—it likely meant he was about to blow himself up, and us with him. If his eyes got wide or he suddenly pulled his hands from inside his robe, that was another bad sign.

Without taking my eyes off the man, I eased my Beretta from its holster—ever so slowly, so he wouldn't know what I was doing. I pushed the barrel against the inside of the door, pointed right at him. I couldn't see his hands, and he couldn't see mine. The door was thin enough that a bullet would go right through it. *Well,* I thought, *if he does anything, I'm going to shoot him.*

Just three feet apart, me sitting in the truck and him standing next to it, we continued to stare at each other. The seconds ticked by. It was like we were two Old West gunslingers facing off, waiting to see who would draw first. I tried nodding at him. Then I tried a slight smile. He didn't move. He gave me nothing, just that same murderous look.

A minute passed. Then another. Nothing demands your complete attention quite like the prospect of imminent violence or death. I was as fully present as I'd ever been in my life. All of my senses were on high alert. I mentally ran through the action steps I would take if necessary—controlling my breathing, pointing my weapon, site picture, trigger control. I was one sudden move away from potentially killing someone or being killed myself.

Despite my anger at terrorists and what had happened to my country, however, I wasn't looking for a fight in that moment. *Please don't do anything,* I thought. *Please don't do anything.*

Then, finally, the man slowly backed away a few steps so that he stood with the rest of the crowd. He was only six feet away and still stared at me, but it was enough. He'd "blinked" first.

A minute later, another Army sergeant pounded on the driver's door. "Forget it. We're leaving this truck. You guys get into that van up ahead. Let's go."

The sergeant and I exchanged relieved glances. "Thank God," I said. "Let's get the fuck out of here."

I'll never know if that guy carried a gun or a grenade or what would have happened if I hadn't had my eyes on him. But I'm thankful I didn't have to find out.

I saw a lot of suffering in Afghanistan, but what always got to me most were the kids. I couldn't imagine living their life.

On a cold, wet day in December, we visited the hospital, the university, and an elementary school to assess their medical and educational needs. Every time we stopped, children swarmed to greet us. We passed out candy and flyers warning people about the dangers of land mines. If the mob of kids got unruly, as often happened, the Afghan soldiers and old men near our vehicles started smacking the hell out of them with the butts of their AK-47s. They continued to do it even after we protested and asked them to stop. They looked at us as if to say, "Relax, you clearly don't know how to handle kids." After a few minutes of peace, the kids would swarm around us again and the process repeated itself.

Child abuse was apparently rampant. At the hospital, I saw a little girl who'd been burned terribly from her head to her toes. "Somehow" she'd been doused in boiling water. Through Salim or directly to those who spoke broken English, I asked doctors and nurses what happened. I never got a straight answer. Equally horrific was the level of medical care I witnessed, which wasn't far advanced from the Stone Age. Tuberculosis was common. A boy had a simple infection on his foot that wasn't treated. I was told he would lose his leg due to gangrene. It was so depressing. I heard that one out of four Afghan children wouldn't reach their teen years. These people knew only violence, fear, and pain.

The elementary school we visited had fifty to sixty kids per class. No desks, chairs, pencils, pens, notebooks, or chalkboards. The windows were all broken. The students sat on dirt floors in cold rooms and soaked up everything the teacher had to say. They had to soak it up because they had nothing to write it down with. The Taliban had closed almost every school in town. Women were forbidden from taking classes or teaching, so some studied and taught in secret. They risked their lives to study and learn. Now there were classes filled with young girls and women teaching them.

I couldn't help thinking that I'd had the greatest schools and the best teachers, and I took it all for granted. I was encouraged to study and learn, yet I so often resisted. Needless to say, I felt a little ashamed. *It's such a gift,* I thought, *to live in America. I am so lucky to be from a free country. I can study whatever I want, choose to be a comedian if I want. If I'm in trouble, I can pick up the phone, dial 911, and high-quality medical help or police or firefighters will be there in minutes to help or protect me. Over here, they're on their own.*

As a society, we in the United States have lost perspective. God forbid that our latte isn't hot enough or foamy enough or arrives two minutes late. The stuff we choose to get upset about would be laughable if it wasn't so sad. We forget that millions around the world live in war zones and count it a success if they make it through one more day.

Salim once said to me, "I want to move to America, where even the poor people are fat." Compared to most places in the world, I lived in a land of almost absurd abundance. I could go to a store and choose from fifty breakfast cereals. I could buy an apple or orange any time of year. I could easily purchase gas for my personal car that would take me wherever I wanted to go. I could sleep comfortably in my own bed, and if I wasn't comfortable enough, I could go out and buy a memory foam mattress. No one had a memory foam mattress in Afghanistan . . . well, maybe some Air Force guys?!

Like everyone else, I had my down days, but I was and am incredibly fortunate to be an American. I never want to take that for granted.

Christmas away from home is tough. Christmas in Afghanistan sucks! I missed my wife and family. Near midnight on Christmas Eve, I stepped into our headquarters courtyard with Gunny and an Air Force combat photographer to sip some weak tea and look at the stars. *There's Orion's belt*, I thought. *It looks just the same as it does back home in Kansas City.* Somehow that provided a bit of comfort.

A couple of Brits who were also part of our contingent at the school stepped into the courtyard. These were SAS guys, the British equivalent to our Navy SEALs. They ambled our way.

"Hey, gents," one said, holding up a half pint bottle of rum, "we got a little something here if you want us to gas up your tea."

That brought on smiles all around our little circle. "Wouldn't that be lovely," I said. "I believe we will."

US servicemen weren't even allowed nonalcoholic beer, but these guys were given a rum ration as part of their equipment issue. For them to share it with us meant a lot, especially on this night. We all would have rather been curled up on a couch in front of a Christmas tree with a special someone, but tonight at least, we could be with brothers in arms.

The first SAS man poured out what amounted to half a shot each for the five of us, then raised his glass. "Happy Christmas," he said. "Here's to success in Afghanistan."

"Merry Christmas," we each responded, also raising our cups and glasses.

"Fuck the Taliban," Gunny added.

A couple of weeks later, January 11, was the four-month anniversary of the terrorist attacks on America. On that day, I rode in a convoy with nearly twenty American personnel plus a handful of interpreters and Northern Alliance soldiers to the former Taliban military headquarters in Mazar-i-Sharif. This was a place where al-Qaeda members might have plotted and trained. Sometime the previous fall, our alliance had bombed out the headquarters. Many Taliban were killed and the rest captured.

When we arrived, I saw a two-story, square building that still stood despite many missing parts. All the windows had been blown out. We moved into the ten-thousand-square-foot courtyard at the building's entrance. It was filled with rubble. As we spread out, a Green Beret glanced my way and said, "Hey, Captain, look down." I saw that I stood on something white. Then I realized what it was—a human pelvis bone. I looked around and began to recognize other white objects in the rubble and dirt—spinal cords, rib cages, skulls. There were human remains everywhere. The wild dogs that roamed the countryside had picked the place clean so that only bones remained. It was a macabre scene.

Justice, I thought. *American justice is swift. Four months ago, I was standing on top of rubble piles at Ground Zero that included the body parts of close to three thousand murdered Americans. Now I'm standing on top of the sun-bleached bones of some of the people who may have helped carry out those plans.*

The job wasn't finished. The fight was just starting. We'd already lost people and would surely lose a lot more. But there was some satisfaction in punching back at these cowards. Being here felt like closing a circle.

Our senior officer and my commander at the time, Lieutenant Colonel Max Bowers, gathered us around and removed a piece of paper from a pocket. "We remember the tragedy that our nation suffered four months ago," he read aloud, "and we honor the innocent lives that were lost. We are here now, not primarily to avenge those deaths but to ensure that such a tragedy never happens again."

No one spoke or moved. The only sound was the distant growls and barks of the feral dogs. I felt the weight of the moment.

I don't know who brought it or how they obtained it, but someone produced a bent and burned metal hinge about the size of a human hand. It was a piece of the World Trade Center. The hinge and the paper read by Lieutenant Colonel Bowers were placed in a body bag and buried several feet deep in the courtyard.

I'd been confronted with so much violence and death over the previous four months. This wasn't a movie. It was real, a part of my life now. Among other things, I'd discovered what it felt like to hate. I didn't like it.

As I stood there in the former Taliban HQ, I tried to bury my hate with that metal hinge. I didn't want hatred to poison my life. I was a blessed man—blessed to have an amazing family and friends, to have my health, to have the opportunity to live in a country that cherished freedom for all.

PART FOUR

LEARNING TO BE ME—A GENERALLY HUMOROUS KNUCKLEHEAD FROM KANSAS

EIGHTEEN

Are You Gellin'? Or, The Day They Broke My Sole... I Mean, Soul

Sooner or later we all reach a breaking point. If you're trying to accomplish anything worthwhile at all, you're going to hit walls and you're going to get discouraged. When those walls start getting taller and thicker, one after the other, like you're trapped in some endless *Super Mario Bros.* video game? That's when you want to quit. It's also the exact moment when you find out what you're made of.

As our military presence in Afghanistan grew, the powers that be decided I was needed most at the Joint Operations Center of Central Command (CENTCOM) back in Tampa. I returned to the US in late February 2002. Because of my previous deployments and work, I had a top secret Sensitive Compartmented Information Facility (SCIF) security clearance. What does that mean exactly? Just that I got to go into certain rooms where there was secret stuff happening. Nothing conspiracy worthy, just operational security secrecy. Sorry to disappoint... but I don't know who killed Epstein. At CENTCOM, I provided information to the media about our predeployment activities and helped coordinate the media's activities in combat zones.

I made a second trip to Afghanistan during July and August. I served on an investigation board looking into a raid on Taliban fighters that also killed Afghan civilians at a wedding party. It's truly terrible when innocent civilians lose their lives. It's also terrible and cowardly when the enemy uses civilians as human shields, hiding antiaircraft weapons among them so that they can claim to be victims if you shoot back. The details in situations like this are so often more nuanced than they appear to be in the next day's media headlines.

My one-year tour of duty officially ended in November 2002, but I hadn't taken any leave, so I was able to go home to New York in October. Although my reasons for returning to active duty were awful, it was fulfilling to have such a strong sense of purpose for that year. I'd done work that truly mattered. I'd served my country during a time of great need. It was an honor to serve.

Just as after my previous deployments, I dove back into comedy and felt like I hadn't missed a beat. It was actually a little weird. For everyone except people in the military and their families, it was as if nothing had changed. If you didn't read the newspaper, you wouldn't even know a war was going on. Don't get me wrong: People were gracious and respectful to me. It was a little like, "Hey, Rob, so glad you're back! Thank you for your service. Okay, everybody, gather round, we've got a sketch to write!" The focus was elsewhere, which I understood. It was a blessing that people didn't have to worry about American streets turning into combat zones.

Besides jumping back into comedy, I also ran in the New York City Marathon a couple weeks after I got home. Why does a guy who'd just survived two deployments in war zones decide to punish himself by running up and down hills, on pavement, with a mob of smelly and sweaty endurance athletes, through all five New

York boroughs for twenty-six miles? Was I looking for new ways to torture myself? Did I just want a tour of the city?

Not really. I'd been running daily in Tampa, sometimes up to fifteen miles per run, so I was in great shape. I'd always wondered how I'd do over a long race like a marathon. I'd been putting my name into the lottery for a few years, and this year my name came up. I thought, *Why not? It would be like an engine check. What's my oil pressure? Any coolant leaks? How's my mental toughness? How's my physical toughness? If I say I'm gonna finish, can I actually do it? What will happen if I hit my breaking point?*

The biggest test would come at mile seventeen. That's when the route would take me near my apartment and right by the Blue Moon Café, my favorite Mexican food place. My worst-case scenario was that if I was hurting bad at mile seventeen, I'd quietly drop out, slip into the Blue Moon for some fajitas and a beer, and slink home in shame.

The race started on Staten Island. I have to admit, I got caught up in the moment. *Look at me!* I thought. *I'm running the New York Marathon with all these amazing athletes! Sign me up for the Olympics!* I ran at a brisk pace for two or three miles before reality set in. *This is stupid. I can't maintain this. I'm gonna die before I get out of Brooklyn—I gotta slow down!* I backed off to a relaxed jog. Then I got into a rhythm. I was like Forrest Gump . . . I felt like running and I just kept on going.

I *was* hurting at mile seventeen. The Blue Moon was calling me. *Wow, a beer sounds sooooo good right now. But I've come this far. How can I stop now? I'm finishing this fucking thing!* Over the last few miles, I alternated between walking and running. But I never stopped. I got it done, clocking in at about four and a half hours. I wasn't going to be threatening the world record anytime soon, but I'd done it. I'd challenged myself to do something I'd never tried before and made it happen. Mission accomplished.

During the following summer, I faced a different challenge that really did push me to my breaking point. I continued to work in an office by day and practice my comedy at night, trying to make my mark and wondering if I was wasting my time. I *was* getting some traction. I was gaining great experience and exposure in the *ASSSSCAT* shows. But it had been nine years since my decision to quit flight school and try for a career as a comedian and actor. I was thirty-three years old. My younger comedy castmates had started calling me *sir*! (Okay, not really, but sometimes it felt like they might.) The clock was ticking. My wife wanted to start a family. So did I. We weren't getting any younger. This was our window. Even though my future career was up in the air, we made the decision to go for it.

If we did have kids, we realized it made more financial sense for Tiffany to stay home with them. We'd be paying just as much for daycare as she made from her job at the time. Which meant the responsibility for supporting our family would be on me. I was fine with that. But at the same time, the pressure to get my show business career established felt like a crushing weight. In the late hours, when I lay in bed and couldn't sleep, I stared at the ceiling and wondered, *Is this all a big mistake? Should I give up the dream and focus on climbing the corporate ladder? Should I be trying to buy a home?*

I had corporate job offers. Or I could just stay in the Marines for the rest of my working life and earn a good living. In an instant, I could walk away from my dreams and solve all our financial worries. But doing that would feel like betraying who I was. It would be like killing my soul.

In the summer of 2003, my commercial agent called to say I'd been invited to audition for a TV ad about gel insoles for Dr. Scholl's, the footwear and foot care company. I was looking for a "foot" (rimshot!) in any door that might open, so I agreed to go.

On a hot and humid Monday afternoon, I put on a civilian suit, took a subway to Times Square, took another subway to the Meatpacking District, and walked nearly a mile—sweating profusely—toward the Hudson River till I found the right office building. The trip took over an hour.

When I got there, I realized it was a cattle call—I had to jam into a waiting room with a hundred other guys who'd showed up to audition. It was standing room only. I waited for what seemed like hours to appear before three people behind a desk so I could deliver these momentous words: "I'm gellin'. Are you gellin'?" They had me repeat it once. My audition took about a minute. Then came the long journey back through the heat to my office to finish my workday.

My agent called at the end of the afternoon. "Hey, Rob, apparently you killed it at the audition today. They want to see you again tomorrow, same time, same place."

I was not overjoyed. "Well, shit," I said. "Do I have to wear the suit again?" I did.

On Tuesday, I went through the same routine. This time, my suit was wrinkled and smelled of sweat from the day before. Even worse, on my walk to the audition, it began to rain, hard. At least the wait was shorter this time. I repeated the line: "I'm gellin'. Are you gellin'?" Back through the rain. Back on the subway. Back to my office.

Late that afternoon, my agent called again. Dr. Scholl's wanted me to report a third time. I couldn't imagine what new insights on my acting skills they expected to learn from another one-line audition. My agent tried to get me to look on the bright side: "Since it's a third audition, they have to pay you!"

"How much?"

"Seventy-five bucks."

That wasn't even enough to cover the cost of dry cleaning my suit! But I sucked it up. If I wanted a career in the arts, I had to pursue every opportunity. Whatever it took. For the third straight day, I made the trip to the southern tip of Manhattan. And once again, my agent called me after. It was down to three guys for the commercial, and I was one of the three. They wanted me back for a fourth audition.

Again? I thought. *This is ridiculous. I'm spending my whole week on this. It's one fucking line!* Still, it was an opportunity. If I was in a commercial, someone might see me and want me for something bigger. I had to go.

This time was different. The room was filled with Dr. Scholl's representatives, ad agency executives, and members of the production crew, nearly thirty people in all, most of them sitting behind desks and sipping lattes. By this point I couldn't have forgotten my line if I tried: "I'm gellin'. Are you gellin'?" They wanted to hear it different ways. A happy version. A sad version. An enthusiastic version. I gave them what they wanted.

The company reps and ad execs passed notes and talked with serious expressions among themselves. I couldn't believe the hyper-analysis this decision was getting. It felt like it was the White House situation room and they were deciding if they should go to war, not trying to choose who would say one line about shoe insoles. Was it really this hard? Finally, they thanked me and sent me home.

My wife was away from our apartment that evening when my phone rang. It was my agent with news I didn't want to hear.

Dr. Scholl's had chosen one of the other two guys.

Something inside of me snapped.

"Are you fucking *kidding* me?" I yelled at the walls after I got off the phone. "Fuck this. Fuck this business. Fuck everybody in this town. I'm gellin', are you gellin'? *Four days* I had to take that subway and walk in that heat and rain and wear that stinky-ass suit, *four days* they had to hear me say that shit, and they still can't make up their minds?"

I paced. I shouted. I was running hot! I was Peter Finch from the movie *Network*, ready to go to the window and shout, "I'm mad as hell and I'm not gonna take it anymore!" The other people living in my apartment building must have feared for their lives.

"I've got job offers! I don't have to do this shit! I could start a family and get a house in the suburbs like *all* my friends are doing. They're moving forward with their lives, and I'm stuck here doing 'I'm gellin', are you gellin'?' and being told I'm not good enough for it? I hate show business. I hate comedy. I hate everybody!"

More times than I could count, I had walked the streets of New York and heard someone scream in agony. Now I knew what that was about. It was a fellow actor who for some bullshit reason had just been rejected for the two hundredth time. It was the unmistakable howl of a soul being broken.

"Fuuuuuuuuuck!"

I had hit the wall. I was at my limit. My breaking point. I was ready to turn away, give up on my dream, and become that guy who gave it a shot but couldn't get there. That's how I felt for the rest of that sleepless night.

By the next morning, though, I'd calmed down a little. I got up, went to get myself a cup of coffee, and sat down in a bustling Starbucks to think. I knew no one else really cared about all the years of struggle and sacrifice I'd been through to this point. It was up to me. I had to make a decision.

Well, Riggle, I asked myself, *what do you want to do? Do you really want to quit? Is it time to accept that you're not going to make it in show business? Is the decision of a bunch of smug Dr. Scholl's executives drinking venti pumpkin spice lattes with triple shots of espresso going to be the final nail in your coffin?*

It was tempting to walk away, to stop fighting for something that seemed so out of reach. Yet even as I had the thought, I remembered another truth: Anything worth having is going to push you to the limit—and then beyond it. It's how you respond when you've reached your "limit" that matters. It's a powerful feeling to discover you're willing to keep going. It teaches you that you really do want it, that you're willing to sacrifice, and that you're ready to succeed.

I'd learned about commitment, sacrifice, and discipline in the Marines. I knew I was capable of just about anything if I believed and persevered. I also knew that so many people turn away from their dreams just before achieving the big breakthrough they've been working for.

I do feel close, I thought. *I feel like something's about to happen.*

I took a deep breath. "All right," I said aloud. "I'm not quitting. Let's see what else is out there."

I'm so glad I made that decision. My Dr. Scholl's breakdown wasn't my last setback, not even close. But it did help me to dig deeper and discover a strength and resolve I didn't know was there. It was a hard lesson, but worth it.

You have your own dreams. Some people might call them crazy. I understand the doubt and fear that come with that. But I'm here to tell you that if you're willing to go for it, those dreams can become reality. Keep working, keep laughing, keep believing. Your moment is coming.

I am sooooo gellin'. Are you gellin'? I hope so.

NINETEEN

Finding My Unicorn

I sit at a corner table in McSorley's, New York City's oldest saloon, finishing the best and funniest story I've ever told in my life. Crowded around me, hanging on every word, are a few of my closest friends: Bill Murray, Jennifer Aniston, Bono, and Lorne Michaels.

"And then," I say, pausing to look each of them in the eyes before I deliver the punch line, "the cheetah licks my balls!*"*

Bill, who'd just taken a gulp of ale, explodes with delight, spraying his drink all over Jennifer, who is suddenly laughing so hard she doesn't even care. Bono jumps to his feet in disbelief, spilling his own ale across the table. "Riggle, that's fooking hilarious! You're killing me!" he shouts. "You gotta join me on my next tour!"

"Fuck that, Bono!" I say. "You know I ain't got time for a tour!"

Lorne, meanwhile, can't stop giggling. He shakes his head. "The balls?" he manages. "Rob, you're the best! America needs to hear this. How would you like to be next week's host on Saturday Night Live?*"*

"Saturday Night Live?*" I say. "Now you're talking! I've wanted to be on that show since—"*

"Reveille! Reveille! Get up! You're late! Time to go! Get moving, Marine!"

I blinked my eyes. Who was the idiot shouting at me? Then I remembered. I smashed my hand down on the object making all the noise. It was my alarm clock, a fourteen-inch-tall mutt dressed in a Marines uniform that barked out orders like a drill sergeant. What can I say? It was a Christmas gift from my sister and nieces.

It was dark. I was in bed. The magic scene at McSorley's faded into the mist. I wasn't best friends with Bill Murray, Jennifer Aniston, Bono, or Lorne Michaels—that was just a dream. Next to me, my wife turned over but didn't wake up. I looked at the clock: 5 a.m.

Ugh.

I hauled myself out of bed and grabbed my wallet. I was already wearing my workout shorts and T-shirt. It was time for calisthenics and a five-mile run in New York's Central Park with the Marines from my reserve unit. I tiptoed past my newborn daughter's crib in our one-bedroom apartment toward the front door. Yep, I was a dad now—my doc had been right about my high-performance sperm!

It was a Wednesday in July 2004. I felt the weight of my new responsibilities—Abby was now three months old. Driving her home from the hospital had been one of the proudest—and scariest—moments of my life. I was supposed to know how to feed, dress, and change the diapers of this miniature human being who had just entered my life? Not to mention love and support her for the rest of my days? I wanted to be a great dad, but I was nervous . . . okay, if I'm being honest, probably a little terrified.

Besides trying to figure out which end of my baby daughter was up, I had a few other things going on too. I'd now been an active-duty or reserve Marine for the last fourteen years and had been promoted from captain to major. I had an office job and was still in the reserves, which meant occasional training on weekends. Nearly every night and weekend, I was still pursuing the career I really wanted—a life in the arts as an actor and comedian.

That's a lot of nights. Even if they weren't saying so, I'm sure more than a few of my family and friends thought I was a lost cause.

It wasn't hopeless, though. I was still performing in *ASSSSCAT* shows at the UCB and there'd been more short appearances on *Late Night with Conan O'Brien*. Thanks to my size and Marines haircut, I played a lot of security guards, like in a bit where the Kids in the Hall comedy troupe pretended to sneak into the show and I started beating on them. Another time, I sat in the audience with Jamie Denbo, a fellow UCB alumnus. We played a couple who got into a fight that was so distracting to the audience that Conan had to stop the show.

"Excuse me, what's going on?" Conan asked.

"Aw, don't worry about it, Conan," I said. "My girlfriend's just being an idiot. I've got it under control."

"Well, hold on," Conan said. "I don't like the way you're talking to her. You shouldn't treat a lady like that."

That was my cue to be offended. "Oh, yeah? What are you going to do about it?"

"I think maybe you and I should step outside."

"All right, you got it!" I jumped up and began stalking down the aisle toward the stage.

Conan, meanwhile, egged on the audience, which was now hooting and cheering his bravado. "Don't worry, guys," he said to the crowd. "I'm going to handle this guy."

I got to the stage and we moved to a door at the end of the set as the cheers and catcalls grew even louder. Conan gave the audience a final "I've got this" wink, then we stepped out of view, though a cameraman followed us into the hallway so the audience and TV viewers could still see everything. As soon as that stage door closed, Conan's smile disappeared. He fell to his knees in front of me and begged, "Please don't kill me! Please don't kill me!" Of course, the studio audience roared with laughter. It was a funny scene.

The Conan appearances were only short bits, but they were valuable experience and got my name and face out there on network TV. Besides that, I'd formed a comedy partnership with Rob Huebel. We'd created a two-man show that was popular enough to earn us an invite to an important comedy art festival in Aspen, Colorado, sponsored by HBO. That led to us signing with a prestigious talent agency, International Creative Management. Amazing, really—I was actually seeing signs that this comedy thing could work.

Yet I still had to wonder how much longer I could keep it up. Another year had gone by, and now I had a family to think about. Putting in the comedy work day after day, week after week, was draining. Would it ever pay off?

My dream of dreams—the goal I'd set for myself when I wrote it in the back of the Tony Robbins book on the beach at Corpus Christi—was still to become a cast member on *Saturday Night Live*. So many of the great comics went through *SNL*. It's what everybody associates with success in the comedy world. I grew up with that show! I mean, who could resist Eddie Murphy as James Brown in "Celebrity Hot Tub Party"? *I could be the next Buckwheat or Mr. Robinson! (Hi boys and girls, can you say "Scum bucket"?)*

I almost made it in 2003. Along with about twenty other hopefuls who were starting to make a name for themselves in comedy, I was invited to audition for a cast opening. I made the first cut to the final six, but after the last round of tryouts, I didn't get the call. I was heartbroken. I mean it hurt more than hiring a mariachi band for a marriage proposal and the girl not just saying no, but grabbing a band member's guitar and hitting you over the head with it. Yet somehow, I still believed I could do it. Even at that point, I didn't lose the faith.

The good news for me was that I'd heard *SNL* might have another opening for fall 2004 and might still be interested in me. On that Wednesday morning, however, I didn't have time to think about any of that. I had to go get sweaty in the predawn darkness so I could work off my stress (not to mention all the fajitas I'd downed in the last week).

I sighed. It was going to be a long day.

Seventeen hours later, at 10 p.m., I dragged myself out of the UCB office space in lower Midtown Manhattan and onto the sidewalk. The evening heat—along with that familiar fragrance of garbage and urine—was so bad. It was like walking into Satan's armpit.

I was exhausted. My early morning workout had been followed by a full day of preparing for an upcoming East Coast media symposium, where our Marine reserve unit would host high-ranking officers from across the armed services branches to conduct media training. I had time for a quick dinner at my favorite low-budget (okay, cheap) taco place—hey, you can't beat three steak tacos for five bucks in NYC. Then I was off to UCB headquarters, where for the next three hours I coached a group of ten improv performers in their twenties. I loved mentoring these guys. It was so rewarding to demonstrate the collaborative rules of improv and see the light come on in their eyes.

But oh man, was I wiped out by the end of it. I looked and felt like I'd been "rode hard and put away wet," as my mom would say. When I stumbled toward the corner of 31st Street and Seventh Avenue to catch a taxi, all I wanted was to go home, scarf down a snack, talk to my wife for a few minutes, and collapse into bed—which was exactly what I planned to do.

Except I had a problem.

The deal was that if I did get a call to audition for that fall opening on *Saturday Night Live*, it would be soon—and I wasn't ready. You'd think I'd have been so jacked that I would spend every waking minute practicing and preparing characters for my potential audition. And this evening was the perfect opportunity to do that, because starting at 11 p.m. was Hump Night at the UCB Theatre, which meant anybody could sign up for five minutes onstage in front of an audience to work on their material. But for the past couple months, I'd been putting off my preparation. The truth is, I was scared of failing. I'd already fallen short once. *If* I got the call for a second chance at *Saturday Night Live*, I knew there wouldn't be a third. My dream was about to either come to life or disappear for good. I did not want to face the negative side of that equation. Stuffing my face with a taco and burrowing into my couch sounded mighty appealing right then.

Maybe you've been there? You want something so bad, you sacrifice and sacrifice to make it happen, but then as you get close to achieving it, you begin to doubt and feel paralyzed. You end up sabotaging yourself. That was me in summer 2004. Everyone knew how badly I wanted this. I was afraid to give it everything and end up embarrassed, hurt, and devastated.

Sometimes you just have to coach yourself into the right perspective—even if you look like a crazy person while doing it. Which is exactly what I looked like on that street corner when my inner drill sergeant and Couch Potato Rob started getting into it, with me providing the voices for both sides, out loud.

COUCH POTATO ROB: *I'm too tired. I just want to go home. I can do my* SNL *prep work tomorrow.*

INNER DRILL SERGEANT: *Are you fucking kidding me? You want to go home? Did you quit flight school, put in all those extra years in the Marine Corps, get yourself to New York, take those stand-up classes, find UCB and take all their classes, do 1 a.m. improv jams in front of drunk idiots, and give up every weekend for the past seven years just so you could go home and sit on your lazy ass?*

CPR: *Well . . . no . . . but I don't have anything to say. I don't have a character.*

IDS: *Hey, big guy, you're an improviser—so improvise it! Just go down there, pick a character, and make it up.*

CPR: *But I have to get up at 5 tomorrow for another workout—I need my sleep! Do you know how comfortable it is to sleep in a warm bed, with a sheet and blanket and down comforter over you, at just the right temperature? It's like being in a soft, furry cocoon. It's like having fluffy cotton all around you. It's like floating on a cloud of cozy marshmallows that—*

IDS: Cozy marshmallows??? *What the hell, Marine!! Get a grip on yourself! You've gone days without sleeping before. You've been to war. You're a Marine! Not some fucking cozy marshmallow! Now get your ass right down to the UCB and do something on that stage. I don't care what it is, just do it! Fucking* marshmallows???

As I paced on the sidewalk and the pitch and volume of my voice kept rising, I was only dimly aware of the figures around me giving me a wide berth. I can only imagine what they thought of the deranged dude in the dress shirt and crew cut who was shouting at himself. Probably that I'd had too many sips of the local Kool-Aid. On the other hand, this was New York City, so they might not have thought anything at all.

"You need to do the fucking work!" my drill sergeant continued. "You have to commit! It starts tonight. I mean, why the fuck did you come here?"

Couch Potato Rob finally gave in. "You're right. You're right! The whole reason I'm here is to try to get on *Saturday Night Live*, and I'm not getting on if I don't do the work. Okay, you win. I'm going."

With that, I found myself stomping down Seventh Avenue toward the theater.

The current UCB Theatre—they'd switched locations multiple times—would not be confused with Radio City Music Hall. It was on 26th Street beneath a Gristedes grocery store. You had to duck under an awning to slip downstairs into a dingy black box space with a stage the size of a small living room. Exposed piping ran the length of the ceiling. Trash bags were wrapped around pipes that had burst a few nights earlier. Gristedes employees used our back hallway to take out their garbage, so the theater possessed its own unique aroma. Yet, for all that, it was awesome. I've done more shows on that little stage than anyplace in the world. It's where I figured out my funny. Our little crowd of aspiring comedians was a kind of family, and the UCB Theatre was our home.

There was no second-guessing once I got there. I quickly wrote my name down for two five-minute slots. I'd chosen my characters on the short walk to the theater. Soon, I was up onstage. The audience was small, made up mostly of people I knew, comics perfecting their craft like me. If I could make this group laugh, I was golden.

My first character was a Marine Corps recruiter who wouldn't take no for an answer. My attitude was "You're a triple amputee and you hate America? Okay, let's talk about how that might fit with the Marines." I picked out a young guy sitting near the stage and started my pitch. "How are you paying for school, son? Why don't you take the burden off your family and be your own man. The Marines are a great way to pay for an education." He played along and gave me straight answers, saying he wasn't interested in the Marines and didn't want to fight.

"A lot of people are scared by combat," I said. "You don't need to be scared. Most Marines won't tell you this, but combat is actually a lot of fun." That bit got some good laughs. I felt better already. I had a character.

A few minutes later, I was back onstage. I based my new character on my junior high gym teacher, a sweet, gentle, grandfatherly man named Dewey Cundiff. I remembered that poor Dewey was tasked with teaching sex education to me and my friends, a bunch of seventh grade boys. As soon as that lesson started, we realized that sex was the last thing Dewey wanted to talk about. Even after giving us the shortest, most by-the-numbers lesson in the history of sex education, he was sweating. "And then the woman gets pregnant," he concluded, wiping his brow. "All right, men"—he always called us *men*—"that's about it. Do you have any questions?" He clearly hoped we didn't.

Do you remember what seventh grade boys are like? They show no mercy. With Dewey, we were like sharks circling an innocent victim in the water. Even though we already knew the answers—or thought we did, anyway—we had many, many questions.

"Coach, what does *erect* mean?"

"Coach, what is a vagina again?"

"Coach, I've heard there are places where they use whips on people—what are those for?"

Dewey's face turned pale. He was horrified. He couldn't end that lesson fast enough. So, when I was up onstage at the UCB, I replayed that scene for the audience, with my gym coach nearly dying from embarrassment every time he had to explain something. The small crowd loved it.

As soon as my time was up, I retreated to the greenroom backstage. It wasn't much more than a space with two couches, a grungy bathroom, and two closets, one filled with costumes, the other with beer. The walls were literally green—a fluorescent, shocking green—and were mostly covered with posters for old shows.

I sat on one of the couches, pulled out a small notebook, and began writing down what had worked best with my characters. I was feeling pretty pleased with myself. I'd made the decision to work on my material and found two characters that had real potential.

What I didn't know about the audience that night was that it included Adam McKay, former head writer at *Saturday Night Live*. Adam had cowritten and directed the just-released comedy hit *Anchorman: The Legend of Ron Burgundy*, which trailed only *Star Wars: Episode III* at the box office. A few minutes after I sat down, Adam poked his nose into the greenroom. We had met only briefly before.

When Adam saw me, his face brightened. He walked right over and put out his hand. "Rob, I love those characters," he said. "They're hilarious!"

"Thanks, man," I said. "I appreciate that."

We chatted for a few seconds, then Adam headed for the door. In the doorway, however, he turned back.

"Hey," he said, "you know what might be good for the old coach? Give him a really bad physical ailment."

"Sure," I said, immediately seeing the humor potential. "That's a great idea, thanks!" From that point on, my gym coach character coughed so much he nearly had a heart attack when he had to talk about sex, which did get more laughs.

Wow. Now I had not only made great progress on my characters, but I'd also connected with one of the leading people in the industry and received valuable advice to boot. I was higher than Snoop Dogg on top of a Ferris wheel in Amsterdam.

After that night, I was on a mission. Whenever there was an open mic, I was down at the UCB Theatre or some other venue, getting in stage time and developing more characters. Every day left me feeling a little more prepared, a little more confident. I had that sense of fulfillment that comes from putting in the work to be the finest version of yourself. I told myself, *I can go in and give this my best—and if they don't want me, they don't want me. At least I've made the journey from that beach on Corpus Christi to New York to being ready to show them what I can do. Even if it doesn't happen, I've made massive progress on my dream.*

Then, a few weeks later, *SNL did* call, inviting me to audition for the cast a second time. I would have another chance to join Amy Poehler, Tina Fey, Seth Meyers, and so many more of my comedy heroes. I was thrilled—and scared again. I knew that getting invited was only the first step.

For the second time in a month, I paced on a New York sidewalk, looking like a lunatic. I grinned from ear to ear—not because I'd just been named Sexiest Man Alive, but because I was practicing smile therapy, psyching up. My audition might be only minutes away.

The process of trying out for *Saturday Night Live* is nerve-wracking. The chosen few, around twenty, are flown into New York and asked to stand by on the evening of the initial audition. You wait for a phone call telling you where to go and when. By keeping you in the dark, they prevent you from lining up a bunch of friends to stack the audience in your favor when you perform. Personally, I could have done without the cloak and dagger. I was surprised they didn't have a mixed martial arts fighter waiting to ambush me at the entrance to the club.

I waited for my call at a Starbucks in Manhattan. I ordered a cup of coffee and downed it in about two seconds. I started pacing, first in the coffee shop, then on the sidewalk. I kept glancing at the cell phone in my hand. *Have they called? Nope, not yet. When are they going to call? Why are they torturing me like this?*

My adrenaline was pumping—or maybe it was the caffeine. Either way, I felt excited and ready. My job now was to coach myself into a positive frame of mind. I needed to believe.

Let's go, I told myself. *Let's do this. You're here to win.* I had my head up and shoulders straight. Every step and gesture were purposeful. I was getting into that comfortable, confident zone.

My cell phone rang. I jumped and nearly dropped the phone.

"Hello!" I said, trying to sound poised and cool.

"Rob," said the voice on the line, "the audition's at Comic Strip Live on 81st Street and Second Avenue. You've got thirty minutes to get there."

"Great!" I said. I thought of D. H. Sweeney and my first stand-up comedy class there seven years ago—a familiar place. Even better, it was in Manhattan. Even with a cab—and I was definitely splurging for a cab—it took about thirty minutes to get *anywhere* in Manhattan, let alone to some other borough. *Thank God I'm close*, I thought. It was a good sign. Of course, I'd just put myself into a space where everything was positive. If a pigeon had used my head as his personal outhouse, I would have seen it as a good sign.

After the cab ride, I found myself in the club's lobby, sizing up the competition. *Oh, I know that guy, he's really good. Uh-oh, she's good too. Hm, there's Jason Sudeikis. When we both auditioned last year,* SNL *hired him as a writer, so he's obviously talented.* Already my confident zone was being challenged.

All twenty of us put our names on a piece of paper and into a hat. An *SNL* production assistant stuck his arm into the hat and pulled one out. "All right, here we go," he said. "First up . . . Rob Riggle."

My confident bubble burst. *You've got to be kidding me! I don't want to be* first*!*

In a situation like that, leading off is like the kiss of death. When you're first, the audience has just arrived and isn't ready to relax and laugh. Even worse, by the time the night is over, few people will remember the guy who went first. It's why show schedulers build the anticipation by saving the top bands and acts for last.

But complaining and lamenting wasn't going to change anything. I was going first—so I quickly tried to turn the situation on its head. *Maybe this is good,* I thought. *I'll go up there and destroy it, and everyone else will be so intimidated that I'll be the obvious choice. I'm just going to get out there and rock it. Here we go. Who's in my way? Prepare to get run over!*

There is a mindset that comes from being a US Marine. It's instilled in you from the first day. You hear it from the drill sergeants, the classroom instructors, the officers. You're taught to attack, to lead, to find a way. It's never a question of *if* you will accomplish the mission, only how and when. There's a reason that Marine Lieutenant General Lewis "Chesty" Puller once said about the enemy during a battle, "They're on our left, they're on our right, they're in front of us, they're behind us . . . they can't get away this time." I don't believe he was being rah-rah or phony. He saw being surrounded as an opportunity. That was simply his mindset.

Thanks to the Marines, that "advancing in a different direction" attitude became my mindset. I didn't always know just how and when, but once I set a goal, I felt I had the ability and tenacity to find a way and get it done. I might face plenty of roadblocks. It might take longer than I wanted. And don't get me wrong, I still had plenty of moments when I felt like I was looking at an obstacle three times my size and wanted to say to someone, "Sir, I think there's been a mistake." But once I got my head squared away and got my mental armor on, I was ready to do battle. Sooner or later, I would get there.

I absolutely had to put on that armor for my audition at Comic Strip Live. Just a few minutes after my name got pulled from the hat, I was onstage. I did impersonations of country music's Toby

Keith, pro football tight end Jeremy Shockey, and Paul Lynde. I did original characters—a street preacher named Leviticus and my old gym teacher. For seven minutes, I gave it everything I had. People laughed, so it seemed to go well. And just like that, I was done. I got out of the club and paced on the sidewalk some more while the rest of the performers did their routines. I didn't need to watch somebody else killing it.

Near the end of the night, I slipped back inside. *SNL*'s head producers and writers were all in a booth in the back: Steve Higgins, Michael Shoemaker, Tina Fey, Harper Steele, and, of course, the top dog, Lorne Michaels. After the last performance, they all came out, waved to the crowd, and left in their town cars. An *SNL* assistant gathered us hopefuls and said, "Okay, guys, if you get a call from us, we'll see you tomorrow. If not, thank you so much."

I didn't know what to expect. I thought I'd done well, but since I hadn't watched the others, I had no idea how everyone else had performed. All I knew was that I'd given it my best.

About an hour later, I did get the call—yes! I was to show up at 30 Rock (officially 30 Rockefeller Plaza, *SNL*'s headquarters) at 4 p.m. the next day for the second and final round of auditions. I was excited, but not over the moon. After all, I'd made it to the final round the year before and fallen short.

I couldn't sleep that night. Neither could our daughter. Abby had started to get the idea that darkness meant time to sleep, not cry and scream like a bullfrog (yes, bullfrogs have an adorable/terrifying scream—look it up!). But my daughter still had fussy nights. In the middle of that night, when Abby began to cry, I went into the next room, picked her up, and gently rocked her. Since I had a captive audience, I decided it was as good a time as any to practice my impersonations. I sang "Rock-a-bye, baby, in the treetop," in a quiet, quivering Paul Lynde voice.

That was surely Abby's first taste of show business, which is either endearing or horrifying, depending on how you look at it. Today, she loves acting and is pursuing it as a possible career, so I give myself and that moment all the credit (or the blame, also depending on how you look at it).

A little after four the next day, an assistant escorted me toward the *SNL* set where the host does their monologue each week. Awaiting me was a cameraman, a stage manager, and Lorne Michaels. The plan was for me to do the same routine I'd performed the night before. Tina Fey and the rest of the writers and producers would watch again from the back of the room. A group of about thirty NBC executives would also watch remotely in Burbank, California.

The frustrating thing about an audition is that it's nothing like a job interview. You don't get to sit down and make your case for why they should hire you. There's no "Hey, listen guys, I'm a little new to show business. I'm still learning and gaining experience. But my growth potential is phenomenal." You just have to show 'em what you've got in seven minutes.

Or in this case, four minutes. On the way to the stage, the assistant walking with me said, "So, Rob, we need you to cut your stuff from last night down to four to five minutes." This was only seconds before the most important audition of my life. I don't think the last-moment switch was someone at *SNL* being unorganized. I believe it was intentional. They wanted to see how I would handle the stress of adjusting on the fly.

I did a quick calculation. I'd never be able to keep track of cutting little bits out of each impersonation and character. I decided to completely drop my Jeremy Shockey impersonation. Problem solved.

Lorne walked up to me. "Rob, very fine performance last night, you did a good job," he said. "Do you have any questions for me?"

"Nope," I squeaked, my voice about an octave higher than normal. Realizing how uncool I'd just sounded, I lowered my tone. "I'm ready to go."

"Okay. Just do what you did last night and have fun."

Holy shit, I thought. *Lorne Michaels knows who I am and said I did a good job. That's awesome!*

I didn't have time to enjoy the moment. Seconds later, I faced the camera and took a deep breath. The stage manager said, "Three, two," waited a beat, and pointed at me. The little light on top of the camera turned red. I was live.

I think most performers experience something like this—when you're onstage, your brain splits in two. I'm not talking about Steve Martin's *The Man with Two Brains.* What I mean is that as I started my routine, part of my mind was focused on telling jokes, but the other part was thinking, *This is it. This is my last shot. I'm actually onstage, right now, auditioning for everything I want. My dream is* this *close! I can touch it. I can feel it. I can see it. But never mind that! You need to relax. Just focus on your lines and the timing and giving it your best.*

The next thing that hit me? Silence. Except for my jokes, the room was dead quiet. I couldn't hear the response of the execs in Burbank and there was no audience present on the set other than Lorne and the head staff. They'd all just seen my routine, so they weren't laughing.

My mouth kept saying words, but my head thought, *Oh, shit—what the fuck is going on? Why is it so quiet in here? Why is no one laughing? Is this funny? I thought this was funny last night. Does this still work? Did it ever work? I hate this character! Why is it—oh, right. They already saw it, they already know the routine. Calm down, calm down, CALM THE FUCK DOWN!!!!!!*

The stage manager, Gena, saved me. She was a lovely woman who'd been at *SNL* for years, a little Italian fireball who ran that stage and show with good humor and great energy. She stood next to the camera and silently mouthed "Yes!" followed by a long-distance fist bump. I relaxed a bit. She did it again for the next joke, which gave me another shot of confidence.

Gena became my audience. I performed for her.

Before I knew it, I was done. Lorne thanked me, and I exited the building. I walked across Sixth Avenue, found a fountain, and sat down.

Wow. That was it. That was my best shot. My dream either happens or it doesn't. It was a surreal feeling. Once again, I felt good about my performance. But I knew it could have been better. Was my timing okay? Had I been too busy freaking out and judging myself to come off as confident and funny?

Anything was possible. Maybe they were looking for a different style of comedy. Maybe they thought they needed another woman on the team more than some big Marine.

As I sat by that fountain, I offered up a heartfelt prayer that the *SNL* staff discussions would go well, that they would see my potential, that they would see what I had to offer. Now, all I could do was trust.

Nine days after the audition, I stood in a line of a dozen people at a deli, waiting to order a takeout dinner for my family. I was nearly to the counter when my cell phone rang.

"Hello, is this Rob Riggle?" the caller asked. "Stand by for a call from Lorne Michaels."

I stepped out of the line, losing my place. I didn't care. This was the moment I'd been waiting for. I hurried outside and onto the sidewalk.

"Hey, Rob," Lorne said in his unmistakable, authoritative voice. "We loved your audition the other night. You did a good job. It was very original stuff."

I held my breath, not wanting to interrupt.

"We were wondering," Lorne continued, "if you would like to join this year's cast on *Saturday Night Live*?"

I didn't want there to be any doubt. "Yes! Yes!" I shouted. "That's what I'm talking about! Lorne, I'm going to work so hard for you. You made such a good decision."

In that moment, my dream materialized. Suddenly, all the late nights, the endless classes, the lost weekends, the missed vacations, the improv sessions in tiny venues in front of tinier audiences were worth it. Almost a decade of grinding had actually paid off! When I'd written down my goal ten years earlier, the chances of some unknown, unpolished Kansas dude with a funny name getting on *SNL* were about the same as getting up in the middle of the night and finding a unicorn in my bathroom—maybe less. But I'd done it! It felt soooo great, so validating.

I was joining the cast of *Saturday Night Live*.

I was tempted to race home to tell my wife, but I was supposed to be bringing dinner, so I went back into the deli and started over at the back of the line. It was eleven grumpy New Yorkers waiting to get their grub and one guy with the goofiest grin on the East Coast.

I couldn't wait to call Bill, Jennifer, and Bono.

TWENTY

My Way

Remember in *Dumb and Dumber*, when Lauren Holly explains to Jim Carrey that his chances with her are about one in a million? His face lights up and he says, "So you're telling me there's a chance!" That's how excited I felt on the first day I reported at 30 Rock to get my *Saturday Night Live* security badge.

It had been so much fun telling family and friends I was going to be on the show. A lot of people I knew didn't pay that much attention to late night television, so if I mentioned I had a guest appearance on *Conan* or Comedy Central, the reaction was often along the lines of "Oh, that's nice." When I told my parents I was going to be on *Conan*, they looked at me like I was a rack of yard tools. It meant nothing to them. But everyone knew *Saturday Night Live*—even my parents. This was the place that made John Belushi, Dan Aykroyd, Chevy Chase, and Bill Murray household names. When I told Mom and Dad I was going to be on the cast of *SNL*, the response was "Oh my gosh, Rob, that's big time!"

That first day at 30 Rock didn't feel real. After getting my picture taken, I rode an elevator to the seventeenth floor. The *SNL* offices for cast members, writers, and producers were arranged in a horseshoe shape, with Lorne Michaels's office at the back in the center of the shoe. I walked down one of the hallways and saw group pictures on the wall of each *SNL* cast, starting with the first one in 1975. Then I saw individual pictures of every cast member who'd ever appeared on the show, whether it was for a decade or just four episodes, as was the case with Ben Stiller. That's when it hit me: *My picture is going to be up here!*

I even had a large office all to myself, which was unusual. Mine was inside the horseshoe, so I didn't have a window like most everyone else. The bigger drawback was being alone. I wanted to make friends with the writers and other cast members! Nevertheless, this was where I would try to create comedy gold.

As I walked those hallowed halls for the first time, I got another reminder of just how fortunate I was. One of the writers who'd also auditioned for a role in the cast spotted me and poked his head out of his office. "Hey, Riggle," he said. "What are you doing here?"

One thing about *SNL*—they're great about passing on good news, but not so hot on communicating the bad. I'd learned this the year before after my last audition. No one called to let me know they'd chosen someone else. I didn't know for certain I hadn't been hired until the new season started without me.

When the writer questioned me in the hallway, I simply said, "Hey! I got hired."

I'll never forget the look on his face. He smiled, but it was the most hollow smile I'd ever seen. I realized, to my surprise, that he was just now finding out he didn't get the gig. I felt terrible.

The bad feeling didn't last too long, however. There was so much to learn. Amy Poehler, who'd been on *SNL* for three years at that point, stopped by my office. "Riggs, welcome!" she said. "I'm so happy for you!"

I had a thousand questions for her. "You guys write on Tuesdays and stay all night? What do you guys do for dinner? What's the pitch meeting like?" I barely gave Amy time to answer before I peppered her with another question. It was so great to be able to ask someone I knew about all the little details, because I knew nothing and was intimidated by everyone. Even the janitor intimidated me. He was BTSB (Been There Since Belushi).

It wasn't long after that first day that Amy gave me some of the most wise and important career advice I would ever receive—wisdom that, at the time, I did not understand whatsoever. One day as we talked in her office, she leaned toward me and said, "Hey, listen. Don't give this place too much power."

"Okay," I said, nodding my head. "Yeah." After we finished our conversation, I ruminated on her words for another minute. *Don't give this place too much power. Okay, got it.* But I didn't get it. Amy recognized that even though we were nearly the same age, I was inexperienced and naïve about the ways of show business compared to her and the rest of the folks at *SNL*. She was trying to help the rookie navigate his first full-time job in the arts. It was a wonderful gesture, one I appreciate to this day, but I wouldn't understand what she meant until it was too late.

I'll never forget my first show—October 2, 2004. It was a thrill to hear Don Pardo, the legendary voice of *SNL*, say ". . . and Roooob Riiiiiggle!" when the cast was introduced to the audience at the beginning of the show. Ben Affleck was the guest host. My first line was in a sketch where Ben and other cast members were on an escalator that stopped moving. What made it funny was that we played it as if they were trapped on an elevator, complete with all the movie tropes. People were panicked because they thought they'd never get off. There was a pregnant lady who started to deliver, a claustrophobic, and a guy who confessed to a murder. I played a firefighter coming to the rescue. From the bottom of the escalator, all of ten feet away, I called up, "Hello, can anybody hear me?" I was nervous as hell, but the line got a decent chuckle.

The other thing I remember from that show was the ending. As you'll know if you've ever watched *Saturday Night Live* all the way through, the program ends with the guest host, full cast, and band gathering onstage. The host thanks everyone, mentions something about their week at 30 Rock, and says good night. Even as a kid, I'd always loved watching the sign-offs and rolling of the credits. You saw the whole cast at once, some still in their costumes from the last sketch. The crowd cheered and everybody hugged. The cast members talked and laughed with each other. They looked like a family. You knew they were all about to go to the after-party, which was legendary. You saw the start of it right there onstage. It was just so cool.

For my whole life, I'd been looking through my television at the people on that stage. Now, suddenly, I was on the other side of the camera. I was *on* that stage, waving goodbye to the studio audience and viewers around the world. It was like *Alice in Wonderland.* I'd fallen through the rabbit hole into another dimension. As we all waved, Ben Affleck turned and called out thanks to a few cast members. Then he spotted me. "Hey," he said, "great job, Riggle!" I was part of all this now. It was special.

I have plenty of other great memories from that year. Playing a scene with Liam Neeson where we were a pair of redneck truckers in an Appalachian emergency room. Meeting Bono (yes, part of my McSorley's dream did come true!) and the rest of the guys in U2. Going to those after-parties and having conversations with people I'd been a fan of for years. I didn't even care that most of those conversations were drunken babble that you could barely hear over the music.

I didn't feel I'd "arrived," but I did think being on *SNL* meant I'd be good for a while. I looked forward to several years on the show. I anticipated creating lots of fun characters and building my career through appearances on other shows and movies. I saw

Saturday Night Live as the foundation for all the wonderful things I planned to do. This was happening, baby!

Only that's not quite how it turned out.

On *SNL*, the week started with a pitch meeting. Everybody—cast members, writers, producers, the celebrity host—jammed into Lorne's large office. Recent hires like me sat on the floor because there wasn't enough couch space for everyone. After introductions, Lorne asked for ideas for that week's sketches and went around the room. We were pitching to both Lorne and that week's guest host. If the host was Ben Affleck, a cast member might say, "So, Ben, I've got an idea where you and I are astronauts lost in space. You're trying to figure out what's wrong with our ship and I'm trying to get the Wi-Fi working so I can look at porn." And on it went. Even if the guest host has no experience with comedy or live television, after hearing fifty absurd and hilarious premises for sketches, they walked away feeling they were going to kill it that week.

I wanted to help create and be in some of those sketches, obviously. So, I went to the writers and producers to ask for their advice. Several of them recommended building relationships with all the writers and cast members and offering to work on sketches as much as possible, even if that meant being involved with six sketches a week. Tina Fey, meanwhile, suggested I focus like a laser on just one sketch and make it really great. I didn't know who to listen to. Remember, I didn't know shit; that's why I was asking for advice.

To use a military metaphor, I chose the shotgun approach over the sniper rifle. I came from a collaborative background, after all. I wanted to work with and please everybody. The problem, however, was that I ended up with twenty masters and spread myself too thin. It's like I was trying to cook the steak, mix the martini, serve the hot fudge sundae, and juggle seven hamsters all at the same time—my attention was so divided that I couldn't please anybody. Hindsight being 20/20, I would say now that Tina was right. I probably should have focused on one sketch a week and crafted it really well. Tina is very smart, very tough, and very talented. She's a natural leader. I wish I would have had more time to learn from her.

I also lost track of what got me onto *SNL* in the first place. Early in the spring, a writer approached me and said, "Rob, I'm writing a military sketch and thinking you'd be great as the featured guy. Do you want to join in?" Of course I did. As the new kid, I wasn't offered many chances to be the lead in a sketch. The problem was that when I read his script about soldiers out in the field, it didn't make sense to me. The jokes seemed clichéd, and it didn't make me laugh.

I asked the writer a few questions and suggested some changes, which seemed to upset him. He thought his script was funny the way it was. Which made me question myself. *If an SNL writer thinks this is funny, maybe he's right and I'm wrong. Am I just missing it? Do I still know what's funny?* I started to lose trust in my comedic instincts.

The result was that I backed off. Like I said, I wanted to please. Even though I felt indifferent about the script, I agreed to have my name on it and it went to a table read.

The table read was the moment of truth for sketches. The cast sat around a long table and performed the voice parts for each submitted script, which took a full day. Out of fifty or so sketches, ten were chosen for dress rehearsal, after which Lorne and the producers picked the best seven for the actual show. Even then, there wasn't always time to fit in all seven sketches when the show aired. When you were competing with so many talented people, you obviously had to nail it at the table read to even have a chance to get your script on the air.

At the table read, it wasn't hard to figure out which sketches worked and which didn't. The best ones drew big laughs from everybody. The ones that bombed brought on looks of confusion or the most dreaded response of all: silence. When the time came for our military sketch, I read my part with enthusiasm. I truly tried to sell the shit out of it. It still bombed. No one laughed. They didn't understand it. It was garbage. I felt terrible, like I'd stolen five minutes from people's lives that they would never get back. Even worse, I'd attached my name as a cowriter to a script that stunk. It was a classic example of my problem that year. Basically, I tried too hard to be what I thought people wanted me to be instead of trusting myself and being myself.

I nearly broke out of that with one of my original creations. I'd invented a character named Leviticus, a wild-eyed, over-the-top street preacher who saw evil lurking in every corner. I got to play him on a "Weekend Update" segment with Tina and Amy. Leviticus stood at the news desk and shouted, "Lord, hear me now, Satan has sent forth legions of demons to destroy yours truly! Help me, help me now to crush the wicked into a fine powder! Allow my hands to become some sort of, I don't know, stabbing weapon or slashing weapon so that I may destroy the legions of evil!"

As Tina and Amy fought to keep straight faces, I continued: "At least grant me the power of flight, Jesus, or the ability to become invisible so that I may sneak up on the demons and snap their reptilian necks!" I finished by cocking the Bible in my hand like it was a shotgun, blasting it at the audience, and saying, "You've just been blown away by the Word."

We had fun with Leviticus and he got laughs from the audience, so we tried to bring him back in other sketches. One of those made it to dress rehearsal before getting axed. Another time, my Leviticus sketch made it to the top seven and was supposed to air, but the show ran long—my sketch was one of two left, and we only had time for one. Hilary Swank was the guest host that week, so she got to choose. In the other sketch, she was supposed to play a runway model who wore sexy clothes and acted like Heidi Klum.

In my sketch, she was supposed to play a teenage tomboy who was confronted by Leviticus. For some reason, she chose being a sexy model over having a street preacher yell at her—go figure.

Near the end of the season, I had one last shot at getting Leviticus on the show. He was in a sketch that made it to dress rehearsal, but at the rehearsal I was so desperate to make him stand out that I overplayed it. I rushed the timing and pushed way too hard. In comedy, being outrageous is funny as long as the audience gets the subtle "wink, wink" of your character's words and actions. But in this case, I turned Leviticus into just plain obnoxious. I wasn't funny.

As soon as the sketch was over, I realized that I'd pissed away my chance. While I sat sulking in the dressing room, Amy came in. She shook her head and said, "Aw, man, you really went for it, huh?" We both knew.

Moments like these created more self-doubt for me. They also created doubt about me in the minds of the producers. I started getting a weird vibe. One time near the end of the season, a producer ran into me in the hall and asked, "Hey, did you get a sketch on the show this week?" I said no. "Oh, okay." He just walked away. It was that feeling you get when your girlfriend is about to break up with you. You can't quite put your finger on what's wrong, but you know something's changed for the worse.

Even so—maybe because I was in denial—I anticipated being renewed for another season. No way my dream could end that abruptly. And I had received *some* positive feedback from Lorne and other producers, which also led me to believe things were good.

That summer, I was at my parents' lake house in Missouri when Amy called. She would call occasionally, as friends do, just to check in. "Hey, Riggs," she said, "how's it going?"

"Hey," I said, "it's so good to hear from you! I'm really getting excited for next season!"

Amy was quiet for a moment before we resumed our chat. I didn't think anything of it at the time. That should have been another clue . . . but again, denial.

The next day, my agent called. He got right to the point: "I'm sorry, Rob, they're not extending your contract." Suddenly, I couldn't deny what I'd feared deep down. It all caved in on me. The dream job I'd fantasized about almost my whole life, the one I'd worked so hard to achieve for a decade, was gone. This was why Amy had called. She was calling to console me. She thought I already knew.

I went out on my parents' porch and sat there in stunned silence. It hurt so bad. I was definitely in shock, like a car accident, for real, shock. I felt like a failure. I cursed a few people and felt sorry for myself for a good thirty minutes. *It's over. The dream is over.*

Then I remembered that I had a wife and a daughter who needed me to get back to work. Pity party done! Honestly, that was it—at least in the sense that I was already thinking of new ways to make a living. Don't get me wrong: I agonized about what happened for years after (if I'd unburdened all that in therapy, I could have financed some Hollywood psychiatrist's new swimming pool). The regret, the pain, the shame, the sadness, the desperate desire to get one more chance is still in me to this day. (Lorne, you still have my number, right?)

I did a lot of reflecting that summer. Even before the call, I'd realized that I'd gotten away from being the confident, funny guy that *SNL* had hired. I hated the tentative, people-pleasing person I'd become at the end of my first season. I finally understood what Amy had tried to tell me and saw that I'd done exactly what she'd warned me about—I'd given that place too much power. I had decided I would be fearless for my second season. If I was going to fail, I would fail being myself (cue Frank Sinatra singing "My Way"). I would no longer put my name on sketches that didn't make me laugh. I wasn't going to try to please everyone. I wasn't going to suck up to people who probably weren't fans of mine to begin with. I felt excited and ready to kick ass—I would be Leviticus, using my hands to crush every obstacle into powder!

Except now there was no second season. Now I just hoped somebody else would give me a chance to apply what I'd learned.

That fall of 2005 was tough. I didn't have a job, and I wasn't getting any comedy or acting offers. I'd already moved my wife and daughter to my parents' house in Kansas because New York was too expensive for all of us to live there. Meanwhile, at least for a few weeks, I was halfway across the country on the West Coast. Since I was still a Marine Corps reserve and because of my promotion to major, I was now a field grade officer. It meant I was required to complete coursework at the Corps' Command and Staff College in San Diego.

On the first day of October, I turned on the TV in my cramped base quarters and watched the season opener of *Saturday Night Live*. Everybody was there—Amy, Tina, Seth Meyers, Horatio Sanz, all of 'em. Steve Carell was the guest host. It was heartbreaking.

I was on *that show! Those are my friends! How did I end up back here, studying a Carl von Clausewitz book about war in this cinderblock-walled room that makes Motel 6 look like paradise? What the fuck happened to my life?* I'd worked so hard to reach one of the pinnacles of comedy, had actually beaten impossible odds and done it—and then in the blink of an eye, lost it all. Watching that show, I don't think I'd ever felt more sad or defeated.

Still . . .

Damn it, Riggle, you're a Marine! Grit, spit, and never quit! Push through that wall! You will find a way!

At least, I hope so.

TWENTY-ONE

Back in the Game

By 2006, my comedy career seemed to be going down the toilet. I was renting a duplex in Los Angeles with my wife and daughter and going to auditions, but I still wasn't getting any jobs, and my funds were rapidly running out. The situation was looking bleaker than Joe Biden's chances of winning a rap contest.

But that summer, I learned that *The Daily Show* on Comedy Central had an opening for one correspondent and they wanted me to audition. *Fantastic!* I thought. *I still have a chance to get back in the game!* *The Daily Show* was hosted by Jon Stewart, already a comedy icon who'd won multiple Emmy and Peabody awards with the show. It was one of the best and most intelligent shows on television, known for its biting political comedy and satire. I wasn't a political warrior, but I knew that guys like Steve Carell, Stephen Colbert, and Matt Walsh had been correspondents on the show, which boded well for my future. I also loved that two of the current correspondents, Ed Helms and Rob Corddry, were friends of mine.

Next to *Saturday Night Live*, *The Daily Show* was about the best place I could imagine for expanding my comedy chops. But at this point, I wasn't worrying about what made the most sense as a next step—I was desperate! I would have played a teenage girl on

Hannah Montana (or a dolphin getting double-teamed) if it meant having another shot at working in the business.

I auditioned with some *Daily Show* reps in LA. I thought I did okay, but not great (by the way, I *never* feel like I do well in an audition). Even so, I got a callback. They wanted me and three or four other guys to fly to New York for an audition with Jon in the studio. That got my hopes a little higher. In truth, I had to land this job or my comedy career was definitely gonna be put on hold. We were so broke, our bank was sending us sympathy cards. Meanwhile, the War on Terror was in full swing. I knew the Marines would welcome me back to active duty with open arms. I'd probably be deployed quickly, most likely to Iraq. That's what my life had come down to. I was either going to New York to make people laugh or going to Iraq to help fight terrorists.

The audition had two parts. One would have me speaking in front of a green screen, and the other would be me doing a bit with Jon at a desk. In both, I was to read from a script on a teleprompter. I'd never worked with a teleprompter before, so when I got to the studio, I asked if I could practice in front of the green screen for a few minutes. I didn't realize that the faster you read, the faster the teleprompter scrolled. I sounded like Robin Williams after he'd sucked on a helium balloon. I was like a dog chasing its tail—I was in a race I would never win.

Wow, I thought. *I fucked that up. But it was just practice. Now I've at least got a feel for it. I'm ready to lay one down.*

What I didn't realize was that Jon had snuck into the studio, sat down at the news desk just twenty feet away, and watched me. When I finished, he said, "Hey, Rob, that was great! Come on over and let's do the desk bit."

I was horrified. "Oh, no, I was just playing, just practicing."

"Nah, you were fine," Jon said, waving me over. "Let's go to the desk."

I'd never met Jon, so I walked over, shook hands, and made small talk. "It's great to be here," I said with a nervous smile.

"Yeah, man, thanks for coming in. You living out here?"

"No, I'm out west now."

I kept on smiling and talking, but at the same time, I thought, *Holy shit, go back to the teleprompter, go back, you've got to do that over! That wasn't your best. You're going to blow your chance!*

We sat down at the desk. I was even more nervous. I still wasn't comfortable with the teleprompter, and I was sure I'd just pissed away half of my audition.

"Really, I was just kidding around over there," I said. "Can I do that again?"

"Nah, nah, it was great. Let's do this."

I had to let it go. Jon was the captain of the ship and he wanted to do the desk piece. This wasn't the time to argue.

We started the bit. My instinct was to make eye contact with Jon, but I couldn't because I had to watch the teleprompter behind his head. I wasn't used to that. It felt unnatural because I couldn't play off Jon's reactions. I again raced through it, trying to keep up with the words on the teleprompter and totally blowing off any comedic timing. I was rougher than an Irish whiskey filled with sawdust. And the whole time, I was still mentally yelling at myself about the first part of the audition. *They're not going to see the real me! They're going to look at the tapes and say, "Yeah, these other guys are better."*

Jon seemed not to notice. "That was great, man," he said when we were done. "You're awesome." He thanked me, and that was it. I liked Jon right away. He was so encouraging. But I was deeply disappointed with my audition. I hadn't shown anything close to my best. It just felt like another defeat. I was lower than Danny DeVito doing the limbo.

I asked to step outside for a minute. I called my wife. "Hey," I said, "I think I screwed up. I'm really sorry. Don't worry, we're gonna be fine. I'm going to go back on active duty. We'll have medical, and we'll have a paycheck. We're not going to be on the street. We're going to be okay."

I was sad, but you don't always get what you want in life. I was ready to accept my fate. *I got further than most*, I thought. *I can't complain. I got my shot.*

Back inside the studio, I was asked to wait in a greenroom. I wanted to get out of there, but I said okay. I was sitting on a small couch when three producers stepped into the room and took the remaining seats. I'd already braced myself for the "kind letdown"—you know, the "Thanks, Rob, we thought you were fantastic, but we've decided to go in a different direction." I would thank them, then go get a drink somewhere, and try not to cry. I just wanted to get it over with.

No one spoke for a moment. Then one of the producers cleared his throat. "Well," he finally said, "Jon loved you. We thought you did great. We would love for you to be a correspondent."

Wait, what did he just say?

I can't remember my exact words because they burst out of me in a vomitus blast. They were something to the effect of, "Holy shit! For real?! Thank you! Oh my God! I'll do my best, I promise! Seriously?! Holy shit!!!!" I didn't cry until I was on my way back to the hotel. I got out of the taxi a few blocks from the hotel and walked the rest of the way. I was in a suit, and it was hot. As I walked, I thanked God and the tears flowed. I took another moment to be grateful. Then I called my wife and told her my next mission assignments weren't going to come from Uncle Sam; they would be from Jon Stewart.

I was thrilled to be on *The Daily Show*. It was a second chance. This time, I would not give the place too much power. For better or worse, I would be myself, Rob Riggle, the generally humorous knucklehead from Kansas, trusting what *I* thought was funny and not worrying about what everybody else thought.

It didn't take long for my new philosophy to be put to the test.

At *The Daily Show*, correspondents acted similarly to their counterparts on a real TV news program—that is, they went out in the field to interview people and investigate stories. My first field piece involved flying to Arcadia, California, and interviewing a man whose credit report identified him as the son of Saddam Hussein. He wasn't, mind you. This was a sweet man who worked hard to provide for his family. Mr. Hussein's problem was that he'd been put on a no-fly list. The hoops he had to jump through to fly on a plane were just ridiculous.

We did our pieces ironically, so in the interview I said things like, "How dare you, sir? You're not fooling anyone! I know the son of a dictator from Iraq when I see one!" Mr. Hussein was not in on the gag, so to speak. He kept trying to explain to me that there had been a mistake. "I'm not him," he said, showing me his driver's license. I wasn't having it.

I felt bad for the guy. He was frustrated that I didn't seem to believe him. I kept wanting to lean over and whisper, "It's okay, I understand, we have to do it this way." To get an honest reaction, I had to play it straight. We'd sent video clips of the show to him ahead of time, but I don't think Mr. Hussein was into the satirical comedy we offered at *The Daily Show*.

For the piece, I did a follow-up interview with a civil rights attorney in California. At one point in the interview, I stumbled over my words during a question. I tried again and screwed it up a second time. Then I botched it a third time. I was so frustrated that I stood up and exclaimed, "Excuse me, would you?" I just walked away from everybody. Glenn Clements, my field producer for this segment (and as it would turn out, for several more future segments) was confused.

"Rob," he said, "what are you doing?"

"I have an idea," I said. "I want to come back and film something later." After completing our little discussion, I returned to the attorney's office and finished the interview.

Later, I got Glenn to film me in a bathroom screaming "What are you doing?" in front of a mirror and shouting "Hyaah!" as I did karate chops in the air to pump myself up and get my confidence back. It seemed like a way to turn my fumbled lines into something comedic. In the editing room, Glenn interspersed the bathroom scene with film of the attorney sitting alone, waiting for me to come back, with my karate screams in the background.

I laughed out loud when I watched Glenn's edited version. The question was, would we actually show it to Jon? This was very meta, not the normal style on *The Daily Show*. It broke the imaginary "fourth wall" that separated the viewer from what was happening on camera. It would be taking a big swing. If Jon liked it, great. But if he didn't—if it made him say, "Riggle, you actually think this is funny?"—it could be the first step toward me being unemployed again. And I needed this job. My family needed this job. I did not want to blow it.

Then I remembered my promise to myself—this time, I was going to lean in to the skills that got me here, trust my instincts, and damn the consequences. Glenn thought the idea was funny. More important, *I* thought it was funny.

We kept the bathroom scene.

A day or two later, I sat in the studio in New York as Jon prepared to watch the edited video of our field piece. I felt like my career was on the line. I was dying a thousand deaths.

I watched Jon lean forward as the video began and the interview progressed. Then came my flubs. Jon frowned. When I walked out of the frame, he leaned back.

Uh-oh.

When the video cut to me walking into the bathroom, Jon looked mystified, like he thought we'd left it in by accident. But when I started yelling at myself in the mirror, he leaned forward again. A grin began forming at the corners of his mouth. Suddenly, he burst out laughing.

"Stop! Stop!" Jon shouted, waving his arms. "I did not see that coming. That's awesome. Go back, go back, I want to see it again!"

He loved it. With only a couple of minor tweaks, our version made the final cut. When it aired in front of a live audience, Jon still couldn't keep from laughing. The audience roared too.

The whole experience was so validating. It made me feel like I understood comedy again, that I could do this job, that I belonged. I think Jon appreciated that I was willing to take a chance and have fun.

Maybe more important, I learned a critical lesson. Of course, I needed to continue to listen to people who had more experience and wisdom than I. But I also needed to be me. I needed to trust the unique blend of abilities and instincts that I brought to the table. If I stayed true to myself and kept working hard, I would be okay. I wouldn't try to make everyone happy and be what everyone else expected me to be. Instead, I would be the best version of me and let the chips fall.

Hyaah!

Guitar Picks and Goodbyes

If you're old enough, you might remember "Stormin' Norman" Schwarzkopf, who commanded coalition forces in the Gulf War against Iraq. In 1991, General Schwarzkopf gave the nationally televised "Mother of All Press Conferences," using military maps with big arrows to describe in detail how various coalition groups overwhelmed Iraq's defenses.

I sometimes visualize my life like a military map. To achieve my dreams and goals, I have to attack them strategically. On one flank, I send in a big arrow of *faith*—a belief in myself and my ability to get the job done, backed up by my faith in God. On the other flank, I send in *courage*, which doesn't mean I'm fearless, but that I'm committed to overcoming my fear. (Believe me, I have battled fear many times, whether it was going into a combat zone or doing stand-up comedy in New York City or betting a hundred bucks when I only had a twenty in my pocket.)

My main thrust—the biggest arrow—is *perseverance*. If I learned anything from the Marines, it's that if you apply consistency and discipline to any goal or problem long enough, you will achieve your objective. I also believe that any dream worth achieving is going to push you to your limit—you will *need* perseverance (and probably a whole lot of tacos) to get there.

I often hear from military veterans on social media, which is great. Quite a few will write something like "Hey, Rob, I appreciate what you've done. I'm getting out of the Army [or Navy or Marines or Air Force] and I want to be an actor. Do you have any advice?" I get the same question from many of the young people I meet.

I know what most of them are really asking. They want to know "Is there a shortcut?" I understand exactly where they're coming from because I used to have the same question. I would regularly corner someone who was famous—or at least on the way to famous—and in a roundabout way ask about hacks to making it in showbiz.

Guess what? There are no hacks. It takes years to master your craft.

The guy that really hammered this idea home for me was Harvey Keitel. Besides being a highly acclaimed actor, he is a fellow Marine who hosted an annual birthday ball for the Marine Corps when I lived in New York. I used to help him organize the ball, so we'd have lunch at Bubby's on Hudson Street. When I told him I wanted to be an actor and comedian, hoping he might let me in on some secret back door to the top, he squinted at me the way gangster Mickey Cohen—the role Harvey played in *Bugsy*—might have squinted at Bugsy Siegel. "There are not shortcuts to a career in this business," he said. "You have to do the work. It takes about ten years."

This was not what I wanted to hear. At the time, I was already past thirty—old, bordering on decrepit, for an up-and-coming comedian. I was sure I needed to make it right away, or it would be too late. Ten years? I didn't have ten months!

Except that Harvey was right. When I joined the cast of *Saturday Night Live*, it was almost ten years to the day after I first wrote down my dream of getting on *SNL* while sitting in my car on the beach at Corpus Christi. As you know, I spent most of those years performing on small stages in front of smaller audiences, learning how to actually be a comedian and actor. I had to keep at it, week after week, month after month, and do the work.

Today, I'm so glad I stuck with it. I've had unbelievable experiences working in comedies like *The Hangover*, *21 Jump Street*, and *Step Brothers*. I had a blast doing "Riggle's Picks" on *Fox NFL Sunday* for eight years and appearing on shows like *Modern Family* and *Holey Moley*. But I want to keep stretching and growing, which is why in recent years I've also taken on dramatic roles, including playing my old boss, Lieutenant Colonel Bowers, in the movie *12 Strong*.

I have other dreams. I want to get behind the camera as a director. I have an idea for a one-man theatrical show. I'd like to devote more time to the Riggle Foundation, a nonprofit I established that focuses on issues that help veterans, first responders, and children. I would also like to master hatchet throwing. It's such an intimate and intimidating weapon. You just never see a guy with a hatchet. It would be memorable . . . You know I'm right.

I also want to keep growing as a parent. I was married for twenty years and had two fantastic children—Abby and George—with my ex-wife, but sadly, our relationship fell apart. Despite that pain and all that's happened since, I prefer to stay positive and look to the future.

It's easier to look to the future when you can make peace with the past. My *SNL* year was such a validating, fulfilling part of my life—a part that vanished faster than Jon Lovitz could say, "Yeah, that's the ticket!" It helped that a week after I got the bad news, producer Ken Aymong called to explain. It was an election year, ratings were down, and NBC panicked. Somebody had to go, and as the last hired on, I was first to get booted off. Ken was so kind and generous to call, and I am nothing but grateful for my *SNL* experience. Even so, I've lived with a degree of shame and disappointment ever since leaving the show. I'd hoped for so much more. I never even got the chance to say goodbye!

But I recently got some closure. As an alum, I was invited to the *Saturday Night Live* fiftieth anniversary celebration in February 2025. I was nervous. Would anyone even remember I'd been on the show? Would they think I was trying to crash the party? But on that first night at Radio City Music Hall, a page greeted me as soon as I walked in the door: "Hi, Mr. Riggle, I'm so glad you're here! Can I help you with anything? Where would you like to go?" I started to relax—I felt welcome.

I had a great time that weekend. I got to say hello and goodbye and share stories with the writers, producers, and castmates I'd worked with on the show, many I hadn't seen for twenty years. Amy and I shared a hug. I introduced myself to Eddie Vedder, the Pearl Jam lead singer, who also recognized me. When I told him I was a fan, he said, "Oh, that's cool. I'm a fan too, man."

"Thanks," I said, "but really, I *am* a fan. I saw you on the KU campus back in ninety-two and later in two thousand at the Thomas & Mack Center at UNLV."

"Oh my God," he said, "you're not kidding!" We talked some more, shook hands, and parted ways. But a couple minutes later, he hurried over and handed me a bunch of guitar picks with SNL 50TH printed on them. "We're playing later, and they gave us a ton of these," he said, "so here you go!" Now those picks are cherished souvenirs.

The other great thing about that weekend was being back in Studio 8H at 30 Rock, this time as part of the audience, and watching so many incredible performers return to that familiar stage. For me, the passion for comedy is always there, but there are times when the flame is lower than at other times, you know what I mean? Yet when I saw Eddie Murphy, Will Ferrell, and Kenan Thompson in the "Scared Straight" sketch, with their wigs, dyed hair, and convict costumes, trading one-liners, screaming weird shit at three young offenders, and trying not to crack up, I got fired up about comedy all over again. *Oh, man,* I thought, *I would love to be onstage, hooking and jabbing with those guys right now. They're having so much fun!*

That weekend was so good for my soul. I got to catch up and share laughs with people I admired and cared about. I finally felt like part of the family. I got to watch some of my comedy heroes do their stuff. I felt renewed and inspired.

The *SNL* anniversary event reminded me that in so many ways, I've lived a blessed life. I have had the honor of serving my country as a Marine and learning what I'm capable of in the process. I've also had the privilege of working and often laughing with some of the most fun and talented people in the world of show business. When you throw in an amazing family and great friends, that's a recipe worth celebrating.

I hope something in these pages has made you want to celebrate, or feel a little bit renewed or inspired—or at least made you chuckle. Here's hoping all your dreams come true. If you stick with it, they just might.

Pow!!!

ACKNOWLEDGMENTS

There are so many people that I am grateful for in my life. I'm blessed to have people around me that I love tremendously. So please bear with me as I throw down this list of gratitude. After all, "No man is an island."

Allow me to start with my children, Abigail and George. I thank God for you every day. Sincerely. I pray for your happiness, growth, and wisdom every single day. I pray for your protection and peace. I hope your journey is full of adventure, productive struggle, love, and success. I am always here for you. You guys are the best thing that's ever happened to me. My love for you is absolute and unconditional. I'm always proud of you. I'm so grateful for you. I hope you'll always know how much I love you.

Mom and Dad, thank you for your patience, kindness, grace, and example. I'll never be able to thank you enough or express enough how much I love you and how much your love has meant to me over the years. The greatest blessing of my life is having you both as parents.

My sister, Julie, and her amazing family: Mark, Mallory, Chandler, and Brooke. Thank you for being so consistently awesome. I go to my sister with the big questions. I seek her counsel when I'm in doubt or feel lost. Julie always reminds me of the good in this world. I love you. You're a rock for so many people, myself included.

To Kasia, thank you for your kindness and love. You are stronger than anyone knows. You handle yourself with grace and dignity. Thank you for being so patient during some very trying times. Thank you for being an amazing partner. Thank you for your sincerity, honesty, and love. I'm grateful for you every day. I love you.

With regard to this book, it simply doesn't happen without the collaboration and efforts of Jim Lund. Jim, you're a great writer and a great listener. You ask great questions. I'm eternally grateful for our conversations and your help in uncovering stories and moments of clarity.

Suzanne O'Neill, thank you for your passion and desire to make this book the best it could be. Thank you for demanding a high standard. Thank you for championing this effort.

To Jimmy Franco, Tiffany Porcelli, and all of the publicity and marketing team at Hachette, thank you.

To Rob Greenwald, my longtime publicist and friend. Thank you for always being a voice of reason and looking out for my best interest. You're the best in the business! Thank you.

Artists First—Maggie Haskins and Peter Principato, thank you for believing in me and supporting me. Our journey over the last twenty years has been epic. I'll never be able to express my gratitude enough, but I thank God for you guys every day. No joke.

United Talent Agency, how blessed am I to be represented by you guys! I am beyond grateful that I have the best agency in the world, in my corner. Chris Hart, Jay Gassner, Cara Alpert, Andrew Lear, Martin Lesak, Albert Lee, Byrd Leavell, Brett Duchon, and *all* of their assistants! Thank you!

My business manager, Jeff Wolman (and Patricia Harris), thank you for keeping things on track and done properly. Thank you for helping me through challenging times. I'm forever grateful.

Thank you, Lon Sorenson, for making sure my contracts are fair and accurate.

To my friends from grade school through college and all the way until today: Jeff Robbins, Bill Konen, Jim Davis, and Greg Lausier. Thank you for your friendship all these years. You guys have been there through it *all*! I look forward to every moment we get to hang out together. I love you guys.

To my comedy friends from the UCB Theatre, stand up, *SNL*, *The Daily Show*, *Fox NFL Sunday*, *Riggle's Picks* podcast, and so many other shows and movies, thank you for teaching me and making my life better with your gifts and talents: Paul Scheer, Rob Huebel, Owen Burke, Chad Carter, Seth Morris, Danielle Schnieder, Dannah Phirman, Jackie Clark, Jason Mantzoukas, Matt Walsh, Ian Roberts, Matt Besser, Amy Poehler, Jon Stewart, John Oliver, Glenn Clements, Chris Pizzi, Bennett Webber, Chandler Barbee, Joe Tessitore, Charles Wachter, Sarah Tiana, Darren Leader, Gary Smith, Claire Brown, Ryan O'Quinn, Heather O'Quinn, Dean Holland, and hundreds of others.

My Marine Corps brothers—there's a loyalty and brotherhood no one will understand unless you've been there and done that. I am grateful to know you and to know that men like you still exist in this cynical world. God bless America! I love you. Brent Heppner, Mike Kaminski, Gabe Valdez, Jeff Breslau, Scott "Lucky" Guilland, and Matt Shortal.

To my pledge brothers, thank you for some amazing years that continue to this day. Thank you for continuing to grow and care about each other over the years. Pergé.

To my friend and business partner, Rich Day, thank you. You give me hope every day, and you're an example I respect. God bless you, brother! To my other friend and business partner, Keith Crawford, I'm so proud of our mission. Your dedication to helping and serving others is a daily source of inspiration. You're a good man in a tough world. To Russell and Calum from 2WAI, you guys are an inspiration. I love and admire your work ethic and huge vision. To

Chris Seithel, thanks for your friendship and a great run at success. To Michael Cyrus and Cody Hyde, thank you for your friendship. I'm looking forward to new adventures.

To Pam Swan, thank you for your selflessness when it comes to our veteran community. You're authentic and dedicated. You work tirelessly for so many, and it doesn't go unnoticed, I promise. Thanks for all your help and hard work.

If I didn't mention your name and you're like, "Hey, WTF?!!!"—I apologize, and I mean no harm or disrespect. However, I could literally drive myself insane trying to hit everyone I've been blessed enough to meet along the way.

ABOUT THE AUTHOR

ROB RIGGLE is an American actor, comedian, and United States Marine Corps Lieutenant Colonel. He served in the Marines for twenty-three years, including in Liberia, Kosovo, Albania, and Afghanistan. Riggle has had over 140 roles throughout the course of his career. He has been in feature films such as *Talladega Nights*, *Step Brothers*, *The Hangover*, *21 Jump Street*, *22 Jump Street*, *Dumb and Dumber To*, and *12 Strong*. His television credits include being a cast member on *Saturday Night Live* and Comedy Central's *The Daily Show with Jon Stewart*, as well as roles in shows such as *The Office*, *Arrested Development*, *30 Rock*, *New Girl*, *Modern Family*, *Brooklyn 99*, *Holey Moley*, *Fox NFL Sunday*, and *Curb Your Enthusiasm*. His various voice acting credits include shows and movies from *The Lorax* to *The Simpsons*, *Bob's Burgers*, and *Big Mouth*. He has two children and currently lives in Los Angeles.